POLITICAL PARTY GOVERNANCE

POLITICAL PARTY GOVERNANCE

A PRACTICAL GUIDE TO STUDYING COMPARATIVE
POLITICAL PARTY GOVERNANCE.

MOHAMMED WAKIL

Political Party Governance
Mohammed Wakil

Table of Contents

Acknowlegements

Incontrovertibly, academic accomplishment of this nature is intrinsically a success story cast by different people, playing an assortment of roles. It is therefore fitting to give credit and express profound appreciation to all those who participated in the expedition that crystallised in the actualisation of this book. First and most momentously, I should like to affirm my profound gratitude and immense thanks to the Director General of the National Institute for Legislative and Democratic Studies (NILDS): Professor Abubakar O. Suleiman, for providing me with the platform and enabling environment for this intellectual exercise. I say a resounding thank you for your untiring support and encouragement in the course of my writing and research. I am indeed grateful. I must also appreciate Dr Jake D'Azumi for his valuable contributions in making the book successful. It is also with delight that express my gratitude to Dr. Asimiyu Abiola, the Director of Studies at the National Institute for Legislative and Democratic Studies (NILDS).

As a matter of academic sincerity, i most sincerely wish to express my unalloyed indebtedness to Dr. Adeyemi Agbelusi who was my Consultant in this intellectual voyage. Many thanks for the invaluable suggestions, technical advice and assistance you gave me in this modest effort. It is axiomatic that you had the tedious business of reading through substantial part of this book in respect of which you offered helpful suggestions and intellectual footpaths to success.

The encouraging roles of Dr Mohammed Bashir, Okoli Chidi Esq., Omoluabi Paul Esq., Stanley Umeakuekwe Esq., and Miss Amaka Ozoude cannot go unappreciated. Through the thick and thin of my academic endeavours and other engagements, you kept the faith with me and were bastions of courage and immeasurable support. It is with delight i note the extent of which the vast majority of students of Political Party Governance at the National Institute for Legislative and Democratic Studies (NILDS) relentlessly urged me to author a book on this subject. I am grateful to them all.

Mohammed Wakil
Abuja
5th March,2022.

Foreword

The health and resilience of a country's democracy are often gauged by the strength of its institutions of democracy, including political parties. In addition to their traditional functions of 'electoral structuration' through the recruitment of candidates, providing 'symbolic integration' by means of a distinct ideology, forming government and participating in governance processes as well as aggregating the interests of citizens, political parties also contribute to ensuring political accountability, democratic stability and national unity, among others. The role of political parties in democratisation has been categorised into three stages by Fukuyama (2014), namely to mobilise and oust the old regime, hold free and fair elections and deliver public services and goods.

To be effective, political parties are expected to be inclusive, transparent in their operations and maintain democratic principles, especially as it pertains to their internal procedures. No matter how they are structured, three basic elements are necessary for their success. These include constitutional and regulatory frameworks (including party manifesto), membership of the party, attractive manifesto, financial resources, a transparent electoral process and the competence and acceptability of candidates it presents, among others.

Within the context of Nigeria, political parties have played a dominant role in mobilising to replace the military and the conduct of elections since 1999. They continue to be important institutions in shaping Nigeria's democracy. However, how much they have evolved beyond mere tools for the selecting of candidates for elections has been the subject of major debate. These and other issues are taken up in this book that provides an in-depth analysis of the origin, nature and functions of political parties as well as their structure and operations. It concludes by drawing on the Nigerian experience to show the journey towards political party institutionalisation since 1999. Some of the challenges identified include limited capacity, non-professionalisation, weak party structures, dominance by 'godfathers' and absence of clearly defined ideologies.

The uniqueness of this book is twofold; it draws from the actual political experience of the author who has been a major political actor since the return to democratic governance and the advent of the Fourth Republic in 1999, having served as the first Majority Leader in this dispensation. By virtue of his involvement quite early in the process, he is conversant with the major issues that have shaped political party development in Nigeria in the last two decades being one of the founding members of the People's Democratic Party (PDP), the dominant political party between 1999 and 2015 when it lost its dominance to the All Progressives Congress (APC). Second, the author has also been involved in teaching postgraduate students enrolled for the Master's degree programme in Elections and Party politics offered by the Institute in affiliation with the University of Benin. Through years of teaching on the programme, he has become increasingly conversant with the major issues and questions raised by students and researchers interested in political party development in Nigeria.

This book will fundamentally improve understanding of party governance, especially in Nigeria. The future of our democracy will depend on the consolidation of political parties, deepening of internal party democracy, strengthening of internal structures and processes, increased accountability and development of distinct ideological foundations. Clearly, as identified by the author, some of these institutional reforms and developments are already ongoing. Yet, political parties in Nigeria still have a long way to go in attaining their full potential.

Researchers and practitioners alike will therefore find this book useful in deepening their understanding of political parties and how they have evolved in various democracies around the world including Britain, the United States as well as select African countries including Ghana, Kenya and South Africa. Equally instructive is the discussion on the formation and characteristics of political parties and the various ways in which they organise to acquire power, form government and implement policies.

However, the central thrust of the book is the analysis of political party structures and organisation and the various models for regulating parties, which is presented from a comparative perspective. It equally discusses how legislations are used in different parts of the world to promote the institutionalisation of political parties. This is particularly the case in countries like Nigeria, where parties are characterised by weak institutional and organisational capacity. Whereas there are no fit-for-all solutions and models, the experiences of various countries presented provide useful lessons for Nigeria.

As a politician cum academic myself, I found the discussion on political parties as tools for leadership recruitment most useful. This is particularly relevant within the context of Nigeria where the process of leadership has been identified as a major defect in our democratic process. Political parties can play a significant role in changing the trend and ensuring that candidates put forward for elective positions are competent, capable and credible. They can also invest in capacity building for candidates to prepare them for the demands of leadership. It has been said that "a party that cannot attract and then nominate candidates surrenders its elemental opportunity for power."

It is therefore my pleasure to recommend this important to all those interested in political organisation and governance and hope that this resource will be used widely to improve our party systems and processes towards good governance. The effort of the author is commendable and I encourage this fusion of theory and practice.

Prof. Abubakar O. Sulaiman
Director-General
National Institute for Legislative and Democratic Studies
National Assembly
Abuja, Nigeria

Chapter One

Introduction

It is in the nature of man not to live alone; he lives in human society. This is the reason the famous Greek philosopher Aristotle said, man is a political animal because he lives in a society, he needs to interact with other people, develop rules and regulations that govern his continued existence in the society. It can be safely concluded that man has since engaged in politics. Right from the time of Greek city states, mankind has always lived in communities with various political structures that suit his environment.

There is no doubt that Democracy has since become the bride of nations especially because of its link with development and the self-actualization of the human person. There is a sustained emphasis on the desirability of democracy and the deepening democratic culture in the continent of Africa to produce the needed development.

Political parties are very critical to the sustainability of democratic norms and values. However, the political party institution in most of African Countries are still very rudimentary. A political party, by definition is an organized group of people with at least broadly similar political goals and ideas who strive to influence public policy by electing their candidates to public office. The same purpose, aims and objectives are shared by members of the same political party. Different political parties contend with one another to influence public policy and opinion through their respective ideas, values, and ambitions. The government is administered by the winning party, with the opposition keeping a close eye on how it functions.

The importance of political parties cannot be overstated; the operation of the whole governmental apparatus is dependent on them and the presence of political parties in any nation is one of the good markers of a successful democratic transition. The reality is that democracy is impossible to imagine in the absence of political parties because they are the driving force behind everything the government does.

Adigun Agbaje cites Remi Anifowose (1999, p.192) and puts it succinctly that "Political parties and pressure groups in a supposedly democratic country is worse than tea without sugar, it is like trying to pass brown water as tea. There can be no meaningful democracy without a properly functioning party and pressure groups process". It is obvious, therefore that parties and pressure groups constitute the heart of democracy - the more vigorous and healthier they are, the better assured is the health of the democratic process itself.

The above view is supported by Johari, J.C. (2008, p.423) in the remark that "modern democracy has procreated the system of political parties and organized interest pressure groups as an indispensable factor in its operations". It is essential that in any electoral democracy, party system is crucial for easy conduct of elections in this complex nature of today's politics. It will be out of place to talk of democracy without mentioning "participation and representation" (Remi Anifowose, (1999, p.193). We cannot talk of democracy without looking at the concept of participation. This describes the extent of individual participation in the political activity of , a community. There should be opportunity for people to participate in the political system of the society they live in. This can be in form of election or selection. On the other hand, representation is the process by which people are chosen to act on behalf of the community.

They put popular opinion into practice, which they helped shape and articulate. They aid in the formation and expression of a general will, which is at the heart of democratic governance. The party system entails a democratic and representative administration. The government may be made accountable to the people through this institution, and therefore responsive to the requirements of the general public and the community as a whole rather than a segment of it.

The party system is predicated on the notion that people are logical individuals who are capable of sensibly exercising their franchise and electing decent governance. As a result, it provides a mechanism for peaceful government transition without violent revolutions or coups. It gives the governing structure the much-needed flexibility. Political parties ensure that the government's many organs function in unison.

However, in Africa, the quality of democratic practice seems a reflection of the lack of cohesion within the parties. Like it is always said with reference to Nigeria, that the political parties are only differentiated in names and not in terms of ideologies or values. The interests of the parties seem not to be properly articulated and aggregated to foist cohesion on the various political platforms.

This work, therefore, is to examine the governance structure of the political parties and find ways to strengthen the internal democracy of the various political parties such that its positive effect will begin to rob-off on the democratic culture in developing nations.

Despite the interest in issues of (good) governance and the traditional attention of political scientists on the role of political parties, there is, paradoxically, no obvious literature available on political parties and their governance-related activities. In this book, some observations will be made on political parties and their role in (good) governance, based on a reading of recent scholarship on governance.

Notwithstanding the widespread use of the term 'governance', it is by no means easy to find a good definition of the word. When just considering the definitions that have been proposed by international organisations, Weiss (2000, pp. 797–8) concludes that there are eight rather different interpretations because of its rather generic and inclusive nature. However, in this work, the definition of the Commission on Global Governance will be applied. The Commission on Global Governance (1995, p. 2), a 'think-tank' consisting of (former) politicians, defined governance as:

"The sum of the many ways individuals and institutions, public and private, manage their common affairs. It is a continuing process through which conflicting or diverse interests may be accommodated and cooperative action may be taken. It includes formal institutions and regimes empowered to enforce compliance, as well as informal arrangements that people and institutions either have agreed to or perceived to be in their interest.

Attention on issues of governance is relatively recent. Only since the late 1980s or the early 1990s, that the role of (the quality of) governance as a factor in the development process has been on the agenda in policy and academic circles. Some have traced the good governance agenda to a 1989 report of the World Bank on the economic crisis in sub-Saharan Africa (Leftwich, 1994, p. 370; Hoebink, (2001, p. 164). Most of the discussion on governance focuses on the positive contribution of good governance to or the detrimental effect of bad governance on the fate of policies adopted in developing countries, most notably their contribution to these countries' level of development.

Towards the end of the 1990s, the discussion on (good) governance received a new impetus with the publication of two World Bank reports, both of which focuses on the effectiveness of development assistance (Burnside and Dollar, 1997; World Bank, 1998). In these two reports, it was argued that development assistance is effective only in aid-receiving developing countries that possess good institutions and/or implement good policies. However, both features were taken as signs of the existence of good governance in developing countries.

The focus on governance issues during the last two decades have shown that there are at least two quite different interpretations of the role of governance in development, which relate to distinct understandings of the meaning of the concept of (good) governance. In an article on governance, the state and the politics of development, Adrian Leftwich (1994, pp. 365–6) distinguished between two meanings:

- a 'more limited meaning ... associated with the World Bank which interprets [governance] in primarily administrative and managerial terms'
- a 'meaning, associated with western governments, [which] is more political' and 'includes an insistence on competitive democratic politics as well'.

The first meaning of (good) governance, which could be seen as the technocratic interpretation (the term is used by van Cranenburgh, 1998, p. 77; and Hoebink, 2001, p. 188), focuses on the way in which the public sector is managed. Leftwich (1994, p. 372) has identified the following four main areas of concern in technocratic governance:

- accountability, which involves holding government officials responsible for their actions
- legality, which means that there is a structure of rules and laws that provides predictability for the public sector
- the availability of information about economic conditions and government policies

- transparency, which refers to the existence of an 'open government', whose decision-making procedures are clear to everybody who wishes to know about them.

The second, political, interpretation of (good) governance focuses on the way in which the political and legal system of developing countries is organised (Hoebink, 2001, p. 188). In the first instance, this approach seems to stress the existence of a well-functioning legal system, which protects the rights and freedoms of citizens. However, adherence to and implementation of internationally agreed human rights conventions are crucial in this interpretation. Next to this, is that the presence of democratic rules and procedures are emphasised. In particular, multi-party democracy, the existence of a pluralist press, and the functioning of an active civil society appear to be elements that are crucial to this interpretation of governance.

In many respects, the existence of a set of active political parties is a necessity for the achievement of good governance when the latter term is based on a political definition. Multi-party democracy, however, tends to be understood in the contemporary discourse largely in procedural, Schumpeteran terms (Schumpeter's classical definition (1976, p. 269) maintains that: 'the democratic method is that institutional arrangement for arriving at political decisions in which individuals acquire the power to decide by means of a competitive struggle for the people's vote'); also, Abrahamsen (2000, p. 67) has phrased it with reference to African politics and politics in the developing world more generally as: 'the democracy the South should strive for is presented as an institution.

What are Political Parties?

There are several definitions on this important topic and it is essential we examine a few of them. However, in general terms, a lot of people agree that political parties are organized group of people who come together to pursue specific policies and objectives with the motive of taking control of state power, by acting together as a political unit.

Michael Curtis, in (Johari, 2008, p. 423) is of the view that political party is notoriously difficult to define accurately because Liberal and Marxist writers differ sharply on this issue. The definition given by Edmund Burke, an English writer and leader was greatly celebrated; He said a political party is "a body of men united for promoting the national interest on some particular principles in which they all agreed" (Chikendu, 2003, p. 42). One thing that is important here is that a political party is a body of men united to promote national interest that they all agreed upon. (Ofoegbu, 1976) gave a clearer picture and remarked that "a political party is an organization of like-minded citizens which seek to promote and advance certain general objectives on which its members agreed", (Chikendu, 2003, p. 42).

Adigun Agbaje (1999, p.195) maintains that "a political party is a group of persons bonded in policy and opinion in support of a general political cause which essentially is the pursuit, capture and retention for as long as democratically feasible, of government and its offices." He went further and cites (Wilson, 1992, p. 138) "that a political party is a group that seeks to elect candidates to public office by supplying them with a label - a party identification by which they are known to the electorate". In his view, a political party should have three clear variables (1) a label in the minds of its members and the electorates (2) an organisation that campaign for candidates seeking elective offices (3) leaders that control the legislative and executive arms of the government.

It is interesting to note that the views of the Americans are different regarding definition of a political party. They view "political party as an instrument of catching power" (Johari, 2008, p. 424). A political party is a platform or machinery for taking part in the struggle for power. Johari went further and declared that "a political party is an agency to mobilise people's support at the time of elections; it is an instrument for aggregation of interest that demands vociferous articulation" (Johari, 2008, p. 424). Grotty, said that "a political party is a formally organised group that performs the functions of educating the public ... that recruits and promotes individual for public office and that provides a comprehensive linkage function between the public and governmental decision makers". From the definitions above, it is clear that a political party should have three essential features (1) an organisation of individual who have common interest that they all agreed upon (2) it is an organisation that should struggle for state power and (3) the members must make efforts to implement the policies and programmes of the party through constitutional means.

The view of Curtis is quite essential in the definition of a political party. He remarked, "Essentially, a party signifies a group of people who hold certain political beliefs in common or who are prepared to support the party candidate, work together for electoral victory, attain and maintain political power" (Johari, 2008, p. 424). Here Curtis stresses the importance of holding a common belief and support for candidates to achieve electoral success.

In the rest of this book, we shall be examining the historical origin of political parties. How political parties evolved and the various developmental phases. Exploration of the basic features and functions of political parties will be undertaken. we shall also review structure of political parties, recruitment patterns and mobilization, and campaign strategy. Within the framework of good governance, we shall examine internal democracy of the parties in terms of decision making and discipline. The book will review party administration highlighting the day to day running of political parties. The book will conclude with some recommendations on how to improve party governance in Nigeria.

Chapter Two

Origin of Political Parties

The political party is a creature of modern and modernizing political systems. Whether one thinks of Anglo-American democracies or totalitarian systems such as the old Soviet Union, Fascist Italy, and Nazi Germany; emergent African states in their earliest years of independent evolution or Latin American republics that have hobbled along for over a century; a mammoth ex-colonial area such as India groping toward democracy or an equally mammoth Communist power such as China seeking to mobilize a population through totalitarian methods, the political party in one form or another is omnipresent.

According to Joseph LaPalombara, (1966, p .3), political parties are primarily phenomena of the 19th century. In England, the modern party really got underway with the organization of the local registration societies favored by the Liberals after the Reform of 1832. In France and other places on the continent, the transformation of legislative cliques or political clubs into mass-oriented organizations is associated with the revolutionary year of 1848. In the United States, although modern parties with substantial following and stable structures appeared in the 1790's with the Federalists of Hamilton and Adams and the Republicans of Jefferson and Madison, it was not until the era of Andrew Jackson in the 1830's that party organization developed to include strong centers of local power on a substantial mass base. In Japan, the first of the Asian countries to transplant major Western political institutions, parties in the sense that we are using the term did not emerge until after the Meiji restoration of 1867 and perhaps not even until the First World War.

Duverger (1954, pp. xxiii–xxiv), argues that, 'the development of parties seems bound up with that of democracy, that is to say with the extension of popular suffrage and parliamentary prerogatives. In Duverger's view, the more political assemblies see their functions and independence grow, the more their members feel the need to group themselves according to what they have in common, so as to act in concert. Hence, he asserts that the rise of parties is thus bound up with the rise of parliamentary groups and electoral committees.

There are three types of theories which have been suggested concerning party origins: institutional theories focusing on the interrelationship between early parliaments and the emergence of parties; historical-situation theories that focus on the historical crises or tasks which systems have encountered at the moment in time when parties developed; and finally, developmental theories that relate parties to the broader processes of modernization.

Institutional Theories of Parties origin

It is customary in the West to associate the development of parties with the rise of parliaments and with the gradual extension of the suffrage. One broad historical formulation of this gradual process is Max Weber's division of party evolution into the stages of aristocratic cliques, small groups of notables, and plebiscitarian democracy.

Duverger notes too that parties are related to the evolution of national parliaments and the growth in the size of the electorate. He suggests that parties grew out of political assemblies as their members felt the need of a group to, act in concert. As the vote was subsequently extended, these committees began to organize the electors. Duverger's theory thus postulates stages in party development: First, the creation of parliamentary groups, then the organization of electoral committees, and finally the establishment of permanent connections between these two elements

The parliamentary circumstances under which some European parties emerged might more usefully be viewed as simply one type of historical circumstance, not as the general case from which all others are deviants. However, the European cases do call our attention to the fact that parties often grow out of crisis situations. Under some circumstances they are the creatures of a systemic political crisis, while in other circumstances their emergence itself creates crisis for the system.

The Historical Situation Theories

This approach to looking at political development sees crises as historical-situational developments that political systems typically experience as they move from traditional to more developed forms. It has been suggested that the way in which political elites cope with such crises (and in some instances prevent them from assuming serious proportions) may determine the kind of political system which develops.

Such historical crises not only often provide the context in which political parties first emerge but also tend to be a critical factor in determining what pattern of evolution parties later take. There are often historical turning points in political systems. Of the many internal political crises which nations have experienced during the period in which political parties were being formed, three strike us as most salient in their impact on party formation: legitimacy, integration, and participation. Though these crises may be analytically distinct, it is commonly noted that in most of the late-developing countries they are frequently telescoped so that political leadership has the extraordinary burden of simultaneously attempting to cope with political problems which historically in other societies had been spread over relatively long period of time.

The Developmental Theories

Under this theory, parties emerge in political systems when those who seek to win or maintain political power are required to seek support from the larger public. There are at least two circumstances under which such a development occurs: (i) A change may already have taken place in the attitudes of subjects or citizens towards authority; individuals in the society may believe that they have the right to influence the exercise of power. (2) A section of the dominant political elite or an aspiring elite may seek to win public support so as to win or maintain power even though the public does not actively participate in political life.

The appearance of new social groups as a consequence of larger socio-economic changes, and in particular the appearance or expansion of entrepreneurial classes and the proliferation of specialized professional classes. Increases in the flow of information, the expansion of internal markets, a growth in technology, the expansion of transportation networks, and, above all, increases in spatial and social mobility appear to have profound effects upon the individual's perception of himself in relation to authority.

Political parties play very significant roles in electoral democracy. In many countries, they characteristically serve as key transmission channels for organizing representation, helping to translate popular demands into legislative initiatives, and acting as gatekeepers which determine which candidates have a chance of being elected. They often serve as vehicles for popular mobilization, and as actors with the capacity to selectively distribute resources and professional expertise; they can leverage all these assets to help politicians obtain and retain electoral offices. This is because parties' choices are consequential for which interests and ideas get represented, parties' organizations can also be arenas for internal disputes, with different factions vying to select leaders, control party manifestos, or get their representatives on party executive boards

The introduction of electoral democracy brought the idea of political party and party system but before the advent of electoral democracy, there existed in the advanced nations of the world, i.e., USA, Britain, etc. different types of public offices for smooth administration of these nations (Shively, 2008, pp. 248). These public structures were mayors, parliamentary members, etc. and they were filled by heritage, outright purchase, and even bribery (Shively, 2011, p. 256). There was no yardstick or standard for filling these offices. However, with the introduction of electoral democracy, a new dimension was introduced, and people were elected to public offices.

It is pertinent to note that political parties developed in the late 1600s. The ancient Greeks that pioneered the idea of developing democracy had no organised political parties as we know it today. Two groups represented people of different interests in the senate of the ancient Rome. These were the Patricians and they represented the noble families while the Plebeians represented the rich and the middle class. In most cases, these two groups often mingled and voted differently or as parties on issues that were considered relevant to the groups they represented. After the fall of Rome, (AD476) the people of Europe had no tangible voice in politics. In this way, there were no true political parties and only groups or factions that supported one noble family or the other. It can be concluded that political parties developed as representative assembly gained power and eventually this change started in England after Popish plot of 1678.

Origin of Political Parties in Britain.

There has been a lot of debates regarding when political parties came into existence in England whether it was during the period of exclusion crisis 1679-1681 or when the terms Whig and Tory were first used as party labels or not until after the glorious revolution 1688-1689 or over the types of the relationship that existed between the court and countries identities and partisan political loyalties. However, the period of Exclusion Crisis in England is usually considered the time political parties came into existence and the struggle between the Whigs who wanted total exclusion of the Catholic heir James II (ruled 1685-1688) from succession on the grounds of his religion and the Tories championed divine right monarchy. In this regard, some believed that the first Whigs were truly a party while Tories were not. Some were of the opinion that neither grouping was a true party because they lacked universally recognisable leader and ideological coherence.

It should be noted that the difference between Whigs and Tories in the 16th century was their view of what government should do and how strong it should be. The Tories favoured and wanted rule by a strong king, while the Whigs wanted ordinary people to have access to the control of the government. As events unfold, the parliament had greater control and both the Whigs and Tories eventually emerged into organised political parties.

It is against this backdrop of the various theories of political parties' evolution that this work is examining the history of the political parties in the USA and Great Britain to situate them within the various theoretical framework.

Origin of Political Parties in the United States

The first political parties emerged in United States during the period of the country's first president, George Washington. The parties were the Federalist and the Democratic-Republicans. The Federalist Party was created by the Alexandra and Haniton, Secretary of the Treasury in the administration of George Washington. The anti-federalist were then in the opposition and it was organised by Congress men James Madison and Thomas Jefferson.

In the history of United States, there have been two main political parties namely the Federalist and the anti-federalist and the two parties have metamorphosed into what we know as Democrats and Republicans. There is absolute freedom to create new political parties and the newly created parties focus on specific issues even though they lack the capability to win national election. This is because voters believe their votes will count only when they use it to elect a candidate from one or the two major political parties. The Federalists strongly believe in central government backed by the constitution, they equally supported industrialisation, national bank, government aids to build roads, canals, etc. While the opposition or the anti-federalist held opposite views and they supported the right of the state.

In 1854, the anti–slavery forces and free-soil forces formed the republican parties. The Republican presented their first candidate, John C. Fremont in 1856. There were four major parties in 1860 and the voters had a wide choice. These parties were - Northern Democrat, Southern Democrat, Republican and the Constitutional - Union party that draw some ex-Whigs. The great anti-slavery emotions favoured the Republican to capture the presidency for Abraham Lincoln. However, in 1861 the Southern state separated, and it resulted into the civil war. The United States has a two - party system and nothing in the constitution stipulates two parties. The Democrats and the Republicans have alternated power before the civil war simply because they presented candidates and policies that appeal to the American while the minor political parties focus on specific issues and ideas. In some cases, they draw substantial support that affect the outcome of elections.

The Spread of Political Parties to other Nations

The Emergence of Political Parties in Africa

As we have seen, the development of political parties worldwide has its roots in the desire of citizens to participate more fully in their political systems and have leaders whose power derives from the will of the people. The underlying issue has been what makes a regime and its leaders legitimate. In Africa, the development of political parties was a revolutionary process based on excluded groups. As in Europe, the essential issue was the legitimacy of the rulers, but in Africa the rulers were foreign colonialists, and the excluded groups which consist of the whole African population. Racism played a key role, as the colonialists used pseudo-scientific theories of racial superiority to argue that Africans were incapable of self-government. Political parties in colonial Africa therefore began as nationalist movements whose ultimate aim was to restore 'the sovereignty of the indigenous people. They generally started out as small groups trying to open up opportunities for indigenous political participation and to resist specific instances of colonial racism and exploitation. However, when the colonial administrations refused to make reforms, these groups became more and more radical and populist. They broadened their support among the people and gradually developed into mass movements and eventually into fully-fledged political parties. Most of these nationalist parties were centered on strong personalities who were pioneers in the struggle for freedom and founders of their parties. In many cases, these individuals had also served long sentences in colonial jails and had become embodiments of the freedom struggle. Notable examples include Kenya"sJomo Kenyatta, Algeria"s Ahmed „ Ben Bella, Kwame Nkrumah of Ghana, and South Africa"s Nelson Mandela. Note well that, the formation of parties around strong personalities is not a new phenomenon nor is it peculiar to African independence movements. In Europe, some of the oldest parties, including the Conservative and Liberal parties in Britain, were founded and dominated in their early years by outstanding personalities such as Robert Walpole and William Pitt. Even during the modern period, a strong party leader like Margaret Thatcher has sometimes been able to dictate a party's policies and approaches. In the United States, the Democratic and Republican parties have often been dominated by strong willed leaders such as Thomas Jefferson and Abraham Lincoln and, more recently, Bill Clinton and Newt Gingrich. This phenomenon is often repeated in emerging democracies, where political movements and parties, especially new ones, tend to be centered on an influential personality, often the leader of a particular community. This is not necessarily detrimental either to the development of democracy or the development of the party. Indeed, in many cases, the opposite is true. On the other hand, the phenomenon has risks, especially in countries where society is unstable due to mass poverty or tribal and regional tensions. Another important feature of anti-colonialist nationalist movement, both in Africa and other regions, was their internal fragility. To pursue a credible nationalist agenda, these movements had to become genuine mass movements. This meant uniting diverse social elements into an effective political force. In most cases, these movements held together during the pre-independence period as a result of a common dedication to the goal of national independence. However, among both the leadership and the grassroots, there were conflicting interests which were submerged for the sake of the common struggle. At independence, most African countries had multiparty political systems as a result of a deliberate colonial policy to bequeath political systems to their former colonies which resembled as closely as possible the system in the mother country. However, after independence, these structures were quickly dismantled, giving way to one-party system. African leaders sought to justify the imposition of one-party rule on many grounds. For example, Julius Nyerere of Tanzania argued as follows: Where there is one party, and that party is identified with the nation as a whole, the foundations of democracy are firmer than they can ever be where you have two or more parties each representing only a section of the community. The argument here is that a two-party system can be justified only when the two parties are divided over some fundamental issue. Otherwise, it merely encourages factionalism (Nyerere, 1962). In effect, Nyerere was putting the case that under the conditions existing in Africa – dominated by imperialism - an "African democracy" could only be created under a unifying single party system. Re-echoing the same sentiments, Mugabe of Zimbabwe had this to say: We feel that a multiparty state is an oddity. It is a strange phenomenon to us, and we say this in all genuineness. We feel that it makes unnecessary division in Kenyas society that Kenyas own traditional style of oneness - we are a family, under one chief with various headmen under him and if we can use this concept to create one political society, allowing for expression of opinions of various kinds, that would be better than a multiparty state and its divisional nature (The Herald, December 31, 1986) Like Nyerere, Mugabe is oversimplifying the African situation to justify his political standpoint. The traditional Zimbabwe which he advances as his model did not have a single chief before colonialism, and the social Organisation was not similar in all communities. The argument that single-party rule has its roots in African tradition is difficult to sustain. Not only were political institutions in Africa very varied and full of internal contradictions themselves, many were destroyed under colonialism and new ones created to make it easier to rule the continent. Even if the one-party system is capable of providing democratic governance in theory, the African experience over almost thirty years has been to the contrary. In almost every case, the one-party state degenerated into one-man rule. Divergent political opinions were ruthlessly oppressed. Political dissidents were harassed or thrown into jails. This was true of Kenya, Malawi, Zimbabwe, Zambia, Ghana, and Nigeria, to mention only a few. Ironically, this intolerance then gave impetus to new movements clamouring for broader-based political participation and genuine competition. The ultimate result has been the transformation of previously single-party states into multiparty ones in most parts of Africa over the past decade. In the next section, we discuss the historical development of political parties in Kenya. Focus will be on the salient trends and features of the colonial era (when African participation in governance was officially repressed), the nationalist movements of the 50s and 60s, the single party era of KANU monopoly in the first three decades of independence, and the rebuilding of political pluralism since 1991.

It was not too long that other countries that are electoral democracies copied the idea of political parties. Political parties had spread to eastern European State; an autocratic state like Egypt has the National Democratic Party and Zimbabwe African National Union - Patriotic Front, etc. In West Africa, political parties developed as a result of self- improvement associations with the sole aim of influencing colonial government to grant independence to various countries. The National Congress of British West Africa (NCBWA) was formed in Accra, then Gold Coast now Ghana in the early 1920s by Joseph Casely Harford and Dr. Akinbade Savage of Nigeria. The main demand of this body was granting elective principle to various countries. They sent a delegation to London to meet the Secretary of State, Lord Milner. The request was turned down and they came back home with disappointment but the Clifford Constitution of 1922 granted elective principle to the legislative council of Nigeria which was subsequently approved by the new British Secretary of State for colonies Winston Churchill. This gave Nigeria the unique opportunity to adopt the elective principle in 1922. The Clifford Constitution of 1922 created conducive atmosphere for the formation of political parties. Herbert Macaulay seized this opportunity and he formed the Nigeria National Democratic Party in 1923. He was regarded as the father of Nigerian nationalism.

It is however clear that modern political party in Africa is generally off-shoot of parties formed during colonial regimes. One interesting thing about the formation of political party is that beside the original aim of some office holders to maintain their jobs, it has served unification function that binds members of similar views together which Shively calls "miracle glue."

Chapter Three

General characteristics of Political Parties.

In every country, there are various types of political parties within various ideologies and they want somehow to enter into government. They have national interests and a definite goal that may be favorable or not for country. Basically, Political Party is a group of persons organized to acquire and exercise political power.

Also, political party is defined as an organized group of people with at least roughly similar political aims and opinions, that seek to influence public policy by getting its candidates elected to public office.

Besides, A political party is a group of people who come together to contest elections and hold power in the government. The party agrees on some proposed policies and programs, with a view to promoting the collective good or furthering their supporters' interests.

Sigmund Neumann (1969, p. 5), surmise that 'political party' generally as the articulate organization of society's active political agents, those who are concerned with the control of governmental power and who compete for popular support with another group or groups holding divergent views. As such, it is the great intermediary which links social forces and ideologies to official governmental institutions and relate them to political action within the larger political community.

In the words of David Apter, (1969, p. 86), There are good reasons why political parties are so hard to define. Their genesis is difficult to disentangle from the evolution of the modern society and state; the role of a party often changes substantially as political conditions in a country change (particularly in modernizing societies, where various political developments may bring about an elaborate and complex polity from a rudimentary one) ; and in developing countries, a peculiar relationship exists between state and society-they are linked together by party solidarity. It is this last aspect more than any other that establishes the general basis of agreement on the rules of the polity.

In many countries, they now routinely serve as key transmission channels for organizing representation, helping to translate popular demands into legislative initiatives, and acting as gatekeepers which determine which candidates have a chance of being elected. They often serve as vehicles for popular mobilization, and as actors with the capacity to selectively distribute resources and professional expertise; they can leverage all these assets to help politicians obtain and retain electoral offices.

According to MacIver, "A political party is an association organized in support of some principle or policy which by constitutional means it endeavors to make the determinant of government."

Moreover, a political party consists of a group of like-minded people who work together as a unit to influence the general public, contest elections to gain control over the government. Members of the same political party share a common goal, aims and objectives. Different political parties compete with each other with view to influence the public policies and opinion with their philosophies, ideals, and objectives.

A political party operates and seeks political power through constitutional means to translate its policies into practice. It is a body of like-minded people and a means to translate its policies into practice. Also, It is a body of like-minded people having similar views on matters of public concern.

Political Parties are characterized by:

1. To attain power: It is the main objective of all political parties. They compete with each other for the same; there is nothing wrong with objective of gaining power as long as the competition is fair.

2. To pursue an ideology: A party's stand on certain social issues define its ideology. In modern times, most political parties have similar ideologies which make it difficult for the common voter to decide whom to support.

3. To have a common agenda: On basis of their ideologies, parties prepare their agenda. They aim to garner public support for their agenda in other to win elections and implement them.

4. To establish a government: The political party which gets majority of votes in the elections forms the government; the parties with lesser votes form the opposition.

5. To act as a link between people & the government: Political parties are the connecting link between people and the government. They communicate the demands and the complaints of the people to the elected leaders and on the other hand, the government tries to get support of the people for its policies and programmes through the channel of political parties.

Parties and political power

Whether they are conservative or revolutionary, whether they are a union of notables or an organization of the masses, whether they function in a pluralistic democracy or in a monolithic dictatorship, parties have one function in common: they all participate to some extent in the exercise of political power, whether by forming a government or by exercising the function of opposition, a function that is often of crucial importance in the determination of national policy.

The struggle for power

It is possible in theory to distinguish revolutionary parties, which attempt to gain power by violence (conspiracies, guerrilla warfare, etc.), from those parties working within the legal framework of elections. But the distinction is not always easy to make, because the same parties may sometimes make use of both procedures, either simultaneously or successively, depending upon the circumstances. In the 1920s, for example, communist parties sought power through elections at the same time that they were developing an underground activity of a revolutionary nature. In the 19th century, liberal parties were in the same situation, sometimes employing the techniques of conspiracy, as in Italy, Austria, Germany, Poland, and Russia, and sometimes confining their struggles to the ballot box, as in Great Britain and France.

Revolutionary methods vary greatly, clandestine plots by which minority groups seize the centre of power presuppose monarchies or dictatorships in which the masses of people have little say in government. But terrorist and disruptive activity can serve to mobilize citizens and to demonstrate the powerlessness of any government. At the beginning of the 20th century, leftist trade unionists extolled the revolutionary general strike, a total stoppage of all economic activity that would paralyze society completely and put the government at the revolutionaries' mercy. Also, rural guerrilla activity has often been used in countries with a predominantly agrarian society; urban guerrilla warfare was effective in the European revolutions of the 19th century, but the development of techniques of police and military control has made such activity more difficult.

The various processes of selecting candidates do not, however, differ significantly in their results, for it is almost always the party leaders who play the essential role. This introduces an oligarchical tendency into party politics, a tendency that has not been overcome by the congresses of the mass-based parties or the U.S. primaries, which provide only a partial limitation on the power of the governing committees.

Participation in power

Once a political party has achieved electoral victory, the question arises of how much influence the party is to have on the government. The influence of the party on members in elective office is frequently quite weak. It defines the general lines of their activity, but these lines can be quite hazy, and few decisions are taken in the periodic meetings between officeholders and their party. However, each member of the legislature retains personal freedom of action in his participation in debates, in his participation in government, and, especially, in his voting. The party may, of course, attempt to enforce the party line, but parliamentary or congressional members cannot be compelled to vote the way the party wants them to. Such is the situation in the United States, within most of the liberal and conservative European parties, and within cadre parties in general. The question of how disciplined a party is, of the extent to which it will always present a united front, enables a distinction to be made between what may be termed rigid and flexible parties that is, between those that attempt always to be united and disciplined, following what is most often an ideologically based party line, and those that, representing a broader range of interests and points of view, form legislatures that are assemblies of individuals rather than of parties. Whether the parties operating within a particular system will be rigid or flexible depends largely on the constitutional provisions that determine the circumstances in which a government may continue in office. This is clearly illustrated by comparing the situation in the United States with that in Great Britain.

Power and representation

It is difficult to envisage how representative democracy could function in a large industrialized society without political parties. In order for citizens to be able to make an intelligent choice of representative or president, it is necessary for them to know the real political orientation of each candidate. Party membership provides the clearest indication of this. The programs and promises of each individual candidate are not too significant or informative, because most candidates, in their attempt to gain the most votes, try to avoid difficult subjects; they all tend to speak the same language-that is, to camouflage their real opinions. The fact that one is a socialist, another a conservative, a third a liberal, and a fourth a communist provides a far better clue as to how the candidate will perform when in office. Democratic political systems, while performing the function of representation, thus rest more or less on the competition of rival oligarchies. But these oligarchies consist of political elites that are open to all with political ambition. No modern democracy could function without parties, the oligarchical tendencies of which are best regarded as a necessary evil.

Features of Political Parties

A political party must have certain features and characteristics that will differentiate it from pressure groups. As political associations develop, they metamorphose into political parties in today's politics. A political party should have clearly stated ideologies. An ideology may be defined "as an action-oriented system of ideas or beliefs that identifies the problems besetting the structures and process of a society, and the alternative programmes and strategies for establishing another system that will overcome the observed deficiencies" (Akeke Ayeni,

2008, p. 168). Note that all ideologies are expected to bring about positive social change to the present condition of the society and even in the future. Some ideologies aim towards changing structures and process of society into something new and better, while others aim at maintaining and preserving the ones on the ground.

Apart from ideology, political parties should aim at contesting elections in order to gain political power and subsequently govern the country. A political party is supposed to air their views on topical issues affecting the country. People who share similar political opinions, interest and beliefs normally come together because political parties are supposed to be associations of people of like-minded interests. It is normally said that birds of a feather, flock together. Political parties should be organized in such a way that everybody in the society will be aware of. In addition, they always employ persuasive techniques when they want to appeal to the electorates. Rather than using coercive means, they organize rallies, congresses and conventions as part of their normal duties.

Conclusion

Parties remain central to modem democracy and undertake a wide range of functions and any consideration of the health of parties must therefore evaluate systematically the panoply of activities that parties engage in, both cross-nationally and longitudinally. Our evidence-necessarily limited in time and coverage-shows that parties remain a crucial link between the citizen and the government. And while there has been a decline in some aspects of partisan politics, there is at least as much evidence of adaptation, as parties transform themselves in order to meet the challenges of ongoing political change.

Chapter Four

Functions of Political Parties

Having looked at the main features of political parties, let us now look at the functions they perform. In any society, political parties perform the function of interest articulation. They channel the interest of their members and encourage them to contest and win election and ultimately form government. Political parties harmonize interest of their members in the political process and make efforts to satisfy these various interests so that people would know the direction of voting.

Political parties also arouse interest of their members before and during election. In some way, they serve as a bridge or link that connects people with the government. They also educate the people about government policies and disseminate vital information to the members of the public. It must be noted that political parties mobilize public opinion in favor or against a particular policy of the government. They perform this function by means of mass rallies, flags uniform/vests, slogans and other symbols of unity in order to show the relationship between the people and the party, i.e., the spirit of togetherness.

In socialist states, political party is one of the important organs of mobilizing the people in favor of government policies. Whereas in liberal democratic states, parties that are not in support of government policies use the same method to mobilize the people against any policy (Akinbade, 2008, p. 199). It is an avenue for changing government. In a cabinet system of government, the party that wins the majority of votes is asked to form government and the party that fails to win forms the opposition. Besides, in the presidential system of government, the candidate that wins the highest number of votes in the general election is elected the president. A political party that wins in the general election seeks to implement policies and programmes stated in the manifestoes and generally provide national direction of the affairs of the country.

Closely related to the above stated function are the issues of political recruitment. It is a known fact that "no modern political system can function without the mobilization and deployment of highly qualified and dedicated individuals of various kinds of engineers, teachers, scientist, doctors, administrators and soldiers to operate the institutions of the state". (AyeniAkeke, 2008, p. 152). These professionals serve in the administrative cadre on merit.

Political parties help the electorate to actively participate in election. To achieve this, political parties educate the people about crucial issues relating to the political system. Parties may nominate candidates that have very good chances of winning election. They often do this by sponsoring candidates with money, campaign materials, etc. (AyeniAkeke, 2008, p. 131). "In sum, parties contribute immensely to the vitality and stability of governments, particularly in competitive, democratic political systems where parties alternate power" (Johari, 2008, p. 424). This enables the smooth transfer of political power from one party to the other in the electoral competition. Political representation is another major function. In view of the fact that modern states are generally too large in size, population and complex to Political parties also perform welfare, social and humanitarian functions like provision

29

of jobs for its members and building recreational centers. Some parties even establish business enterprises like hotels, newspapers and other business ventures in order to generate funds for the party. It must be emphasized that without political parties, conduct of elections would be tedious, rowdy and outrightly uninteresting.

In the contemporary world, democracy is unworkable without having any political parties. The functions of the parties have become a crucial factor in stabilizing the state. In modem and democratic societies, fighting to gain power usually is the perfect function of political parties. Mostly, political parties, present programmes that the society can decide to support or refuse. It is the party leaders and members who decide upon special policies and rules while sticking together and sharing their ideas, in addition to, taking suggestions from their society. The basic aim is to present these ideas to the government for the good of the citizens. The function of political parties can be classed under the following subheadings:

The governing function:
Without political parties, this multifaceted modem civilization would become unmanageable. Political parties make easier the creation of governments. They also give stability to the government; particularly if members of the authority belong to a party. Political parties usually collaborate between the two main areas of government the legislative body and the administrative. In all, parties provide a very important opposition and criticism, from within as well as out of government.

The electoral function:
Election in democratic societies is dependent on political parties. Political parties generally select candidates at elections. They offer funds and services for election campaigns. Recent electoral investigation has discovered that the common man has some problems in making the right selection in elections because complication of matters and the

diversity of choices confuse voters. For this reason, one of the strange functions of political parties is to make politics more reachable to citizens. Political parties need to organize the vote bank to get votes and also to protect the election of their candidate to parliament or other public office. On other hand, all political parties try to find ways to persuade voters that their candidates are more reliable than those of its rivals. They set up policies which the voter is required to support. Parties supply a tag with which the electorate can identify and take responsibility, since the voter is capable of holding them accountable for policy achievements or disappointments.

The representative function:
Political parties facilitate the formation of ideas of people to be understood and they guarantee issues of social concern in the political scheme. They are the main input mechanisms that guarantee the fulfilment of the needs and desires of the society. This kind of function is, one of the basic and essential functions of a party.

The policy, or goal setting, function:
While performing their representative functions, political parties try to create some policies. They are one of the agencies through which people of a country try to attain their joint goal. While doing this, political parties gather support of the common people and through this, they ultimately gain political power. This helps them, get into the parliamentary system of a specific state and there, they make and implement the policies they had promised the common masses. Political parties also introduce ideas and matters; they clear other goals for the society in ways that could improve the chances for selecting those values.

The recruitment and participation function:
In modem and democratic societies, most political campaigners are members of parties. In these countries, political parties perform the

main function of giving confidence to people to become political activists. They are in charge of supplying to the states their political principals. Leaders gain office because of their high profiles and participants in a presidential selection are generally political party leaders. In the parliamentary system the head of the majority in parliament usually becomes prime minister and other place of duty are generally filled by most important party members. Sometimes, political parties offer a training class for policy makers, and equip them with information and skills. Otherwise, in societies where political parties are powerless, power is generally in the hands of traditional leaders like that of military institutions or ruling families.

Ideological function of Political Parties
Ideology refers to a set of ideas that tries to link thought with action. That is, ideologies attempt to shape how people think—and therefore how they act. As we shall use the term, then, an ideology is a fairly coherent and comprehensive set of ideas that explains and evaluates social conditions, helps people understand their place in society, and provides a program for social and political action. An ideology, more precisely, performs four functions for people who hold it: (1) explanatory, (2) evaluative, (3) orientative, and (4) programmatic functions.

An ideology offers an explanation of why social, political, and economic conditions are as they are particularly, in times of crisis. At such times, people will search, sometimes frantically, for some explanation of what is happening. Why are there wars? Why do depressions occur? What causes unemployment? Why are some people rich and others poor? Why are relations between different races so often strained, difficult, or hostile? To these and many other questions, different ideologies supply different answers.

The second function of ideologies is to supply standards for evaluating social conditions. There is a difference, after all, between explaining why certain things are happening and deciding whether those things are good or bad. Are all wars evils to be avoided, or are some morally justifiable? Are depressions a normal part of the business cycle or a symptom of a sick economic system? Is full employment a reasonable ideal or a naïve pipe dream? Are vast disparities of wealth between rich and poor desirable or undesirable? Are racial tensions inevitable or avoidable? Again, an ideology supplies its followers with the criteria required for answering these and other questions.

An ideology supplies its adherent with an orientation and a sense of identity of who he or she is, the group (race, nation, sex, and so on) to which he or she belongs, and how he or she is related to the rest of the world. Just as hikers and travelers use maps, compasses, and landmarks to find their way in unfamiliar territory, so people need something to find their social identity and location. Like a compass, ideologies help people orient themselves to gain a sense of where they are, who they are, and how they fit into a complicated world.

An ideology, finally, tells its followers what to do and how to do it. It performs a programmatic or prescriptive function by setting out a general program of social and political action. Just as doctors prescribe medicine for their patients and fitness trainers provide a program of exercise for their clients, so political ideologies prescribe remedies for sick societies and treatments designed to keep the healthy ones in good health. If an ideology provides a diagnosis of social conditions that leads you to believe that conditions are bad and growing worse, it will not be likely to win your support unless it can also supply a prescription or program for action that seems likely to improve matters. This is exactly what ideologies try to do.

Political ideologies perform these four functions because they are trying to link thought-ideas and beliefs to action. Every ideology provides a vision of the social and political world not only as it is, but as it should be, in hopes of inspiring people to act either to change or to preserve their way of life. If it does not do this if it does not perform all four functions—it is not a political ideology. In this way our functional definition helps to sharpen our picture of what an ideology is by showing us what it is and is not.

A political party's ideology is a set of principles that lead to a certain set of policies, sometimes called the party "platform." The ideology and the policies that flow from its ideology are put down in writing in a party manifesto (or blueprint or action plan). This manifesto is a statement of the goals and principles the party promises to pursue if voted into power. As a contract with voters, the manifesto spells out the party's perception of the country's problems and states how the party proposes to address problems and help achieve the collective aspirations of the nation if elected. The manifesto sets out the measures which the party proposes to take in order to improve public services such as health, education, and transportation, promote national development issues such as trade, industrialization, employment, and address public concerns in areas such as technology, the environment, and crime. However, for a responsible and effective political party, it is not enough to propose policies. A credible party manifesto must also justify the party's plans, prove its commitment to them and persuade the public that these plans are feasible. Political parties that have had Previous experience in government can do this by spelling out their achievements and accounting for their failures. However, a party's abilities and the efficacy of its policies can only be fully tested when it forms the government-and attempts to implement its programme.

Membership Base

Another essential characteristic of a political party is the membership base. Generally, political parties try to build as large and broad-based a membership as possible. The larger the membership base - and the more varied in terms of age, gender, education, occupation, social class, ethnicity, region, and so on - the more credibility the party will have and the more successful it is likely to be in winning elections. In addition, the membership base is vital for the internal functioning of a political party. A political party recruits' people who are committed to its ideology and principles and who will be able to participate in party governance, policy formulation, and campaigning. From among these members, the party leaders are elected. The membership base is therefore vital to the future of a political party. The membership base of a political party is also an important aspect of citizens" participation in national politics. People who join political parties are usually more politically aware and activist than the average citizen. By joining a political party, members of the public achieve a higher level of political participation than those who merely vote. Therefore, the level of membership in political parties among the voting population of a country is an important indicator of the political maturity of the people. Members of parties are able to shape the ideology and policies of their parties. They can demand more accountability from their leaders and even become party leaders themselves. As party leaders, they have a better chance of being nominated as candidates in national elections and therefore of participating directly in policy making and governance. In other words, political parties make a contribution to the overall development of responsible citizenship by building their membership base. However, regardless of the nature or breadth of the membership base of a political party, the ultimate responsibility of the party should be to the nation as a whole. A truly national political party is interested in the welfare of the nation, not the welfare of its own members or supporters only. Otherwise, it is really only a political faction whose aim is to advance the restricted interests of its members whether or not such interests promote the common good.

Another Significant characteristic of Political Parties in democratic societies is orderly competition for power. Parties offer ideologies and programmes that the public can choose whether to support or not.

Party members and their leaders have certain common aspirations, principles, and policies, and they join together in a political party mainly in order to sell their ideas to their fellow citizens. The ultimate goal is to put these ideas into practice in government for the good of the nation. Parties field candidates in elections so that the aspirations, principles, and policies of the party can be implemented through government programmes.

Political Parties and Governance
It is important to emphasize that whether or not they win control of the government, political parties participate in governance. There are two ways political parties participate in governance either directly as the party in power or indirectly as the opposition. The government, of course, is constituted only by the party or parties that control a majority of seats in the legislature, but the losing parties still play - or should play a vital role in the overall governance of the nation. When elected to participate directly in government, party leaders are expected to promote their party's ideology and carry out its legislative agenda. They do so by taking the appropriate actions according to the constitution of their country, such as appointing officials, setting up commissions and task forces, and drafting and passing laws. Also, being in government is a political party's opportunity to implement its programmes. In some cases, such as coalition governments, a political party will support policies of other parties if these ensure that some of its own goals are achieved. When political parties fail to be elected to form the government, they form the opposition. The role of the opposition is to criticize government policy and prevent abuse of power. This role is essential for ensuring good governance, minimizing mistakes and corruption, and protecting the rights of citizens. Without an effective opposition, there is no ongoing check on the power of the government. On the other hand, an active, vigilant opposition keeps the government "on its toes" and not only prevent abuses from arising but also encourages more efficient policy making

and implementation. The key to both good government and effective opposition is free competition for power. This requires a constitutional and administrative framework that enables competing political parties to freely market their ideas and policies to the people. It is this framework that distinguishes competitive, democratic political systems from non-competitive ones: In noncompetitive political systems, the only party in the country places and maintains people to be in control of government machinery without any formal competition from any other quarters. In other system however, each party seeking to gain power must compete for popular support with another group or groups holding divergent views (Newman, 1956). However, for political parties to participate effectively in competitive politics they also need the internal capacity to bring their ideas and project public attention and influence public opinion. At election time in particular, they require the machinery, infrastructure, skills, and resources to campaign throughout the country and make good use of whatever instruments available. Therefore, political parties are also channels of communication which circulate political ideas, principles, and policy options among their members and entire society. As such, they perform a vital educational role in the maintenance and development of democracy in a country. However, if political parties distort their messages, mislead the public, or incite ethnic or racial animosity in order to influence public opinion, they undermine democracy.

Chapter Five

Political Paties Organisational Structures.

A political party may be guided in its structure and functioning by external regulations, such as the Constitution or laws and regulations, by internal party rules, for example, the Party Constitution, or by both. Practice, however, may differ from written Party Constitutions or internal rules. Given that political parties perform such important tasks in democracies today, their internal functioning becomes very important. Aspects of this include the policy-formulation and general decision-making process of the political party, the involvement of members and party groups, and the accountability of the party leadership.

National leadership committee - The National Executive Body
This is usually the "party government" making and implementing decisions on a day-to-day basis. The decision as to who is to be a member in this body determines much of the party functioning. The composition of the national executive body varies between political parties: sometimes just a few party leaders form the leadership, while in other cases, representatives of party wings, such as the women's wing, members of local branches, or auxiliary groups are represented in the leadership committee. How members of this committee are appointed differs between political parties and countries: some parties

hold elections for leadership committees where for instance delegates from the party organizations, such as regional and local groups, are entitled to vote, while others do not. When elections are held, quotas for women or ethnic minority groups may be applied. There is also a difference between countries and parties as to whether the members of the national executive body are paid by the political party or not. This may have a great influence on the professionalism, responsibilities, and dedication of the leadership committee.

National Conference, Congress, or Convention

The National Congress is usually the highest decision-making body of the party and meets one to five times a year. Attendance at the conference may include delegates from regional and local branches, auxiliary groups, the women's wing, and the youth wing of the party, if any. Ordinary members may also be welcomed. Sometimes, Congress resolutions are binding upon the party leadership, while in other cases they are just suggestions or guidelines.

State party organization

Political parties prepare for statewide elections. Party activists are named as electors in the Electoral College if their party carries the state in a presidential election. Candidates for state office may be chosen through a primary election, state convention, or caucus process. At a state caucus, party members select their candidates. However, in many states, the executive officials - governor, lieutenant governor, treasurer, and attorney general - are elected as individuals. Although the party's slate, its candidates for office, is listed on the ballot, voters can vote for any candidate they want. In such states, it is not unusual for voters to elect a Democratic governor and a Republican lieutenant governor or vice versa.

Local and regional party branches

Most political parties try to have local and regional party branches, sometimes in up to five layers below the national level. Internal party rules determine who is in control of the decision-making process – the national level or the local levels of the party. Local and regional party branches can be more or less independent from the national party organization in leadership, budget, and campaigning. The local levels often play important roles in connecting with the electorate, nominating candidates, and carrying out local election campaigns.

Auxiliary groups
Youth wings and women's wings are the most common auxiliary groups in political parties all over the world. They are usually part of the party organization and lobby the party leadership on issues of specific concern to their members. The independence of the auxiliary groups differs in terms of rights to have their own membership registers and budgets and to make independent decisions. Auxiliary groups often have the right to send their own delegates to National Conventions and are sometimes even represented on the National Executive Committee. The degree of internal fractionalization in the political party denotes how heterogeneous the internal party structure is. In some political parties, distinct factions are independently organized and they elect their own leadership.

Affiliated groups
Affiliated groups are usually not formally part of the party organization but constitute independent organizations with strong links to the party. Trade unions or employer's organizations are typical examples of affiliated groups. At times, membership in the affiliated group automatically gives membership in the political party, and even if large and regular donations between them are common, the organizations' budgets are separate.

State Regulation of Political Parties
The Constitution of a country and a number of relevant laws and by-laws, such as those regulating political parties and elections,

provide the legal framework for the operation of political parties. Relevant constitutional provisions would normally provide a definition of a political party and prescribe a multi-party system and protect the usual list of civil and political rights without which elections cannot be free and democracy cannot be true. Party leaders and activists ought to know and seek to improve these laws and regulations. Although the behaviour of parties in the party system is of far greater consequence to the performance of the party system than the legal framework, we have to acknowledge that such behaviour is influenced, constrained or encouraged as the case may be, by the law and by the structures that the law creates or heavily influences. The electoral system demonstrates its significance both directly, through strategic alliances and strategic voting that the electoral system may encourage, and indirectly, through the number of parties that it helps to spawn. Some analysts view parties as elite-owned instruments for seeking and maintaining political power but this may not necessarily always be correct. In a democracy, parties are not personalized, and limited to serving only the interests of the elite. Rather, they have structures, rules, procedures, norms and principles. Also, they are institutionalized coalitions, not just for elites but for the mass of members as well.

Their formal machinery or structures are found at all levels of political activity- national, regional, district, constituency, ward, and indeed all the way down to the grassroots. They operate within specified legal frameworks that define their membership, composition, roles and functions, financial base, and operational rules and discipline. Two of the many ways that states regulate political parties are by establishing requirements necessary to create a new political party and dictating party processes. A primary way individual associate to advance their political goals is by creating a new political party. Although third parties challenge the political mainstream and could be viewed as contrary to the state's interests in political stability, citizens have a federal constitutional right to create and develop them. Depending on the state, a group may be required to demonstrate it is a bona fide political party with a local and state party structure before it is permitted to run a candidate under a political party label. States may also require the party to hold party conventions or meetings and demonstrate the public's support of the party. In general, once political parties are established, states may not regulate their internal structure, governance, or policymaking. However, if a state can posit a relationship between its regulations and "fair and honest" elections, a state may usually

(1) Enact laws that set voter eligibility requirements, including eligibility to participate in a primary election,

(2) Require that candidates be citizens, and

(3) Specify whether the party must use a primary election or nominating convention to select its general election candidates.

States may generally regulate these areas even though the party might prefer to make other choices. When the state-required selection process for a party nominee conflict with national party guidelines, the latter prevail, at least when the selection of the party's electors to its presidential nominating convention is at stake. For example, states cannot require political parties to select their presidential electors in an open primary, which allows non-party members to vote, when the national party rules limited participation to party members only. In addition, states may not tell a political party which individuals will serve as its delegates to the party's presidential nominating convention. Addressing the distinction between internal party rules and external state regulation of parties, Richard Katz cites (Janda, 2000, p. 3) and notes three objectives of state law concerning political parties:

(a). To determine what constitutes a political party. This determination often spawns additional party laws: who qualifies for ballot access, who benefits from public resources (such as subsidies or broadcast media), who participates in the government and how, and so on.

(b). To regulate the form of activity in which parties may engage. This umbrella heading covers the raising and spending of funds, campaign activities, issue stands in party platforms or manifestos, and more.

(c). To ensure appropriate forms of party organization and behavior. This is held to be the most controversial objective, because it intruded into internal issues of party leadership and social relationships. Laws could require parties to elect officers by party members, but a party might prefer to choose them through a party congress. Laws might also demand gender or ethnic equality or require maintaining party organizations in various national regions. One can imagine other policy goals that nations seek to implement through party law.

Nassmacher, (2001, p.32) discusses three broad strategic options relating to the regulation of party finance

(a) the autonomy option, which emphasizes the freedom and privacy of political parties, minimizing the need for regulation and relying largely on self-regulation and the self- correcting mechanisms of party competition.

(b) the transparency option, which highlights the disclosure of information on party finance to enable the individual voter to assume his or her responsibilities and prerogatives and make an informed choice on election day; and

(c) the advocacy option, which foresees a set of detailed regulations on party finance, monitored and enforced by an independent agency. A combination of the three is possible and indeed desirable.

43

Nassmacher (2001, p.) also puts forward the diversified regulation option which combines "benign neglect, precise regulation, public incentives and occasional sanctions". It is clear that no one model of regulation can fit all circumstances. Every country will need to develop its system according to its political values and culture, its political and electoral system, the stage of development of its democracy, its institutional capacity and so on. There will undoubtedly be a mixture of motives and tools. However, the issue of political finance can scarcely be treated in isolation, since it reflects more broadly on the role and regulation of political parties in general and on the potential for reform and development of the party system as an essential component of sustainable democracy.

In Nigeria, political parties are formed and operated mostly by those Nigerians who possess or have access to the enormous funds required to comply with the guidelines. This in turn leads to the creation of political parties based mostly on alliances of convenience between wealthy political entrepreneurs" rather than political parties based on "ideology" or political platforms. Parties and candidates finance their activities and campaigns from funds provided by party bosses and political entrepreneurs in absolute secrecy.

The Nigerian public has no information as to which entrepreneur has provided funds to any political party or candidate. This type of politics contributes to a lack of accountable governance because political leaders are primarily beholden to the party financiers and their electoral machines rather than the electorate. The cumulative result is distortions in Nigeria's democratic development. Bearing in mind that the contribution of political parties to democracy "gets increasingly important as the process evolves and is especially central to successful consolidation", all hope is not lost in making political parties in Nigeria stand the test of time and work on the pedestal of democratic consolidation. The question is, how do we achieve this significant milestone in Nigeria's democracy where the political parties as pillars of democratic sustenance are either not adequately financed or formed primarily in order to get funds from the government, or dubiously financed and hijacked by political entrepreneurs? Although some of these political parties are strong and could survive even without dependence on financial grants from the government because of the contributions from their members, corporate organizations and other groups, they still manifest some worrisome value orientations. One of such orientations is the dominance of "political entrepreneurs" or in Nigerian parlance "money bags" or "god fathers" Furthermore, as some political parties could not stand on their feet without government's financial grant, they become weak and incapacitated in developing new structures outside their local bases. Still others are financially weak to the extent that they become moribund for a long period after the general elections, until another round of elections when they revive their activities.

As we said earlier, parties are usually required by law to have certain organizational structures, such as a constitution, particular officers, and a network of local branches. The specific legal requirements vary from country to country, and different political parties have different organizational structures within the law. The underlying purpose of the organizational structure of any political party is to enable the party to develop popular policies, broaden its support, and campaign effectively in elections. Therefore, political parties require an organizational structure, which leaders and members can use to run the party, choose their leaders and officers, and determine party policies. Usually, this organizational structure is defined in the party constitution. Like other types of constitutions, the constitution of a political party is the party's "basic law." It sets out the principles and operating procedures of the party, specifies the rights and responsibilities of members and officers, and lays down the rules for the internal governance of the party. The ultimate aim of a party constitution is to provide a democratic structure and ensure that this structure is observed in practice. The constitution should therefore be very clear about the party's leadership structures, the rights and powers of the leaders and members, and the nomination and election procedures. It is pertinent to note that democracy, within a political party, can be achieved in various ways. It is therefore up to each political party to decide exactly how it should govern itself. However, the basic principles of democracy - transparency, accountability, and popular decision making by the people, or in this case by the members must be observed. Therefore, the constitution of a political party should be in harmony with the interests of the members in particular. It should ensure that the members are the ones who ultimately choose the party's policies and leadership. A political party should be more than a vehicle for the political ambitions of its leaders. It should be a vehicle for citizens sharing a common political agenda in which the members, not the leaders, are the foundation and the reason for the party's existence. In addition to being democratic, a party's organizational structure also needs to be effective. A political party is much more than a "talking shop." Its mission is action-oriented: to develop policies, sell them to the electorate, and win power in elections. Therefore, its organizational structure has to be efficient in terms of day-to- day management and forward planning (the next party conference, the next election). At the same time, it also has to ensure that party leaders are aware of the views, needs, and problems of the party membership and the entire country. This is normally accomplished through a party branch network that enables grassroots members to be represented in decision- making processes.

In the USA, In the late 19th century through a good part of the 20th century, political machines flourished in several large cities; Tammany Hall in New York, Frank Hague in Jersey City, the Pendergast family in Kansas City, and Richard Daley in Chicago are examples. The political bosses, the mayors, and the party leaders used their control of patronage jobs to reward party loyalty and provide a broad range of social services. Reforms in the civil service and the growth of primary elections gradually brought an end to machine politics. Political parties prepare for statewide elections. Party activists are named as electors in the Electoral College if their party carries the state in a presidential election. Candidates for state office may be chosen through a primary election, state convention, or caucus process. At a state caucus, party members select their candidates. In many states, the executive officials-governor, lieutenant governor, treasurer, and attorney general are elected as individuals. Although the party's slate, its candidates for office, is listed on the ballot, voters can vote for any candidate their choice. In such states, it is not unusual for voters to elect a Democratic governor and a Republican lieutenant governor or vice versa. At the national level, political parties run candidates for Congress and the presidency. Each party has its own national committee made up of party leaders, elected officials, and the chairs of the state party organizations. The chair of the national committee is chosen by the party's candidate for president. The Democratic and Republican national committees do not run the campaigns of their respective presidential candidates; they play a supporting role to the campaign organizations of the candidates themselves. In both the Senate and the House, each party has its own congressional campaign committee, which raises money for congressional elections. The national committee loosely runs the party between national conventions. As noted earlier, a party's choices for president and vice president are nominated at the national convention. The delegates to the convention are already committed to vote for particular candidates based on the results of the state primary or caucus voting. While some delegates are appointed by the state party organization, the overwhelming majority are selected through primaries and caucuses. A party's nominee is often determined months before the convention, which makes the choice official. The party works on and announces its platform at the national convention. The platform is made up of planks that explain how the party stands on the issues facing the country. The terms platform and plank date from the presidential election of 1832, when national party conventions were first held. Developing the platform is often the most controversial part of the convention. The Republicans, for example, have had to work out an acceptable compromise on abortion between pro-choice and pro-life forces within the party.

The East African Political Experience (Contemporary political party systems)

Just like most other African countries, Uganda, Tanzania and Kenya can be classified under the new post "third wave" democracies. The tag "democratic" however needs to be qualified as referring to countries that have undergone transitions into multiparty political systems and hold regular elections. These East African countries however exhibit significant variations in their political party systems.

Uganda and Tanzania can be described as one-dominant-party systems where both CCM and NRM have enjoyed electoral victories and prolonged periods in power. Neither party has been voted out of office since their inception. Kenya on the other hand, has a two dominant party system since the 2002 elections. The party-political environment was then dominated by KANU and the National Rainbow Coalition s(NARC) which dethroned KANU from almost 40 years of uninterrupted rule. The NARC coalition was however to disintegrate two years later and by the 2007 election, another coalition configuration had emerged pitting the Orange Democratic Movement (ODM) against the Party of National Unity (PNU). After the disputed 2007 general election, the two parties formed a coalition government leaving virtually no opposition except for the United Democratic Movement (UDM) with only one member in the parliament.

Uganda has six political parties represented in the country's parliament, Tanzania has five and Kenya has no less than twenty-three (23) almost all under either the PNU or ODM umbrella parties. While Kenya has held competitive multiparty elections since 1992 and Tanzania since 1995, Uganda has only had one in 2006. Its pluralist politcs is therefore still infantile and can be described as a dominant authoritarian party system. Whereas political parties form the mainstay of political organisation and representation, the level of institutionalisation of political parties as instruments of contesting for and attaining political power is still relatively weak. In such circumstances, dominant party systems have a negative effect on competitive politics.

In Uganda for instance, opposition political parties operate under severe constraints imposed by President Museveni and his authoritarian government (Chege, 2007). The lack of institutionalised structures within political parties gave rise to the development of personality cult in politics. Makerere university political scientist Dr. SsaliSimba argues that for instance, president Museveni does not even respect the party he has created by virtue of the fact that during the 2006 elections, he set up parallel structures for his campaigns, ran by close associates from the military. It is these parallel structures, other than the civilian party taskforce that are credited with ensuring his victory in the elections.

Similarly, President Kibaki in Kenya abandoned his sponsoring party NARC and set up a new political party the PNU just three months before the 2007 December general elections. His campaign secretariat was run by professionals drawn from the private sector while politicians associated with his coalition partner parties were shunned leading to numerous complaints, discord and disorganisation. This portrays a system where political elites have scant respect for political parties and only see their value as convenient tools for contesting elections and can be discarded once they have served their purpose. Political parties therefore tend to be dormant after elections only to be revived at the next cycle (Chege 2007, p. 25).

Dominant party systems also pose a challenge to democracy in general and may lead to less intra-party democracy since they dominate the legislature and monopolise the law-making process to promote their interests. In most cases, parliament loses its sovereignty as an independent arm of government; it simply exists to rubberstamp and legitimise decisions by the Central Committee of the ruling party. This scenario is made worse in simple majority or First-Past-The-Post electoral systems that prevail in all three East African countries. In a situation where the vote is divided between numerous parties, it is possible that a party can form government with a minority of the vote. This was the case in Kenya after the 1997 elections in which KANU formed the government with less than 36% of the total votes cast. A proportional representation system would therefore help to redress some of these short comings.

Governments formed by dominant party systems can be less accountable to the legislature and the wider electorate while the opposition is too weak to hold it to account. Party technocrats in Uganda such as DP"'s DeoNjoki and UPC"'s Chris Opoka-Okumu argue that the greatest need is to rebuild political parties along sound ideals and principles, to give its new following a clear world view and direction by entrenching these in clear and relevant ideologies and party programmes as well as building strong structures of inclusion and effective representation. Jimmy Akena, a leading UPC Member of Parliament and son of Uganda's first president Milton Obote stresses the need for a major shift in the social consciousness of Ugandan civil and political classes to truly embrace a multiparty democracy. What he argues for Uganda could apply to the rest of the countries in the region that it will take time and hard work to build a truly democratic pluralist political culture in a society that has been without functioning political parties for more than 20 years.

Political party systems: Legislation and institutionalization
Political parties are by definition voluntary citizens' associations based on free exchange between individual citizens and various communities.

Based on the common assumptions under girding the distinction between the state and society, such forms of association should not normally be the object of government interference (Karvonen 2007, p. 437). In democratic states, detailed legislation defines the spheres of state organs, public bodies and general public power on the one hand while protecting civil liberties and the private sphere of life on the other. The subject of legal regulation of political parties remains a contested matter. Liberal democrats see political parties as an aspect of civil society organization based on the free exchange between individuals and various communities that should not be the object of government interference.

In non-democratic societies however, state power frequently extends over large parts of the civil society sphere. The borderline between state and society is blurred or vanished all together and, in some cases, totalitarian order prevails (Linz, 2000, p. 66). Although East African states characterize themselves as democratic, their treatment of political parties tend towards the undemocratic and authoritarian category as opposed to the democratic. Political parties and party activities are often severely limited, their rights abrogated and, in some cases, outlawed by archaic public order legislation especially during election campaign periods.

The stated goal of political parties to contest and capture public office and form government differentiates them from other civil society organizations. They therefore constitute a zone of transition between the state and civil society (Lipset 2001, pp. 1-3). Given this ambiguity, public regulation of political parties varies greatly across the continent and East Africa is no exception. All three countries have political parties" acts as part of their constitutions that were amended, repealed or wholly introduced with the transition from single to multi-party rule.

In Kenya, the government bowed to internal and external pressure and reluctantly restored political pluralism through the constitution of Kenya Amendment Act, 1991 (Musambayi 2006, p. 31). It was not until 2007 that the Political Parties Act No.10 of 2007 was passed by parliament. In Tanzania, multipartysm was introduced in 1992 by way of a constitutional amendment by which the government created institutions to manage the democratisation process. It became the first country in Africa to enact a political parties' act providing guidelines for the registration and conduct of political parties. Act No.5 of 1992 established the office of the registrar of political parties and Article 74(1) established the National Electoral Commission (NEC) in 1993.

In Uganda, a referendum to return the country to a multiparty political system was held in July of 2005 and subsequently, parliament ratified a constitutional amendment by enacting the Political Parties and Organisations Act number 18 in November of the same year. In general, party law across the three countries provide the constitutional framework within which political parties can function; it spells out the legal guidelines and safeguards underpinning their operations. For instance, it sets conditions and procedures for the registration, regulation and monitoring of the conduct of political parties. The desire to regulate political parties stems in part from an inherent fear of competition from the political opponents on the part of the ruling party and a desire to manage the transition process by ensuring a stable and orderly transition in order to avoid potential social division and disintegration of the fabric of the state. This was more evident in Tanzania and Uganda that still exhibit strong party-state tendencies under a one-dominant party system. This seems to contradict the very tenets of democracy which ought to promote free and fair competition among equal political forces in society. In Kenya, the enactment of the Act more than 15 years after the introduction of multipartyism seems to be motivated by a desire to provide some form of order in a seemingly chaotic party-political environment. The country has no less than 300 registered political parties many of which are personal "briefcase" parties registered for commercial purposes only to be sold at election time to the highest bidder looking for a convenient vehicle with which to contest and seek political office.

In Kenya and Uganda, the registration and management of political parties fall under the Electoral Commission while in Tanzania, the act created an independent office of the Registrar of Political Parties answerable to the prime minister. Under the provisions of the act in Kenya and Uganda, the Electoral Commission has the power to deny registration or in effect recommend deregistration of a political party if it does not comply with the requirements provided under the act. The act also spells out the code of conduct for political parties including stipulations for internal organisation, holding of regular elections, declaration of assets and liabilities and filing of annual financial returns.

In light of the weak institutional and organisational capacity of political parties in the region, legal regulation is seen as likely to encourage intra-party democracy by fostering processes of accountability and transparency through regular elections, financial accountability and inclusiveness. Party law also serves to encourage institutionalisation and organisational capacity of political parties in order to improve their competitiveness in elections. Also, Regulation encourages parties to offer better policy options and more capable candidates emerging from competitive and credible selection processes. It may also increase party responsiveness and accountability to its membership and raise levels of membership participation in party activities and programmes thus reducing oligarchic tendencies and the overwhelming powers of party leaders.

In Tanzania and Kenya, political party laws provide for public funding of political parties. This has been the practice in Tanzania for more than ten years now and is only coming into force in Kenya in 2008. In

Tanzania, funding was first restricted to parliamentary parties, but was later extended to include those that won seats in local government or council elections. With certain qualifications, all political parties will benefit from a percentage of the fund, the bulk of which is distributed proportional to the number of votes a party gets in a general election. At the time of writing, the government of Uganda has tabled "The Political Parties and Organisations (Amendment) Bill 2008" which is meant to introduce public funding for political parties. Its preamble states its purpose being to "enable the political parties be funded in some way so that they can strengthen their bases to provide good governance".

Legal regulation of political parties is therefore becoming a standard norm in the region and is widely seen as a positive development especially where public funding of political parties in concerned. This strengthens the competitive capacity of opposition parties against the ruling parties which often rely on state resources that give them undue advantage over the opposition. The constitutional framework as depicted in the party laws however contains significant short comings regarding the independence of the regulatory bodies and the possibility of state interference in the discharge of their supervisory roles.

A sticking point remains the powers vested in the presidency to appoint senior officers to the national Electoral Commissions and the Registrar of Political Parties without reference to any other regulatory mechanism such as parliament. This casts in doubt the independence of these institutions which are perceived by the opposition to be partisan and pro-government and likely to owe allegiance to the appointing authority which happens to be the leader of the ruling party against whom they have to compete in an election. A case in point is the recent example in Kenya where the Electoral Commission is perceived as having been complicit in the mismanagement and fraudulent conduct of the 2007 general elections in favour of the incumbent (E.U.

2008). This is likely to compromise principles of democracy in the wider society by impeding free and equal competition among political parties.

The current legal provisions are also restrictive in terms of the formation of political coalitions in Tanzania and Uganda where existing parties are required to dissolve themselves before joining or forming a coalition. The situation is worse in Kenya and Tanzania where independent candidates are prohibited by law and one can only contest an election through membership of a registered political party. These shortcomings have led to calls for far reaching constitutional reforms especially from among the political opposition and civil society groups across all three countries. Although recognised by governments and relevant bodies as necessary, implementation has been contentious to say the least. The constitution review process in Kenya has had many false starts culminating in the defeat of a divisive government sponsored draft in 2005.

In Tanzania, the registrar of political parties and the electoral commission recognise these shortcomings and have pledged to push for the reform of electoral laws. The office of the registrar of political parties is in the process of amending the law to allow mergers and alliances between political parties to be recognized in law (Tendwa, 2007).

Conclusion.
Prevailing political party systems have a significant impact on the structure and conduct of political parties. They determine both formal and informal strategies as well as organisational structures that parties adopt in order to enhance their competitiveness in the party-political environment. All these factors do influence the status of intra-party democracy. The shared political, cultural, economic and social fabric that forms the East African region undoubtedly imbues

the party-political environment in the three countries under review. Still, the unique developmental, ideological and socio-economic trajectories that the three countries adopted after independence have led to markedly unique contemporary party-political environments.

The distinction between the one-party dominant systems in Uganda and Tanzania are in sharp contrast with the vibrant multi-party environment in Kenya. In all, opposition and ruling parties therefore adopt different strategies of internal organisation, membership mobilisation and coalition formation in order to remain relevant, competitive and either gain or retain power. These factors notwithstanding, most parties are characterised by low levels of institutionalisation, high centralisation and less inclusiveness of varying degrees which are explored in detail in the following chapter.

Party law has been enacted in all three countries to regulate the party-political environment based on varying motivations and with varying results. Party law is by no means a panacea for low intra-party democracy or weak democratic institutions in the wider society. However, in weak democracies with hegemonic parties, the state machinery can still be employed to thwart the interests of democracy. In countries undergoing democratic transitions however, party law can be useful in the consolidation of democratic gains and strengthening democratic institutions. The following chapter examines in detail the evidence based on empirical findings in order to determine the various factors that influence intra-party democracy in East Africa.

Chapter 6

Recruitment and Membership Organization

RECRUITING AND ORGANISING MEMEBERSHIP.

The conceptualisation of political parties as instruments of collective human action, mobilisation of social forces and aggregation of diverse interests implies a significant place for party membership within its organisational structures, activities and orientation. In East Africa however, political parties are more creatures of political elite to control government and the masses. Consequently, the role of party membership is secondary to that of the elites. One of the significant challenges to the institutionalisation and democratisation of political parties in Africa in general is the lack of distinct and disciplined party membership (Oloo, 2007). Political parties are characterised more by supporters as opposed to card holding registered membership. Party affiliation is thus fluid and membership participation in multiple parties is not uncommon. In most cases, card carrying membership ended with the demise of autocratic single party rule where card possession was proof of political loyalty and patriotism. Membership was in most cases through coercion hence the negative attitude towards registered and card-carrying membership.

Intense competition for votes and support among the multitude of new political parties also places a low premium on the restriction of participation in party activities to registered members. Party elites fear alienating potential voters should they restrict participation for instance in party primaries only to registered members (Muite, 2007). Party law across the region does not make any stipulations regarding party membership and although almost all parties have regulations on party membership, these guidelines are often ignored. However, various party instruments such as party constitutions set out members" rights, responsibilities and obligations and the parties studied refer to the existence of a membership register organised at three levels; Branch, District and National level or headquarters. Interestingly though, none of the parties could actually produce any documentation to support the existence of a membership list or give exact figures.

In Uganda for instance, despite the alleged existence of a national data centre, the NRM could not produce any figures to support this. Some of the figures given are completely arbitrary. The DP in Uganda for instance cites a membership of a hundred in 1962, three hundred in 1980 and a thousand in 2005. FDC on the other hand estimates its membership at seventy thousand and assumes that the 37.5% of presidential vote it received in the 2005 election is a fair reflection of its membership, which may not necessarily be the case. UPC concedes that its membership has declined significantly over the years when parties were prohibited from engaging in political activities including mobilisation and membership recruitment drives. Accordingly, several reasons are given for the dismal membership levels compared to the vibrant 1960"s and 1970"s. Opposition party officials cite the defection of many older members to the NRM for economic reasons due to increased poverty and dependency on state patronage. In some cases, individuals even to date are expected to show NRM membership cards in order to get employment or recommendation from district government officials for employment in the civil service or government sponsored projects (HRW 2006).

Declining and low party membership on the part of old and new parties respectively can be attributed in part to their lack of capacity to carry out effective membership recruitment drives. The parties are limited by their lack of institutional structures and resources for mobilisation and penetration countrywide. With the exception of the ruling parties NRM and CCM, most opposition parties charge a minimum fee for basic membership (either annual or one-off subscription). It is worth noting however that due to massive rural poverty, many voters can not even afford to pay the membership fee and the practice in Kenya for instance is for prospective candidates to buy cards from the national secretariat for distribution among intended supporters in the grass-roots. In Uganda, opposition parties complain about the practice by the ruling NRM to give out its membership cards for free as a further strategy to undercut their appeal among the masses (Njoki, 2007).

The situation varies slightly in Tanzania where most parties give estimates of party membership, though with difficulties in quoting actual numbers because the figures were continually fluctuating. UDP and TLP for instance could not give an estimate of its membership figures, though an earlier report gave TLP membership estimates at no less than one million in 2005. Chadema gave its membership estimates in December 2006 at about 850,000 on the Mainland and in Zanzibar representing an accelerated increase between 2004 and 2006. This included a membership drive during which no fewer than half a million new members were recruited during 2004 in preparation for the expected election in October 2005(Shayo, 2006). CCM gave its membership strength as having risen from just under three million in 2003 to 3.8 million in 2007, an increase of about 30 percent. Opposition parties however cite allegations of CCM use of state resources and administrative structures for more than 40 years to swell its membership ranks. Further concerns were raised regarding the ruling party's ability to pay its officials and staff much higher salaries compared to the opposition parties (Komu, 2007).

Most political parties become dormant after elections and the lack of political activity involving party members adversely affect the external credibility and internal democracy within parties. The role of party membership in the formulation of party policies and selection of candidates is virtually nonexistent. Although stipulations exist regarding the members' roles, rights and responsibilities, these are not implemented in practice. In Uganda for instance, most parties have had only one delegates' conference since 2005 and these simply served to endorse and legitimise party platforms, election manifestos and office holders who either set up the new parties or those that kept the old ones alive over the years. While membership recruitment is delegated to the branch or district levels, most parties, except for NRM do not have structures beyond the major urban centres and in some cases only in their regional strongholds (DP in central and UPC in the north and east of the country).

Effective communication between the party and its members is also a key component in ensuring a constant exchange and inclusion of members" views in party planning. This is another significant challenge facing African political parties due to the lack of infrastructural capacity. Although some parties give indications of vibrant communication both ways between the party and its membership at all levels, there is little evidence for this. In Uganda for instance, apart from FDC and NRM; most of the others do not have functioning websites and email addresses by which to communicate with its membership.

Public rallies, party meetings and individual correspondence seem to be the most frequent form of communication between parties and members. In Tanzania, CCM and CUF have party newspapers used for communication with membership and to the wider public. It is pertinent to note that some parties are slowly embracing new technology such as mobile telephony and internet for communication; about half of the parties studied have relatively good websites containing basic party information, though most of them are not up to date. Advertisements in the media, billboards and leaflets to reach out to the wider public are usually used during election campaigns, but do not form part of regular party communication strategies.

Conversely, members may communicate with the party during public meetings and rallies as well as individual postal mail, petitions and by telephone. Members who have filed petitions against election results communicate with party leaders in order to receive administrative guidance and support. Although parties' constitutions and election manifestos are widely available, most party leaders said that few of their members read these regularly. Intra-party communication more often than not tends to be one way as members rarely take the initiative to communicate with the party or party officials.

With limited resources to hold public rallies and delegates conferences, even physical communication afforded through such forums are limited and sporadic. Party caucuses for special interest groups such as women and youth wings are crucial in achieving greater intra-party democracy. These are however not fully developed and in most cases are not operational in most political parties. Except for the DP's Uganda Young Democrats (UYD), CCM's Umojawa Vijana (Youth Wing) and Umojawa Wanawake (Women''s wing), there is not much evidence of a strong focus in revamping and strengthening these institutions which are only mobilised during election campaigns and soon after neglected once they have served their purpose.

The American Political Landscape; as a litmus test.

In a rural county in North Carolina, the poorest in the state, and one in which American Indians, African Americans, and Hispanics made up the majority of the county, a large corporation proposed the building of a toxic waste treatment facility near a river that served as a water supply for several local communities. Some of the residents suspected one of the reasons their county had been chosen was because their demographics were reflective of the politically quiescent and the belief was that their communities would not try to block the proposed facility. However, when a public hearing was held, well over three hundred people showed up, packing the room to overflowing and necessitating the addition of chairs and public address system in the halls. Many of the participants were American Indian, African American, Hispanic, individuals with low levels of education and income, and limited ownership of working vehicles. They not only filled the seats, but were also some of the main speakers against the building of the proposed facility. In fact, they were precisely the types of individuals that the political science literature would have predicted least likely to show up. On the other hand, they were exactly the kinds of individuals that the community organizing literature in the social work tradition argues should be organized and tapped for political participation. There is a puzzle behind this story and one that needs the contributions of both social work and political science. In this paper, I will bring together these two disciplines to highlight what each field can learn from the other, and will utilize data from the Detroit Area Study to further explore influences on who is recruited for political participation. For decades, political scientists have attempted to solve the puzzle of political participation and the continuing disparities in rates of participation between groups categorized by race and class. Recent research has highlighted the key role played by mobilization in explaining some of the disparities in participation. However, research on predictors of recruitment has been fairly limited. Most political science studies have focused on recruitment to politics in general, with little distinction made between recruitment for different activities to issues, or to the influence of neighborhood on who is ultimately mobilized. These are precisely the factors that community organizers are encouraged to consider in their recruitment strategies. Note well that factors influencing participation are complex. To assume that mobilization is less complex or that one strategy is utilized for all issues and activities may diminish our ability to tease apart the participation puzzle. Further, over the last several decades, social science has paid increasing attention to neighborhood effects. However, little of this conversation about neighborhood effects has entered into the literature on recruitment to political participation. Lastly, given the persistence of residential segregation in the United States (particularly in urban areas with high proportions of African Americans), and the fact that blacks are more likely than whites to live in the most resource poor neighborhoods (Massey, 2007), it is time to pay closer attention to the neighborhood context of recruitment.

Recruitment Factors: Rosenstone and Hansen (1993) have argued that political strategists target 1) individuals who are known to them and who are effective when they take action (typically those from the upper echelons of society); 2) who are likely to participate (activists); and 3) those who are socially connected. In essence, what matters are individual resources and characteristics, social connections and past political involvement. The authors' data however, is based solely on responses from individuals about whether they had been recruited for political participation. They did not interview activists to ascertain their recruitment strategies, and thus were not able to provide evidence of what actually guides mobilizers' targeting decisions. We do have some clues about what is in the minds of organizers from the community organizing literature. Rosenstone and Hansen's theory, along with guidance from the organizing literature will be utilized as a starting framework for examining the recruitment literature in the field of political science.

63

Resources and Individual Characteristics.

Greater individual resources (education and income) have been shown to be strong predictors of recruitment by political parties and by other political and non- political organizations, for voting, campaign contributions, and campaign work (Abramson &Claggett, 2001; Brady, Schlozman, &Verba, 1999; Gershtenson, 2003; Kenneth M. Goldstein &Ridout, 2002; Krassa, 1988; Leighley, 2001; Zipp & Smith, 1979). In the few cases where individual activities were analyzed separately, there were some variations in the influence of resources on recruitment to specific activities. Abramson and Claggett (2001) found higher levels of education associated with an increase in the likelihood of contact to vote, give money or work on a campaign, but greater wealth only influenced the chance of contact for the latter two activities. Goldstein (1999) found greater levels of education increased an individual's chance of being contacted during lobbying about Clinton's healthcare reform, but income did not appear to be a factor. In other words, resources may be an important predictor of mobilization, but income and education are not interchangeable. Age and gender also play a role in recruitment to politics, but their influence on likelihood of contact is much smaller and more mixed than is true for education and income. In a few instances older citizens were more likely to be asked by a political party to vote or contribute to a campaign than were younger citizens (Abramson &Claggett, 2001; Gershtenson, 2003; Rosenstone& Hansen, 1993; Zipp& Smith, 1979). In some studies, men were more likely than women to be recruited by strategists to vote or to become politically active (Kenneth M. Goldstein, 1999; Verba, Schlozman, & Brady, 1995), but in the majority of studies, gender was not a significant predictor of contact. Verba, et al (1995) used a summary variable for mobilization that included recruitment to do campaign work, make a campaign contribution, participate in a community activity and to protest. Thus, it was not possible to determine if there was any variation in recruitment by gender for each of the different activities. Several studies suggest that blacks were less likely to be contacted for electoral participation than were whites (Kenneth M. Goldstein, 1999; Verba, et al., 1995; Wielhouwer, 2000). If, as Rosenstone and Hansen (1993) suggest, strategists target the upper echelons of society, this finding is no surprise since race is so closely associated with both education and income in the United States. However, the influence of race on contact was not a consistent factor in all electoral years or for all activities. Abramson and Claggett (2001) found that blacks were less likely to be contacted to contribute to a campaign, but race did not predict contact to vote or to work on campaign. Blacks were less likely to be contacted by the Republican Party between 1972 and 2000, but not between 1956 and 1968 (Gershtenson, 2003). Race did not appear to influence Democratic Party strategies. Leighley (2001) suggests there were minimal differences by race for institutional mobilization (by churches, on the job, and by voluntary organizations), but a clear bias toward Anglos for particularized mobilization. Anglos were twice as likely as African Americans and four times as likely as Hispanics to be asked to contact a government official. There were similar gaps in contact rates by race for those asked to work on a local activity or to do campaign work. In other studies, due to the use of national data and the small sample size for African Americans, SES may have overwhelmed the race effect given its strong link to class. The mixed results for the influence of race on mobilization may be due to different strategies utilized by different types of organizers, particularly if the organizing takes place at the local, rather than the national level. It may be true as Rosenstone and Hanson ( ) suggest that political organizers target individuals with resources (more likely to be white). In the community organizing literature however, it is precisely the poor and marginalized (more likely to be black) who activists are encouraged to bring into the political game (see for example, (Alinsky, 1972; Piven&Cloward, 1979; Yeich, 1996). If neighborhood or civil rights organizations are mobilizing for electoral participation, it might explain some of the differences seen in the racial profile. Individual characteristics and resources were strong predictors of participation, so it is no surprise that organizers might consider these factors in recruitment strategies. As Brady, et al (1999) have suggested, political recruiters are rational actors and want to get the most return on their investment. However, identifying individuals with specific characteristics in large geographic areas is a big task and requires a large investment of resources. Although political parties may have the resources for such a data mining operation, this is not often the case for groups organizing at the community level, particularly for non-electoral activities or issues. Thus, some other method of locating potential activists may be required.

Social Connections and Past Activity.
Past voting and campaign activity, indicators of a propensity to participate and to respond to a request for action, have been shown to be strong predictors of political recruitment (Abramson &Claggett, 2001; Brady, et al., 1999; Gershtenson, 2003; K. Goldstein & Paul, 2002; Kenneth M. Goldstein &Ridout, 2002; Huckfeldt& Sprague, 1992; Parry, Barth, Kropf, & Jones, 2008). Also, Abramson and Claggett (2001) found that past campaign activity was the strongest predictor of contact to work on a campaign, outweighing the influence of education and income. Past campaign contributions and voting were positive predictors of each respective activity, but were less significant than resources. This differential influence of resources and past activity on recruitment by type of activity begins to hint at the use of activity specific targeting strategies, at least by political parties. For anyone who has ever made a financial contribution or participated in a local activity, the relationship between past activity and contact to participate in a subsequent activity comes as no surprise. If organizers are rational as Brady et al (1999) suggest, they will keep lists of individuals who have previously responded positively to recruitment efforts or simply shown up at an event. Lists of previous participants decreases the effort needed to find those who will respond positively to a contact in the future. Indeed, Kahn (1991) in his text on grassroots organizing

recommends that activists keep lists of all contacts they have with individuals, including notes on their interests. There is a reason for the identification of individuals' interests, past participation alone is not a guarantee that in person will be interested in or likely to participate in an unrelated issue or activity. Strategists often need to expand beyond past participants, thus other clues are needed to determine who else might respond to a request for action on a particular issue or activity. Zipp and Smith (1979) found that individuals who knew party members personally or considered themselves opinion leaders were more likely to be recruited than others who did not share these characteristics. Members of groups (typically unions), those who attend religious services, and long-time community residents were recruited more often than non-joiners for political activities, most often electorally related (Abramson &Claggett, 2001; Brady, et al., 1999; Djupe& Grant, 2001; Gershtenson, 2003; Kenneth M. Goldstein, 1999; Rosenstone& Hansen, 1993; Wielhouwer, 2000, 2003). Membership in organizations or residential status may make an individual more visible to organizers, particularly if organizations are targeted as well as individuals. Some community organizing entities, ACORN for example, recruit members by contacting individuals. Other groups, such as the Industrial Areas Foundation (IAF) founded by Saul Alinsky, People in Communities Organized (PICO) and the Gamaliel Foundation recruit organizational members who are in turn asked to bring their members to organizing efforts (Fisher, 2009). Particular types of organizational membership may also serve as indicators of interest in a specific issue. For example, unions and their membership were targeted during lobbying efforts around healthcare reform (Goldstein, 1999) and several authors argue that Black churches were the focus of organizing efforts in support of the civil rights movement (Branch, 1988; McAdam, 1982; Morris, 1984). One of the premises of the community organizing field is that strategists need to recruit individuals and groups who have a stake in an issue, since they are more likely to act if invited (Alinsky, 1972; Bobo, Kendall, & Max, 2001; Delgado, 1986; Fisher, 1994, 2009; Kahn,

1991, 1994; Mondros & Wilson, 1994; Rubin & Rubin, 2008). This is important, since much of the community organizing literature, often —how to‖ manuals, focuses on organizing around issues rather than around elections. Thus, the type of organizations individuals chooses to join provides clues about the issues in which they might be interested, and possibly about the types of political activity to which they are drawn. In a study of associations, Knoke (1990) found differences among unions, professional, trade and recreational associations regarding the type of activity for which they recruited their membership. Unions for example, were more likely to ask their members to contact a government official, write to a newspaper, demonstrate or work on a local or national election than any of the other types of associations. However, there is little research on specific types of organizational membership and recruitment, other than membership in general or in unions, and religious service attendance. If organizational membership serves as an indicator of interest or willingness to participate in certain types of activities or issues, one should expect different types of groups to make a difference in who is contacted for action for specific issues and the activities. In addition to organizational membership, results from a few studies suggest that other factors related to social connectedness or accessibility may be important. Rosenstone and Hansen's (1993) analyses suggest that homeownership and longer residency in a community increase the likelihood of contact by a political party (see also Wielhouwer, 2003). It may be that such factors make an individual less of a moving target and thus more visible to organizers. As with group membership, these factors may also serve as indicators of interest in an issue. Homeowners were targeted in efforts to defeat a ballot issue in San Francisco, in part, because they tend to be reliably moderate to conservative on economic issues relative to renters‖ (McNulty, 2005). The author also argued homeownership served as a proxy for age, SES, and residential stability— potential indicators of positions on the ballot issue. If this is the case, homeownership and residential longevity may matter more on some issues rather than others. Membership in a group and in specific types of groups, length of residency in an area, and homeownership can provide access points for organizers as well as clues about potential interest in a specific issue. However, strategists may miss potential activists if they content themselves with lists of groups and their membership lists. Individuals who are not members of a group may be willing to act if a particular issue impacts their self-interest. Issues do not affect all neighborhoods to the same extent, nor are economic and social resources equally distributed across all geographic areas. To be sure, individual characteristics and resources, past activity and social connections may be factors in who is tapped for political participation, but they do not take into account the geographical clustering of individuals in similar social and economic situations or the continued housing segregation by race. For this, it is necessary to factor into the mobilization story the residential context of individuals.

Neighborhood

Most research on political recruitment focuses on individual characteristics and resources and to some extent, organizational memberships as predictors of contact by activists. However, despite the growth of neighborhood effects on literature in other areas of research (see for example, (Massey, 2007) and (Sampson, Morenoff, & Gannon-Rowley, 2002) for important reviews of this literature) few studies have considered the influence of place of residence on who is recruited. From the national perspective, Goldstein (1999) suggests organizers in lobbying efforts around national healthcare first targeted strategic states and then moved to the individual level. Certainly, more recent elections have highlighted efforts by political parties to target key states and areas within states and cities in order to win campaigns. On a more local level, several authors have argued that strategists target (or avoid) certain neighborhoods depending on their level of educational and income resources or past participation in electoral activities (Cohen & Dawson, 1993; Gimpel, Lee, & Kaminski, 2006;

Huckfeldt& Sprague, 1992; Leighley, 2001). Leighley (2001) examines predictors of mobilization by party chairs and found that party chairs were more likely to target an area for some type of activity if the chair was a Democrat and there was a higher percentage of African Americans or Hispanics, and less likely to focus on an area as the area SES increased. However, black population size became insignificant when areas with less than one percent blacks were eliminated from the analysis. Unfortunately, SES was operationalized as the percent of the white population with a high school degree. It is not clear that black and white educational levels can be equated across the board, or that education is the sole resource party chairs or any other organizer deem important when developing recruitment strategies. Cohen and Dawson (1993) suggest that strategists looking for monetary contributions might avoid neighborhoods with greater levels of poverty or that are perceived to be dangerous. It does not make sense to go where people don't have what is needed. On the other hand, we may underestimate people's willingness to participate based on the preconceived notions of outsiders, particularly if there is a large minority population. The story may be different if organizing is initiated from within a community or on an issue that is perceived to directly impact a community's self-interest. Just as type of organizational membership may matter to political recruiters when organizing around a specific issue, the type of neighborhood and its resources may influence political strategies. Not all issues have an impact on all neighborhoods in the same way or to the same extent. It makes sense that greater levels of organizing would occur in neighborhoods most directly affected by an issue. Since most of the data available comes from national election studies, it is difficult to determine whether there are neighborhood differences in recruitment profiles for other types of non-election related activities or issues. National samples also do not typically include neighborhood or environmental characteristics. It is possible that the importance of individual resources is over estimated in the recruitment literature due to the general failure or inability to include neighborhood characteristics and resources. With current technology, it is certainly feasible for activists to fine tune the areas they wish to target before moving to the individual level, and given limited resources, it would be foolish not to target neighborhoods as well as individuals. Further, in light of the importance of individual resources as predictors of recruitment and the continuing housing segregation by race and class in this country, the role of individual resources may be overestimated if neighborhood characteristics are not considered.

In summary, what is missing in the political science literature is a more nuanced study of the predictors of mobilization. Most of the research is limited by availability of data from national election studies, and therefore to recruitment for voting and in a few instances, to contact by a party to contribute to or work on a campaign. Where there is some attention to other activities, such as contacting a public official or protesting, activities are generally collapsed into one summary variable. It is likely that not all activities require the same kind or level of resources from potential activists, and it is also likely that all issues do not generate the same level of interest. Elections are infrequent occurrences, so to ignore other types of non-electoral activities or issues may cause us to miss important nuances in the recruitment story. Indeed, if the community organizing literature is correct, there is a lot of recruitment occurring on a daily basis, but who is organized and the types of activities and issues for which they are recruited are very different than has typically been addressed in the political science literature. The specification of social connectedness, or what makes an individual visible to an organizer, has been somewhat limited in the recruitment literature. In the same vein, social connectedness is usually limited to only two types of groups in the recruitment literature, unions and religious groups. To a lesser extent, years in a community and home ownership, as with individual resources, it is possible that strategists target different types of groups or forms of social connection depending on the issue and/or activity for which they are recruiting. Affiliations serve not only to make an individual accessible to an organizer, but can also be indicators of expertise or stake in an issue. Thus, to limit affiliations to the groups mentioned above is to assume that no other types of groups matter, regardless of the issue. The other drawback to many of the theories and studies is that such theories usually fail to account for the environmental context or the neighborhood in strategists' decisions. With limited resources, organizers may focus on neighborhoods most likely to have the resources and the interest in an issue and activity to respond to a request for action. Conversely, strategists may avoid particular areas due to either a historically based belief that residents will not respond to a request for action or to biases or fears about particular neighborhoods, possibly based on the racial makeup of the area. Without the addition of neighborhood characteristics and resources, analyses may unduly emphasize the importance of individual characteristics and resources. Race may matter, but it might be at the larger neighborhood level, rather than at the individual level. Lastly, most of the existing studies are based on national data which results in an overwhelmingly white sample. The national studies do not allow for an examination of local context, nor do they allow for a more nuanced examination of the role of race in recruitment. To stop there is to fall into the assumption that one model fits all races. Given historical gaps in black and white political participation, it is not clear one size fits all. Also, given the significant impact of mobilization on likelihood of participation, we need to understand which factors most affect the recruitment of black citizens into politics if the gaps are to be minimized. Since much of the political science research is focused on national and electorally related mobilization, it misses the larger story that occurs in everyday politics at the local level. The community organizing (CO) literature and manuals might provide some of the answers to the local mobilization puzzle. Extensive writing in this field provides guidance on how to organize at the local level. Recruitment in the Alinsky tradition in particular focuses on tapping into and building on the already existing social capital in a neighborhood (Alinsky, 1972; Kahn, 1991; Reisch, 2008; Reitzes & Reitzes, 1987; Warren, 2001). This does not contradict the findings in political science, but it does highlight the importance of social accessibility through organizational membership. One of the key strategies is to bring together individuals, organizations and neighborhoods around common issues and interests, and one of the key avenues is the use of existing organizations—both for the recruitment of participants and the identification of the issues. In many cases, organizers work in poor and politically marginalized communities. These areas are often hardest hit by specific issues, such as cuts in school budgets, public transportation, or police services. These issues will not be the same as those experienced by wealthier neighborhoods. If the CO methods are followed and if we presume that local organizing often occur in communities hardest hit by economic problems, one should see a different profile of the recruited for local issues than is found in national election studies. Thus, the influence of high individual resources as a factor in recruitment found in the political science research may not hold if issue specific organizing is examined. Another key in much of the CO literature is tapping into an individual's self- interest, as well as utilizing non-organizational relationships as access points when recruiting for an issue or activity. If they care and if they can be reached, individuals are more likely to act. While organizational membership offers a clue to issue interest, there are other avenues suggested as guides. Several authors urge organizers to build membership by personally interviewing community residents and keeping notes on contacts' skills, interests, family and community involvements, etc. (Bobo, et al., 2001; Delgado, 1986; Kahn, 1991; Mondros& Wilson, 1994). Some of the noted interests might come directly from the individuals interviewed or from the linkages made by the recruiters during the interview process. For example, individuals with children might be concerned about the condition of neighborhood parks, the level of traffic on their streets, or the quality of the local school system. The children also serve as an indirect access point to the adults. When a parent cannot be reached directly, they might be reached via the schools or organizations to which the children belong. Thus, demographic information about an individual can serve not only as an indicator of interest, but also as a clue to indirect access. Lastly, information about an individual's skills are important for matching the right people with the right activities, and determining who might be potential leaders for the organizing effort.

In all, political science research provides a good starting point about predictors of mobilization, but its story is more national in scope and thus more generic. It may not be nuanced enough for the organizing that takes place at the community level where issues matter. While the CO literature is short on research, it is rich on how to organize at the local level. It might provide some answers to the mobilization, and ultimately the political participation puzzle. It also provides avenues for exploring the differences between national and local mobilization in particular and in terms of the influence of issues and activities on who is mobilized.

A Theory of Political Recruitment Bringing together the fields of political science and community organizing, utilizes an expanded version of Rosenstone and Hansen's theory of mobilization to hypothesize who is mobilized. If political activists target individuals who 1) have the individual resources to participate and to be efficacious in their action and 2) who are accessible via social connections, or a history of participation, then individuals who have the greatest levels of education and wealth, and are politically and socially connected should have an advantage over their counterparts in receiving a political invite. If the CO literature is right, then 3) neighborhood characteristics and resources and 4) the specific activity and issue around which organizing is occurring should shape recruitment as well. Individual resources and accessibility are not new as explanatory factors for mobilization, but neighborhoods may play a greater role in predicting recruitment than previous research has been able to test. If a strategist wants to reach wealthy or highly educated individuals, lacking a list, the most efficient route might be to target neighborhoods with a greater proportion of such individuals. In addition, given continuing housing segregation in the United States by race, disparities in access to resources, such as employment, education, and other services by neighborhood and race, and the differential impact social and economic issues on particular neighborhoods, activists should not be expected to mobilize all individuals in a city. Rather, they should be expected to target those individuals and neighborhoods most directly impacted by an issue and with the perceived resources to act. The idea that recruitment strategies are crafted with an eye toward individual resources and accessibility has contributed greatly to our understanding of recruitment.

However, the argument is that the weight these factors play may not be static across all issues or activities, and that accessibility (group membership) may be more nuanced than previous research has been able to test. Strategists may look for individuals with higher levels of education and income to contact a public official, partly because such individuals may have greater clout when they do act, but also because they may have more of the skills necessary to act on such a request. However, attendance at a community meeting or at a protest may not require such skills. For such activities, it might be important to simply turn out large numbers of individuals, regardless of their perceived clout or skills. If this is the case, getting a positive response to a request to attend a meeting or protest may be more dependent on figuring out who cares about the issue or which neighborhoods have a stake in the issue at hand. However, race may matter, both at the individual and neighborhood levels, because many social and economic issues are strongly related to race. Although past researchers have accounted for group membership in general, and unions and religious groups in particular, other types of groups can give more detailed clues about a citizen's priority concerns. An individual's interests and concerns may not be physically visible to an organizer, but recruiters may be able to target individuals through the groups they join. Members of environmental or anti-crime groups may share some common interests, but their concerns may also diverge quite a bit. To lump these types of groups together may hide key information. For an activist to recruit individuals to write legislators about the issue of water pollution, it is probably a lot easier and productive to locate individuals who are members of an environmental group than to find citizens with greater individual resources or who are members of any group and hope that they will care about the environment. Thus the issue focus of a particular group should be a more important factor for a political recruiter than membership in general. One other type of accessibility has not been adequately addressed. Some studies have included the marital status of a citizen in their analyses of recruitment. I argue that not only are individuals made accessible to organizers through their partner or spouse, but also through their children. Parents or children's caregivers often receive information from schools or groups to which their children belong about events, requests for action or information about particular issues. Children are an access point, but also an indicator to activists of a possible stake in a particular issue. For example, the quality of our educational system should be important to all citizens, but may be a higher issue priority for parents, simply because they and their children are more directly affected by educational decisions.

Questions tested to be clear, available data will not allow the researcher to directly analyze factors that influence strategists' targeting decisions. However, by examining data from individuals about whether or not they were contacted by activists, it may provide us with a dim reflection of the factors that influence strategists' thinking. At the very least, the results should shed more light on who is contacted and who is ignored. In this aspect, four questions are addressed in each chapter. First, given the race disparities in political participation, what role is played by race in the recruitment strategies of organizers? Does race enter as a factor for some forms of activity more than for others, if at all? Since mobilization strongly predicts political participation, the answer to this question not only has consequences for participation, but ultimately for which voices are heard in the defining of policy, particularly at the local level. The quality of our political, social and economic systems tends to disproportionately favor those who are better off, and those who are white. Although the provision of services and access to resources are complicated, part of the reason for some of the local disparities by race may be due to who is invited to influence political decisions and who is ignored. The second question pertains to the extent accessibility and involvement in the community play in the recruitment process. Is it simple membership, membership in specific kinds of groups, past participation or something as simple as having children that makes one visible, and thus accessible to recruiters? Given limited resources, organizers will most likely choose to recruit those who are easiest to find and, if targeting a specific issue focus will be on individuals who are thought to care about the issue. Third, does place of residence play a part in whether or not an individual is invited into the political process? Organizers in the electoral realm can use extensive voting lists to refine their recruitment strategies, but this resource is not available for many forms of political participation or for particular issues. To locate individuals for non-electoral recruitment can be a costly process. If, as some have argued, organizers are rational and strategic, do they minimize their costs by identifying and focusing on neighborhoods with the skills, interest in and resources necessary for political action, as well as on individuals who are accessible through other means? If targeting individuals with the skills, knowledge and resources necessary for participation on the issue of crime, a focus on neighborhoods most directly impacted by the issue, generally poorer areas and with greater numbers of black citizens, might be a far more cost-effective strategy than doing a broad sweep of the populace. On the other hand, organizers might ignore certain neighborhoods, possibly in the belief that there aren't enough individuals living in such areas with the requisite political resources, or because of organizers' biases or fears regardless of the issue. The final question is whether profiles of the mobilized vary based on the type of activity and the specific issue for which they are recruited. My assumption is that strategists use a different individual, social and neighborhood profile when recruiting for attendance at a meeting than they do for urging people to join a protest or make a financial contribution, for example. Different political activities require different skills, knowledge and levels of interest. It would be foolish and costly to expect a positive response to a request for action from all individuals. We should also see a different profile based on the issue for which recruiting is occurring. Not everyone cares equally about all issues. Strategists know this and should vary their strategies if they wish to get a positive response to their request for action. The goal of the writer is to examine political recruitment in the broader context of individual, social and neighborhood characteristics. In particular, this work adds to current research by illuminating differences in targeting strategies for participation in general and on the issues of schools and crime in particular. Much of the current research either focuses exclusively on recruitment in the electoral arena or fails to distinguish the issue for which an individual is mobilized. We cannot assume that strategists believe all activities or issues require the same resources or interest. To do so, is to assume that organizers are irrational and clueless on effective strategies.

Lastly, strategists appeared to recruit younger individuals to contact a public official and to volunteer in the schools. This difference from the apparent preference for older citizens in the electoral arena holds, even when having a child in public school is held constant. It is possible that strategists believe those who are younger care more about school issues, regardless of whether they have children or not. On the other hand, it might simply be that the young are more likely than to rub shoulders on a daily basis with friends and colleagues who have school-aged children, and are thus presented more opportunities to hear about educational issues and activities. In any event, it appears that age, gender and race play out differently in recruitment to school related activities than they do in electoral mobilization, and failing to consider the issue at hand may mean missing the boat on when deciphering the strategies of political recruiters. Moving to the individual resource story, Abramson and Claggett (2001) found both education and income to be positive factors for requests to volunteer on a campaign and for campaign contributions. This is generally true for contact by a political party and for any recruitment in general (Brady, et al., 1999; Gershtenson, 2003; Goldstein and Ridout, 2002; Rosenstone and Hansen, 1993; and Wielhouwer, 2003). In this study however, income was never a significant factor and higher levels of individual education only increased the chances of contact to attend a school related meeting. However, in the latter case, the effect was small compared to the weight carried by the accessibility and neighborhood factors. One of the reasons for the minimal role played by individual resources may be that previous research did not include the broader array of accessibility factors included in these analyses and neighborhood characteristics and resources. It might also be due to a greater willingness to ask for financial contributions for a political campaign than is true for work on educational issues. As in previous research on recruitment in general and in the electoral arena (Abramson and Claggett, 2001; Brady, et al., 1999; Gershtenson, 2003; Goldstein and Ridout, 2002; Rosenstone and Hansen, 1993; and Wielhouwer, 2003), accessibility factors significantly increase the likelihood of political mobilization, and in this case, for every school related activity. Past participation is one of the biggest predictors of recruitment to contact a public official and to protest. Indeed, it along with working outside the home, were the only two predictors of invites to protest. On the other hand, while past involvement significantly increases the likelihood of receiving a request for meeting attendance, money and to volunteer in schools, it is generally dwarfed by having a child in public school and by membership in a school group. Generally, researchers have included a group membership variable in their analyses of predictors of recruitment, and this may be fine if the focus is general or electoral recruitment. However, membership in any group was never significant in the current analyses when membership in a school group was also included. In addition, homeowners stood a better chance of being mobilized than did renters for meeting attendance and money requests. Given the time period this data was collected, it is not clear if homeowners were targeted because they were more residentially stable and thus more accessible, or if they were seen by strategists as having a stake in the continuing presence of school funding through property taxes as a ballot issue. Lastly, members of religious groups stood a better chance of being asked to attend a school meeting than did their counterparts. This might be due to having children in private, religious schools. The broader array of accessibility factors included in these analyses highlights not only the sizable role played by this category of variables, but also the importance of distinguishing the various types of access when considering recruitment to different activities. It is not clear if strategists believe the various types of accessibility are indicators of stake in an issue, knowledge and skill needed for an activity, or simply that, to varying degrees, they make one visible to a recruiter. Brady, et al., (1999) have equated political recruiters with rational prospectors, but much of their focus was on individual characteristics. Indeed, strategists may be rational prospectors, but given the weight carried by accessibility factors, they may be targeting social access points and groups over and above the characteristics of particular individuals. Social movement theorists have argued that organizers recruit participants through pre-existing social ties (Marwell, 1988; Oberschall, 1973; Tilly, 1978). That certainly appears to be the case with recruitment to school related activities. Neighborhood variables as predictors of recruitment were only significant for two activities, but they do provide some interesting and surprising insights. Residents of areas with the greatest proportion of homeowners were almost 45% more likely to be asked to attend a meeting than those living in areas with the fewest homeowners, even when individual homeownership is held constant. Again, it is not clear if this is an accessibility/stability issue or the perception that homeowners might have more of a stake in a property tax ballot issue than would renters. Neighborhood makeup was also a factor in fundraising. Residents in areas with the highest percentage of African Americans were 17% less likely to be asked for money than were residents of mostly white neighborhoods, even while black individuals were more likely to receive such requests than their white counterparts. Part of the story explaining the increased inclusion of individual black citizens may be their relatively high numbers throughout the Detroit metropolitan area, and the continuing imbalance in school quality based on the race of the students. It may be a story of perceived self-interest. On the other hand, the Detroit tri-county area remains one of the most racially segregated urban areas in the country. It may be that there is less fundraising in areas with high concentrations of people of color due to strategists' belief that residents will not or are not able to contribute to school issues, or strategists' own racial biases. Previous research on electoral recruitment has found that individual homeowners are often targeted by organizers and at times, people of color are ignored (McNulty, 2005; Rosenstone& Hansen, 1993; Wielhouwer, 2003). However, failing to include the type of neighborhood in which the individual lives may overestimate the importance of the individual in the recruitment story and paint a picture contrary to that actually played by individual characteristics. Cho, et al. (2006, p. 158), have argued that neighborhood context influences political participation because it structures information flow and affects the exogenous forces that come to bear on potential voters‖. It appears that the effect of neighborhood context goes beyond voting to the more frequent activities of local school politics.

There has been relatively little research on recruitment to individual political activities or activities beyond the domain of electoral politics. This chapter has expanded upon previous researches by examining recruitment to individual, school related activities; by including a broader range of accessibility variables as predictors; by examining the neighborhood as an important context for the recruitment process and lastly, by teasing out the role of race as a factor in political recruitment. However, individual characteristics are important, but in ways that differ from their role in electoral mobilization. Unlike in electoral recruitment, individual resources barely make the cut in explaining school related recruitment. Accessibility, neighborhood race and percentage of homeowners in a neighborhood each predict an individual's chance of being recruited. It appears that the broader social context of recruitment is at least as, if not more important than, individual attributes in the strategies of organizers in the school domain. It is also clear that there is no one mobilization strategy that fits all types of activities or issues. It is crucial to note that accessibility plays a strong role in recruitment for all acts. The recruitment story is a complex one that needs to take into account individual attributes and resources, as well as a broad range of accessibility factors and neighborhood characteristics. Clearly, future research needs to explore this complexity, especially given the important influence of recruitment on actual participation, and examine the effect of the various profiling strategies on actual participation. The apparent over reliance of political organizers on accessibility factors raises some troubling concerns. Understandably, strategists may choose to make efficient use of currently existing networks but continuing racial segregation and biases in the makeup of group joiners toward those who are white and with more resources may only serve to continue in lowering overall political participation rates for those who are already marginalized in our society.(Schlozman &Tieney,1986) We may also be excluding those with the greatest stake in an issue, particularly when it comes to education. If mobilization provides citizens information about an issue, about its potential impact on their lives, and about ways to influence decisions on the issue, targeting those easiest to find may exclude those with the greatest stake in the outcomes. Who is asked to play in the game, may not be the one who most needs to participate?

Conclusion

Past research on political recruitment has been limited in its attention to mobilization on specific issues and specific activities, focusing mostly on electoral and general recruitment. In addition, there has been scant attention paid to the role played by a broader array of accessibility factors and neighborhood characteristics in mobilization strategies, as well as the specific influence of race at both the individual and neighborhood levels. In this chapter, I have explored the mobilization story specific to the issue of crime and the broader array of types of activities to which one might be recruited. It is clear that recruitment on the issue of crime is very different from that found in electoral and general mobilization. The importance of past participation, specific types of group membership and neighborhood factors strongly suggests that recruitment strategists on the issue of crime target individuals who are accessible and already active, as well as neighborhoods perceived to have a stake in the issue. Since crime tends to be geographically localized, rather than widely dispersed, it appears that mobilizers are targeting precisely those citizens most directly affected by the issue. This is a different story than that found in general and electoral recruitment research. It is a story to be expected from the CO literature however, where the focus is on pulling people together around issues that directly affect their daily lives—in this case crime, rather than elections. The question that arises is; who determines which issues citizens are interested in, have a stake in, or should be involved in? If due to limited resources, organizers operate on the belief that people in low resource and black neighborhoods care about and are more likely to respond to contact about the issue of crime, but not about elections or politics in general, they may be unfairly denying residents of these areas the chance to participate on a broader range of issues. That's the benign story, if on the other hand, differences in recruitment are due to the writing off of certain types of people and neighborhoods, then the consequences for the breadth of the voices heard in the democratic processes are significant. Mobilization is essential for participation, and if we fail to consider who is recruited for various issues and activities, particularly the role of neighborhood, we may perpetuate the continuing disparities in political participation.

Chapter 7

Campaign Structure & Mobilization

CAMPAIGN STRATEGIES AND SUPPORT MOBILISATION

Election campaigns are exciting opportunities for candidates and political parties to evaluate what it is they are truly offering the people of their country and to strengthen their relationships with voters. The better a campaign team or political party plans and prepares for an election, the more it will gain and the stronger it will become.

The road to the seat of power is long, expensive, and exhausting: becoming a candidate is only the beginning of the election process. Successful candidates must both persuade voters that they deserve their individual votes and garner the critical votes of electors in the Electoral College as in the case of the USA. Note that persuading voters is the essence of a political campaign. Also, advertising, theme songs, stump speeches, and even negative campaigning have been around for a long time, and each advancement in technology offers new opportunities for candidates to persuade voters.

In this chapter, we shall take a critical look on how political parties in some countries mobilizes for campaigns and electoral victory.

Party Campaign Strategies: Rallies, Canvassing and Handouts in an African Election- the *Ghana Example*

Using post-election survey data from over 6,000 citizens, we document the campaign footprints of Ghana's two major political parties ahead of the country's 2012 elections. While researchers acknowledge resource disparities between opposition and ruling parties in developing democracies, our analysis shows these differences translate into concrete campaign outcomes. We theorize that the incumbent party will use its greater access to financial resources to mount a more national campaign and campaigning outside of stronghold constituencies. This is because the ruling party can use transfers of resources before the election to shore up votes in core constituencies, it can dedicate campaign resources to other types of constituencies, available data confirm these trends. Further, in highlighting the importance of face-to-face mobilization tactics, we document the widespread use of political rallies and canvassing, which dominate the distribution of material handouts. Our results demonstrate how advantages of incumbency impact campaign decisions, with implications for governance and elections in young democracies.

Incumbency and Political Party Campaign Strategies in Ghana

Ghana has held competitive multi-party elections every four years following a return to democratic rule in November 1992. Along with a growing number of African countries, there have been three successful democratic transitions of power, in 2000, 2008 and 2016. Two parties dominate electoral politics, the National Democratic Congress (NDC) and the New Patriotic Party (NPP). Focusing on Ghana's December 2012 election during which the NDC was the incumbent party, and the NPP was the main challenger. The NDC won the election, securing both the presidency and the majority of parliamentary seats. The president is elected in a single national constituency using a majoritarian run-off system while MPs are elected in single-member districts. The need for the president to secure an absolute majority to win office incentivizes political parties to seek votes from across the country. Accordingly, both major parties have a national character, and draw support from "all geographic constituencies, encapsulating different groups, socio-economic backgrounds and perspectives" (Gyimah-Boadi and Debrah,2008, p.147). That said, each party has areas of historic electoral dominance that coincide with ethnic alliances (Friday, 2007). While ex-President J. J. Rawlings popularly referred to the Volta region as the electoral "World Bank" of the NDC, the constituencies in the populous Ashanti region are stronghold areas for the NPP. The Volta and Ashanti regions are two of Ghana's ten administrative regions. At the parliamentary level, voters elect Members of Parliament (MPs) using plurality rule in 275 single-member constituencies.

Rising levels of electoral competition have created an incentive for the ruling party to use public resource to finance the party's campaign. The closeness of electoral contests is exemplified by Ghana's 2008 presidential race which saw the NDC's candidate (John Evans Atta-Mills) beat the opposition candidate with a razor-thin margin of 40,000 votes (out of an electorate of roughly 14 million). Lindberg

(2003) argues that this increased competition has led to an explosion in campaign spending. He estimates that parliamentary candidates spent around $40,000 on their campaigns in 2004, which increased to$75,000 in 2008 (Lindberg, 2010). To put these figures in perspective, the annual salary of an MP was approximately $24,000 (post-tax and deductions) in 2010 (Lindberg, 2010).

This implies that citizens can join both parties and serve them in official roles at the local, regional and national levels. Each party has institutionalized grassroots members into the party structure through the establishment of polling station level positions. Party activists often compete in elections to win these local positions. Both parties also organize competitive local primaries to select presidential and parliamentary candidates, which gives party members a direct influence on the composition of national party elites (Ichino and Nathan, 2013). During the campaign period, which intensifies in the three months before the elections, the mass party network comes to life. Regional offices dispatch resources to polling stations where party mobilizers draw up local campaign plans. The NDC have party positions in each electoral ward, while the NPP have positions for each polling station.

Some Campaign Strategies

Rallies.

Political parties in Ghana adopt a number of campaign strategies, and we focus on the three that are most prevalent. First, as in other countries in Africa and elsewhere (Horowitz, 2016) (Szwarcberg, 2012a), presidential and parliamentary candidates regularly hold campaign rallies. Rallies typically involve both the presidential candidate and the MPs from nearby constituencies. Ordinary voters, and local notables, including traditional chiefs attend rallies. Political parties often bus citizens into metropolitan areas for rallies and provide food or drinks for those who make the journey. At rallies, voters are also given t-shirts, handheld fans and other party paraphernalia emblazoned with pictures of the party's flag bearer. During rallies, politicians take to the stage to discuss their campaign promises and disparage the opposition. In terms of cost, rallies are no doubt expensive to organize; stages and public address systems need to be erected, sometimes large screens are also mounted. In addition, parties must pay activists to bring voters to the rally and provide nourishment to those who attend. Sometimes parties also exchange money with citizens in return for their attendance. Parties weigh these costs against the benefits. One important benefit is the creation of a public perception that the party is popular, in this regard, the larger the rally the better. Second, rallies can be cost effective in that politicians' messages are able to reach a large number of voters – often thousands – in one day.

Door to Door

A second major campaign activity in Ghana is door-to-door canvassing (Nathan, 2016). Here, political party activists visit potential voters at their homes in an effort to mobilize them to turn out to vote when targeting core supporters or to persuade them to vote for their party when targeting swing voters or supporters of the competing party. Nationally representative survey data collected by the Afro barometer shed some light on what happens when political party activists canvass potential voters at their homes. The survey conducted in 2012 (Round 5) included the following country-specific question about party activists: In your opinion, which three main activities would you say grassroots political party activists (or foot soldiers) primarily engage themselves in during election campaigns and elections? This was an open-ended question with enumerators coding responses into pre-defined categories. The data show that the most frequent first responses to this question were:

(1) "Explaining their party's plans, policies and programs during campaign"

(2) "Mobilizing people to support their party during elections". A smaller proportion of people said that the main activity of activists is to distribute gifts to voters and a very small proportion mention intimidation or violence. The idea that party activists are informed about the policies of the party they represent is also documented in the handbooks that parties in Ghana provide to activists. For example, the NPP's "Polling Station Manual" says that "It is deemed very necessary for Polling Station Executives [party activists] to up-date themselves on the policies and programmes of the NPP government so as to be able to proactively defend the Party at all times and at whichever level" (New Patriotic Party,2006). Thus, while party activists do employ a range of techniques when canvassing for voter's door-to-door, it seems that a large component of these interactions involve mobilizing

electoral support through a discussion of plans and policies rather than vote buying or intimidation.

During the election campaigns, one of the major policies that both parties discussed was the challenger's commitment to make senior high school (SHS) free. NPP billboards displayed the slogan "Free SHS Now! Not in 20 years. Your vote can make it happen. "Party activists have the task of convincing voters that the party's proposed policies will have a positive impact on their lives. They also remind voters of the party's track record over the years of democratic rule. For example, NDC activists are often eager to remind voters that their party was responsible for the electrification of the North of the country (Briggs, 2012), while NPP mobilizers are keen to remind voters, especially women, that they introduced the national health insurance scheme, which significantly reduced the cost of maternity care.

MONEY INCENTIVES
The distribution of money and gifts is also common during campaigns. Many voters expect to receive gifts from candidates (Ghana Center for Democratic Development,2016) and put pressure on candidates to distribute private benefits during the campaign. According to Afrobarometer survey data, about 12 percent of Ghanaians were offered money or a gift during the 2004 elections, and about 7 percent were offered money or a gift during the 2012 elections. Much vote buying in Ghana, and elsewhere in Africa, occurs in public spaces such as campaign rallies.

Incumbency Advantage and Campaign Strategies.
First, opposition parties are at a significant resource disadvantage because they lack access to state resources. In Ghana, the incumbent party is in a particularly strong position because the constitution requires that the president appoints the political head of each local government. This provision ensures that both the national and local

bureaucracy, traditional sources of party finance, are in the hands of the ruling party. In contrast, opposition parties have little to offer private firms aside from prospective promises. Accordingly, the opposition struggles to obtain financial capital.

Second, the incumbent is advantaged because it can direct public resources to fulfill its political goals before the election campaign even begins. There is evidence that presidents in some African countries channel public goods and resources to areas where their ethnic and partisan supporters live in high concentrations (Franck and Rainer, 2012; Jablonski, 2014). Briggs (2012) finds evidence of such targeting in Ghana, showing that incumbents have disproportionately delivered electrification to their stronghold areas. These advantages shape campaign strategies in two important ways. First, the incumbent's resource advantage should allow it to invest in more resource intensive campaign strategies. In particular, the incumbent should be better able to distribute private benefits to voters ahead of elections. Indeed, there are some evidence that the incumbent party in Ghana is able to engage in more vote buying (Ghana Center for Democratic Development, 2016).

Second, we expect that these advantages allow the incumbent to pursue a more national campaign strategy. This is largely because each of the main campaign strategies described above is labor intensive. As a result, each party must deploy a vast network of political party activists known locally by Ghanaians as "foot soldiers" to engage in campaign-related work. As in other contexts, political party activists play a central role in mobilizing voters to attend campaign rallies (Szwarcberg, 2012a,b), canvassing potential voters door-to-door (Horowitz, 2016), and engaging in vote buying and gift giving (Kramon,2016; Lindberg, 2003; Stokes et al., 2013).Party activists are motivated to work on campaigns for two reasons. First, some are motivated by a partisan attachment to their preferred party. This is especially the case in each party's stronghold areas.

However, many others work for political parties in return for private benefits (Bob-Milliar, 2012), or because of the expectation that they will receive private benefits should their party win office (Driscoll,2017). These benefits take the form of state employment, the payment of school fees and health care bills, and contributions to weddings and funerals. Given their resource advantage, incumbent parties can more easily attract the type of activists who are motivated by private benefits. It is important to note because they are richer, incumbent parties can offer upfront benefits to these activists and, because they are already in office, their promises of post-election benefits may appear more credible (Wantchekon, 2003). Thus, in addition to having more money to spend on campaigns, the incumbent has a comparative advantage in the recruitment of non-ideologically committed activists.

This advantage is important because each party's pool of ideologically committed activists is likely to be concentrated in its stronghold areas (Friday, 2007). Thus, while both parties should be able to campaign intensely in their own strongholds, the opposition is at a disadvantage with respect to its ability to pay activists to work in other parts of the country. By contrast, the incumbent can use its resource advantage to pay activists to campaign outside of its areas of core support. This implies that the incumbent will be able to invest more effort in campaigning in competitive and opposition electoral districts, while the challenger may be confined to its strongholds. A second reason that the incumbent should be able to pursue a more national campaign strategy is that the incumbent can strategically allocate state resources to fueling its electoral goals well in advance of the electoral period. Discretion over the state allows the incumbent to solidify electoral support in stronghold areas through targeted redistribution of state resources. We expect that this frees up the incumbent to campaign more intensely in competitive and opposition-stronghold areas of the country. It also allows the incumbent to deter insurgencies from within the party (Cox, 2010); that is, to prevent elites from defecting from the party and running against it as independents during the campaign.

In summary, political parties in low-income democracies such as Ghana pursue a range of campaign strategies and these strategies vary in how costly they are, meanwhile, all strategies are somewhat labor intensive. This is because incumbents enjoy substantial resource advantages and the executive enjoys significant discretion in the allocation of state resources before the campaign period begins, we therefore argue that incumbent and challenger campaign strategies will differ in two important ways. First, incumbents and challengers will invest in a different mix, or portfolio, of campaign strategies, with the incumbent being able to invest more heavily in more resource intensive strategies such as vote buying. Second, because the incumbent can use its resource advantage to purchase the labor of non-ideologically committed activists and use its discretion over the allocation of state resources to shore up support in its stronghold areas before the campaign period begins, the incumbent should be able to pursue a more national campaign strategy.

POLITICAL PARTIES, SOCIAL DEMOGRAPHICS AND THE DECLINE OF ETHNIC MOBILIZATION IN SOUTH AFRICA, 1994–99.

Before the advent of democratic rule in South Africa, most people had expected the country to experience an explosion of politicized ethnicity when minority rule was replaced. Yet this has not come to pass, and ethnic political parties have declined in number and influence in post- apartheid South Africa. Instead, between 1994 and 1999 partisan politics developed in a multipolar direction, with some parties embracing racial mobilization and others attempting to build multi- ethnic, non-racial entities. This article explains these developments as a product of the ways that political parties have responded to the incentives established by political institutions, on the one hand, and the structure of social divisions, on the other. The nexus between electoral rules and the level on which parties compete (national, regional, or local) holds enormous implications for the types of social cleavages that political parties will attempt to exploit as they seek political power.

Between 1994 and 1999, opposition politics in South Africa have developed in a multipolar direction, rather than along purely race-based lines. The general political cleavage that has emerged runs along an African minority divide that belies ethnic diversity on both sides. Political mobilization has emerged in this pattern primarily in reaction to some structural factors namely: the electoral system, federal system, and demographic divisions of South African society. In South Africa, the interaction of a weak federal and permissive electoral system created incentives that led parties to construct large electoral coalitions capable of delivering national rather than sub-national level representation. Once the political institutions set this incentive, particular parties set about constructing support blocks out of the most easily manipulatable societal cleavages, given an individual party's situation in the political marketplace. Given these incentives and constraints, party strategists turned away from the long-term goal of stealing supporters away from the ANC, and instead focused on challenging each other for the small pool of voters outside the ANC's traditional support base. Thus, the Democratic Party (DP) and New National Party (NNP) attempted to define political competition along lines based on the overlap of race and class divisions, while other parties, such as the Inkatha Freedom Party (IFP), responded to these incentives by attempting to move beyond a purely ethnic appeal.

The Ethnic Implosion that Never Came.
Many analysts now consider the supposed racialization of post-apartheid South African politics to be a natural occurrence. Yet this assessment can only be made by completely disregarding the

widespread predictions that ethnic conflict would replace racial divisions in post-apartheid South Africa. Analysts predicted that, once in power, the ANC would splinter along ethnic lines, similar to what had happened to the Zambian Movement for Multi- party Democracy (MMD) in the 1980s, and following the pattern witnessed in many African countries in the 1960s. Accordingly, the most intense debates over designing a post-apartheid political system revolved around the issue of how to construct an electoral system that would not exacerbate ethnic conflict. On the one hand, advocates of a proportional, power-sharing system argued that the model's inclusiveness would allay the fears of domination and exclusion that the minority groups would feel once White rule had ended (Lijphart, 1993). Advocates of a plurality electoral system argued that the centralizing tendency of this system would force parties to make broad appeals, resisting the incentives for the reification and Balkanization of ethnic differences that the proportional or consociational approach would inevitably foster (Horowitz, 1991). While differing in their prescription, advocates of both sides proceeded from the common diagnosis of the problem, namely, that South Africa would witness a sharp increase in divisive ethnic mobilization after the liberation struggle was over (Horowitz, 1991, p. 85; Lijphart, 1985, p. 122). The electoral system under which South Africa finally achieved democratic rule could have made these expectations a reality. South Africans ran the 1994 and 1999 elections under an electoral system that employed a closed-list PR formula (the Largest Remainder Droop formula) without a threshold. As a result, in both elections, several parties gained entrance into the National Assembly (NA) with less than 1 percent of the national vote. The ability to win representation in the NA with such small numbers could very well have encouraged parties to mobilize the small ethnic constituencies spread throughout the country. Despite permissive electoral rules, however, the number and influence of ethnic political parties have decreased in the post-apartheid scenario. Most of the small Coloured, Afrikaner, and African parties that existed in 1994 had disappeared by 1999. Even large ethnic parties like the New National Party (NNP – the party that created apartheid and once the staunch advocate of the Afrikaner volk), and the IFP (the political vehicle for the Zulus), shifted their appeals away from their narrow ethnic focus, such that in the campaigns for the 1999 elections both of these parties rarely appealed explicitly to ethnic interests. Instead of ethnic mobilization, race-based mobilization seemed to become the principal dividing line in the 1999 elections. Parties like the NNP and DP, rather than competing with the ANC for the support of African voters, fought amongst themselves for the 'minority vote' – Whites, Coloureds, and Indians. The IFP, which throughout its existence had gained political influence through its ability to mobilize Zulus and control the area that is now the KwaZulu–Natal province, moved away from a purely ethnic-based platform. In place of its long-standing emphasis on the status of the Zulu monarchy, respect for traditionalism and the rights of amakhosi (traditional leaders), the IFP's 1999 election campaign focused on a broad conservative platform (family values, anti-crime, anti-corruption, and a 'revolution' of goodwill), targeting potential supporters in virtually all population groups. The IFP virtually never brought up its traditional issues outside the deep rural areas of KwaZulu–Natal. The trend continued among the smaller and new parties. In its 1999 campaign, the Pan Africanist Congress attempted to shift its 'Africanist' stance from its historically pro-Black position to include anyone whose primary allegiance was to the continent of Africa. The newcomer in the race, the United Democratic Movement (UDM), attempted to build a non-racial coalition, and thus avoided explicitly ethnic appeals in all provinces (though cloaked appeals surfaced in the Eastern Cape). The Africa Muslim Party changed its name to the Africa Moral Party. Thus, the widely feared ethnic explosion did not occur. The explanation offered in this article rests on a number of factors, but places primary emphasis on the ways that party strategists responded to institutional incentives created by the interaction of a federal state weakened to the point of unitarism and a permissive electoral system. Together, these factors created a joint incentive structure that decreased the payoffs of appeals to small ethnic groups. The data for this argument will be presented through case studies of the NNP, DP, and IFP in the period from 1994 to 1999, culminating with an analysis of their campaigns for the 1999 elections.

The debate on the relationship between party systems and ethnic mobilization focuses most often on the choice between a permissive PR system and a centralizing plurality-based system. Permissive electoral systems, by lowering the number of votes needed to gain entrance into legislatures, facilitate the representation of small parties, and thus are considered to provide incentives for political entrepreneurs to cultivate small electoral coalitions based on small and marginal groups. In contrast, systems with more strict standards for representation, such as those requiring majorities concentrated in geographic constituencies, tend to weed out smaller parties, forcing parties to cultivate larger, more encompassing constituencies. Electoral institutions thus directly affect strategies of mobilization. First- past-the-post plurality (FPTP) electoral systems will often induce parties to campaign on issues that will be of concern to a broad audience, since the party needs to win over either a plurality or majority of the citizens in a geographic district. In contrast, under PR systems, if the district magnitude is not too small, parties can seek to mobilize particular constituencies that may be geographically dispersed, seeking to gain seats in the legislature based purely on the number of votes that this group can deliver. In this way, PR can provide incentives for exclusive appeals and mobilization of distinct groups. In this literature, the structure of government figures centrally as a solution to mitigate ethnic conflict, once it has already surfaced. Also, federal systems have received most attention for their potential to devolve power and reduce conflict in countries with geographically-based divisions, such as regional rivalries, ethno-territorial groups, or concentrated religious minorities. Federal systems are viewed as solutions in these situations because creating more tiers of government increases opportunities for groups to obtain representation in government and defuses the intensity of competition for power at the center (Coakley, 1993).

Yet the structure of government and the form of the executive also influence strategies of political mobilization, especially ethnic mobilization, a dynamic that receives comparably little attention in the academic literature. This oversight represents a fundamental neglect, because federal systems can shape party systems in very direct ways. A federal system that genuinely devolves power will cause parties to compete for power at lower levels in the political sphere, fostering the development of regional or local political parties. This dynamic creates incentives for parties to mobilize smaller or larger constituencies, sized appropriately to the level of power for which the party contests. In addition, federal systems could thus increase the politicization of ethnic or other regionally concentrated groups, because at lower levels of political competition, these groups become rewarding support bases. Nigeria serves as a prime example in this regard, where states were created to give ethnic groups increased control over their affairs. The creation of states then led to the political activation of even smaller ethnic groups that had not been relevant when the administrative unit was larger, which in turn fueled demands for further state creation (Ayoade, 1986; Diamond, 1988; Suberu, 1991).

These two factors interact with each other in a dynamic way to shape party system development in divided societies. Taken together, electoral rules and the structure of government create interacting incentive structures to which party elites respond when deciding where to focus scarce resources in the struggle to gain political representation. This joint incentive structure in turn interacts with the dimensions of social cleavages to shape mobilization strategies as parties attempt to craft support coalitions capable of providing the votes necessary to win legislative representation at the designated level.

POLITICAL PARTY GOVERNANCE

Social Divisions

South African society is complex and multilayered, with multiple divisions along the lines of race, ethnicity, class, and religion, to name but a few. In the South African context, race and ethnicity refer to separate concepts. Race groups refer to the four population categories established by the apartheid policies of the former government: Black (used interchangeably with African) refers to people belonging to 'tribes' indigenous to the area; Coloured are those of mixed ancestry; Indians refer to people of South Asian descent; and Whites are Europeans who are 'obviously' white. Whereas racial categories are based on visual (and incendiary) criteria, ethnic distinctions encompass communities grouped by cultural and linguistic differences. Thus, English, Xhosa, Afrikaner, and Zulu are all ethnic groups. South Africans self-identify themselves as members of ethnic groups more frequently than racial. When asked in an open-ended question to indicate the primary groups with which they identify, only 22 percent of South Africans reported racial categories, with more South Africans reporting their ethnic groups (29 percent) and almost as many citing religion (19 percent) as race. The high salience on religion, third overall, was notable, especially because of its non-politicization in national politics. Within each racial category, the primacy of ethnic and religious identification renders their relative non-politicization even more surprising. Given that much of South African political discourse takes place along a White–Black, previously advantaged–previously disadvantaged dichotomy, this primacy of ethnic over racial identification is notable. In part, this social latency arises from the overlap of racial and class groups. Together, they create racially bounded groups that provide easy targets for parties seeking to build support on the national level. For example, consider the relationship between class and race, using occupation as a proxy for class membership. South Africans according to occupational categories roughly corresponding to class groups. Each tier is divided into its racial composition, after which it becomes obvious how Africans cluster in the lower rank, while the professional class is over 50 percent White. These trends, demonstrating a sharp racial basis to class position, are reproduced in education, income, and other socio-economic measures. Each of the four racial groups thus occupies a distinct position in the country's socio-economic structure. This positioning generates similar material interests for each group, making them easily mobilized, large blocks of potential supporters. Meanwhile, the least educated, those employed in the least skilled occupations and those earning the lowest wages, are all disproportionately African. Class composition becomes more diverse the higher the class rank, but even in the highest tier White South Africans are disproportionately represented. The resulting overlap of class and race creates large communities, delimited by race, that share many common characteristics. Other apartheid policies, such as the Group Areas Act, also guaranteed that many South Africans lived in segregated communities. This not only reinforced the perception of shared interests, but also created racially bounded information networks (Mattes, 1995), further adding to the political importance of race as a tool for political manipulation, even if it does not dominate other bases of personal identity. The alignment of race and class also makes it possible to issue cloaked appeals to race groups through carefully constructed messages that raise specific interests, especially important in a society where blatant appeals to race have been de-legitimized. Thus, race combined with other factors renders it one of the most easily mobilized and most encompassing social divisions, one that easily overwhelms ethnic and religious mobilization. Finally, the geographic distribution of South Africans also plays a role in how parties pick and choose from the available menu of mobilization strategies. While Black/African South Africans are spread relatively evenly throughout the country's nine provinces, members of racial minority groups tend to cluster in specific provinces. For example, three-quarters of Indians reside in KwaZulu–Natal. The Coloured population lives almost entirely in three provinces: Gauteng, Western Cape, and Northern Cape. White South Africans are the least concentrated of the minority groups, yet still have concentrations in Gauteng, KwaZulu–Natal, and Western Cape. Parties seeking to court the racial minority vote would thus be more likely to concentrate their campaigns on particular provinces, rather than spreading the message evenly, as would a party focused on the African vote. These provincial concentrations help partially to mitigate the nationalizing effect of the weak federal system. Yet, since only two provinces have populations where racial minority groups are in the majority (Northern and Western Cape), targeting the minority vote in most provinces is not a winning strategy useful for winning provincial governments outright. Taking all these factors together, this article proposes an interactive explanation that in South Africa between 1994 and 1999, parties responded to these institutional and social incentives to turn away from ethnic mobilization as a viable strategy in national and provincial elections. Ethnic groups were too small to present lucrative political support bases when parties were concerned with winning influence at the national level. As a result, no party sought to activate any of the divisions that either cross-cut the racial groups or had the potential to reach into the support base of the ANC.

Parties could have utilized mobilization tactics that worked against the cumulative nature of the socio- economic cleavages by mobilizing people at either extreme: the multi-racial well-to-do, or the increasingly mono-racial rural poor. Courting ethnic, religious, and regional support had the potential to enable parties to build local support bases. Parties like the NNP, DP, and IFP, which could have advanced either ethnic or regional platforms, chose instead to challenge the ANC at the national level on national issues. Given the national focus of power, an electoral system that did not require geographic concentration of support, and the ANC's huge majority in the national parliament, winning just a few seats in the NA did not cede a party any real influence. Parties like the Freedom Front (FF), PAC, and ACDP, all of which had seven or fewer members in parliament between 1994 and

1999, barely made any impact on national policy making. Therefore, in order to win enough seats to have any influence on policy in the NA, when generating campaign strategies for 1999, most parties eschewed small-group mentioning language or ethnic groups were coded as the ethnic category; mentions of 'race' or a specific racial group as the racial categories, and so on. (Analysis conducted by the author). The figures are taken from the South African portion of the Southern African Barometer project. A few small parties did actually organize along regional lines, such as the United Christian Democratic Party, with the explicit purpose of advancing regional interests. A few others, such as the African Christian Democratic Party, advanced religious platforms. These parties, however, were extremely small and such changes were proposed in 2003 after a lengthy national debate by the Electoral Task Team appointed by the ANC government to consider electoral system reform, but the ANC promptly rejected the proposals.

Mobilization and Party Recruitment- the Chinese Example

Definitions of Mobilization
Political mobilization is defined above as "the process by which citizens are selected for involvement in politics". This definition is quite general and can probably be seen as more or less a "common denominator" of past conceptualizations of this term. However, the generality of this definition doesn't necessarily mean that it can be readily applied to the political context of Mainland China or can easily fit into the theoretical framework developed below. Worse still, as Verba, Schlozman& Brady (1995, p. 133) pointed out, mobilization "have multiple meanings and, therefore, might lead to misunderstanding concerning the process we are discussing". "Mobilization" can mean at least three quite different social phenomena. First, in the social economic sense, mobilization, as defined in the traditional "social mobilization theory", may refer to a process of "considerable social and economic development". In this process, large "numbers of individuals have been urbanized, have

become literate, and have been exposed to differentiated economic enterprises" (Almond & Powell 1966, p. 284) and to "the media of communication" (Almond, Powell &Mundt 1996, p.184). Second, "mobilization" can mean the sweeping effort by the totalitarian regime as portrayed in the "mobilization model". Barnett (1962, p. 31), for example, presented the following picture of the Maoist regime in China:

The Communists in China are true believers in, and practitioners of "totalism", involving maximum control and supervision of ordinary people's lives, maximum involvement of the entire Chinese population in state-directed activities, maximum control over people's thoughts and behavior, and maximum mobilization of China's millions to serve the purpose of the nation's new Communist regime.

Third, "mobilization" can also refer to the selective process to involve citizens in politics. For the research discussed in this thesis, apparently only the third meaning of "mobilization" is relevant. The theoretical concern of this study and the political reality of contemporary Mainland China render the former two definitions mostly irrelevant.

Defining Mobilization in China
To avoid confusion, Verba, Schlozman& Brady (1995, p. 133) used the term "recruitment" instead of "mobilization" to denote the process by which citizens are selected for involvement in politics. In this research I shall follow their usage. Another candidate is "activation." Schier (2000, p. 7) made a clear (and useful) distinction between "mobilization" and "activation," which he defines as "the more contemporary methods that parties, interest groups, and candidates employ to induce particular, finely targeted portions of the public to become active in elections, demonstrations, and lobbying". This seems to be a more appropriate counterpart in a liberal democracy of the selection process. Since I regard this issue as more of a word choice than of theoretical

significance, I shall still use the general term "recruitment" mentioned above. However, as with many other terms in social science research, the use of "recruitment" is not immune from problems. Although, generally defined as the inclusion of citizens among political elite, this term appears too narrow to capture the more general process in the theoretical framework that will be developed below, since political elite are not the only group that carry the expectation to be active in politics. In the political context of contemporary Mainland China, political mobilization takes on the form of recruitment of members by the Communist Party. The Communist Party of China is an "elite-dominated" Leninist party (Dickson 1997, p. 2). Although it also recruits power elite at the top of the political system, the Party as a whole is not an elite club. The Party is a mass political organization, with 64.5 million members by the end of 2000 (People's Daily, July 26, 2001), constituting 5.1% of the then total population in Mainland China and 6.6% of the population aged 15 or above, according to the 2000 census.

Recruitment as Party's Choice

Recruitment of members to the Party is in effect a long and deliberate process of decision-making by the basic level organizations of the Party. This implies two things for the theoretical model. First, even though people sometimes talk about "joining" the Party in everyday life, the recruitment of Party members is to a large extent a choice made not by an individual citizen, but by the Party organizations, and in theory it can be modeled that way. Second, in terms of the specific choice of whom to recruit, the Party cannot be modeled as a unitary actor, even though its recruitment policy has been carried out in an impressively consistent way. In the end, local Party organizations, especially the Party branches and their respective superior Party committees, are the decision-makers as regards recruitment. To justify these two theoretical assumptions, we have to turn to a somewhat "thicker description" of how a Party member is recruited at the grassroots level.

Recruiting vs. Joining

Practically, the general aggregate patterns of Party recruitment are largely determined by the Party, not by self-initiated actions taken by individual citizens. First of all, the whole recruitment process normally begins with the local Party organization obtaining some quota and/ or guidelines for recruiting new members from the upper level (Lee, 1991, p. 305). The recruitment work has to follow the Party center's policy of "adhering to standards, ensuring quality, improving structure, and recruiting prudently". Every year we made plans of recruitment for basic level Party organizations. These plans include how many members can be recruited, and the extent of adjustments to those quotas. We also specify the emphases of recruitment. Four areas have preferences, that is, the production frontline, youth below the age of 35, women, and work units where there has been no recruitment for some years.

At the aggregate level, it would be inappropriate to characterize Party recruitment as starting from a citizen's self-selection process of applying to join the Party (Bian, Shu& Logan 2001, p. 814). By the time a citizen formally submits the application to a Party branch, some macro level conditions have already been set. In 1990, the Party promulgated a Detailed Regulations on Recruitment of Party Members [ZhongguoGongchandangFazhanDangyuanGongzuoXize], which starts by stipulating that "basic level organizations shall regard the recruitment of advanced elements with communist consciousness to the Party as a regular and important work" (Article 2). Later on, it states more explicitly:

Article 5 Party organizations shall, through the propaganda of the Party's political stand and in-depth and elaborate ideological and political work, enhance the non-Party masses' understanding of the Party and constantly enlarge the ranks of activists who apply to join the Party.

Recruitment Decision at Local Level/ Basic Level Party Organizations/Hierarchical Relationship

According to the Party Constitution, "basic level Party organizations are formed in enterprises, countryside, organs, schools, scientific research institutions, city neighborhoods, companies of the People's Liberation Army and other basic units, wherever there are three or more full Party members" (Article 29, Chapter 5). In the countryside, according to the Organization Work Rules of Basic Level Organizations in the Countryside [ZhongguoGongchandangNongcunJicengZuzhiGongzuo Tiaoli], Party committees should be established at the town or township level and Party branches should be established at the village level. A village with more than 50 full Party members can set up a general branch, and a village with more than 100 full Party members can set up a Party committee. However, a general branch or committee thus set up is still under the leadership of its superior town or township Party committee.

Recruitment Procedures and Application

As mentioned above, part of the routine work of the Party organizations at the basic level is to enlarge the pool of applicants through contacting and propaganda. In practice, the formal recruitment process at the local level can be generalized like this. At some Party branch meeting, some Party members are assigned to "observe" and talk to prospective candidates. At this stage, those candidates may have turned in formal written applications to join the Party to the basic level organization, but may not in some cases. When a Party member talks to a prospective applicant, it is normally on a very informal occasion, since in most cases they already know each other. A typical scenario is that the Party member starts by almost casually asking about how the candidate is doing in work or study, and compliments or praises are inserted whenever appropriate. Then the subject turns to the candidate's view about the Party, by which time the flattered candidate knows roughly what the talk is actually about. If the candidate has not submitted a written application yet, before the talk ends the Party member normally reminds him or her to do that sometime soon.

Observation and Training

After the application is turned in, the Party branch has to do even more observation, evaluation, training, and education on the applicants, mainly through the one or two full Party members (not probationary) who are assigned as the "contact persons" or "trainers" for each applicant. The Party organization also seek opinions about the candidates from all Party members, and even from non-Party members. (The secretary of a Party committee described to me how that is done in his location:)

Every year we put up the activists' name on a board in the Party committee compound, and both Party members and non-Party masses can see it. We also write down two telephone numbers below the list of names, so that the masses can call to tell us problems with the quality and conduct of the applicants. If the problems are serious, we'll carry out investigations and postpone the recruitment.

Probation and Admission

After at least one year of "fostering" and education, Party branch will handpick some "recruitment targets" and carefully examine their political background. Party committee will organize 5 to 7 days of intensive study of Party documents for the recruitment targets, and then an all-member meeting of the Party branch will discuss and vote on whether to admit the targets as probationary Party members. The admission of probationary Party members has to be examined and approved by superior Party organizations, normally the Party committees. The probation period for a new Party member is normally a year, but can be longer if it is decided that more examination and education are needed. Then a probationary Party member becomes a full member after another discussion and vote session at the Party branch level and examination and approval again at the superior Party organization.

Strategic Rationality

Past research on Party recruitment in Mainland China has mainly focused on such personal characteristics as family background, social relations, education, age, etc., and sometimes political participation is also included as a factor (Lee 1991, p. 306), (Bian, Shu& Logan 2000, p. 809). However, it is the opinion of the writer that, political participation is qualitatively different from the other factors in two important aspects. First, political participation clearly indicates a decision or choice made by an individual citizen, whereas it is hardly sensible to say so for the other factors, which are mostly personal qualities. Second, political participation enters into the Party's consideration mainly as an expectation. For each prospective target of recruitment, the Party organizations implicitly ponder the question: "what will s/he do if recruited?" Although the Party organizations observe participatory activities by the citizen before recruitment, in the final analysis it is the citizen's expected participatory behavior after recruitment that enters the Party's utilities over recruitment. That is, the Party organization's decision of recruitment depends on its expectation of political participation.

As mentioned above, the aggregate patterns of political participation and mobilization are the consequences of the micro-level decision making by the political parties as to whether to recruit an individual citizen and by each individual citizen as to whether to participate in politics. And more importantly, these two decisions making processes are not just choosing from a menu of determinate outcomes fixed by nature. Instead, they are interdependent, in the sense that for either of the two decision-makers which action is the better choice depends not only on exogenous background variables but also on the decision made by the other. That is, the final outcome is jointly determined by the actions of both the party and the citizen. This kind of situation is still within the rational choice paradigm, although it belongs to a special class of cases, that of "strategic rationality" (Little 1991a, p. 52). I shall discuss below the strategic aspects of the party's and the citizens' rational calculations, respectively, and derive hypotheses from these discussions in terms of the utility functions (costs and benefits) of the party and of each citizen. For a political party in general, its decision of whether to mobilize an individual citizen or not depends on a calculation of expected returns and costs for each outcome, as above mentioned. The party has to take into consideration whether this citizen will continue to participate or not, since the outcome also depends on the citizen's action. As a rational actor, the party only mobilizes a citizen if its expected returns from that citizen's future political behavior outweigh the necessary investment of time and efforts to mobilize him or her. For the Communist Party of China, when its local organizations make the decision of recruitment, their choices depend on the expected participatory behavior of the citizens, which has a major impact on their expected utilities over recruitment.

For any political party, if it mobilizes a citizen, it has to pay the cost of mobilization (henceforth denoted as C1, a non-negative value), which depends on the necessary investment of time and efforts to mobilize the citizen. The cost of mobilization is an important factor in a political party's decision whether to mobilize a citizen or not, and this is true both in Western liberal democracies and in an authoritarian system. Indeed Schier (2000, p. 30) explains the rise of "activation" (equivalent to the "targeted mobilization" discussed earlier in this dissertation) with the lower cost of mobilization brought about by technological innovation as one of the most important reasons. For the Chinese Communist Party, the cost of mobilization used to be exorbitantly high during the Maoist mass campaigns. To achieve sweeping participation of the population in voting, meetings, or demonstrations, the party-state usually had to call up all the political activists as "mobilized mobilizers", or to make use of its resources to offer positive and negative incentives. Under the Party's new agenda of economic development since the late 1970s, however, this type of mobilization is simply not sustainable, if only because its cost would be unacceptably high in terms of lost productivity. As above mentioned, in the reform era, the mode of political mobilization has been shifted to the recruitment of Party members, but recruitment is still a very lengthy and careful decision-making process. From the above description of the recruitment procedure, the cost of mobilizing a citizen is apparently not negligible for the Chinese Communist Party. With everything else held constant, the Party certainly prefers to pay less cost in recruiting a citizen.

THE UNITED STATES OF AMERICA MOBILIZATION EXPERIENCE

Introduction of Racial and socio-economic disparities in political participation continue in the United States, both at the national and the community levels. Mobilization as an important predictor of political participation has received much greater attention in recent years. However, not as much is known about predictors of mobilization, in particular about recruitment to non-electoral acts such as attending meetings or contacting a public official. Such acts are the means through which ordinary citizens can attempt to influence the policies and practices that affect their lives. If there are disparities in who is recruited for political participation, these differences could well be reflected in the voices heard or not heard in the political arena. If we wish to understand the continuing disparities in political participation, then it behooves us to understand who is invited to participate in the multiple facets of the political process and who is ignored. There is ample evidence supporting the positive role played by mobilization in increasing electoral focused activities, such as voting, giving money to or working for a campaign (Abramson &Claggett, 2001; Brady, Verba, &Schlozman, 1995; Cohen & Dawson, 1993; Eldersveld, 1956; Ellison & Gay, 1989; Gosnell, 1927; Huckfeldt& Sprague, 1992; Kramer,

1970; Krassa, 1988; Niven, 2001; Norrander, 1991; Rosenstone& Hansen, 1993; Schlozman, Burns, &Verba, 1999; Smith &Zipp, 1983; Wielhouwer, 1999; Wielhouwer& Lockerbie, 1994).8 Some authors have found mobilization to be particularly important for African Americans {Ellison & Gay 1989, p. 260}. Most of these studies focus on voter turnout or other types of electoral behavior, such as contributing to a campaign or putting up a sign. While elections are important, they only occur once a year and nationally important elections occur even less frequently. Citizens can attempt to influence political outcomes throughout the year through such acts as contacting public officials, attending meetings, or participating in protests. However, relatively few studies have examined the effect of mobilization on participation in activities other than in the electoral realm (Brady, et al., 1995; Cohen & Dawson, 1993; Kenneth Michael Goldstein, 1996; Marschall, 2004; Rosenstone& Hansen, 1993). Those that have, found the effect of recruitment to be positive and significant, so much so that Cohen and Dawson (1993, p. 297) have argued it might provide an important leveling effect for people who reside in low-income neighborhoods, given their lower rates of participation. Given the apparent importance of the mobilization factor, what do we know about who is mobilized or the predictors of mobilization? The answer is, —not much. Rosenstone and Hansen (1993, pp. 287-89) argue that political elite, i.e., parties, politicians and interest groups, target those who are well connected, whose actions are effective and who are more likely to respond positively to the recruitment message. Their research suggests this may be the case for mobilization efforts by political parties in general. Predictors of contact by parties in presidential and mid-term election years were wealth, higher educational levels, being older in terms of both age and tenure in the community church attendance and union membership. Goldstein and Rideout (2002) and Gershtenson (2003) found similar results. However, when they included an additional variable, past voting history, its effect was often far larger than those of the variables Rosenstone and Hansen had included. If nothing else, voting in a previous election may give recruiters a clue as to potential effectiveness of a contact. Unfortunately, although the National Election Study data utilized in each of the studies included a question on mobilization, the format of the question was very general. Respondents were only asked if someone from a political party spoke to them about a specific candidate or campaign. We do not know if they were asked to vote, contribute money, attend a campaign meeting or perform some other action. Thus, we also do not know if individuals targeted for the various actions all fit the same profile.

Campbell et al (1960) indicated that likelihood of contact by a political party in 1956 was highest for those in the skilled and semi-skilled professions. Professional level could certainly be viewed by recruiters as a proxy for political resources or effectiveness. Huckfeldt and Sprague (1992) examined contact by party separately in a 1984 study in South Bend, Indiana and maintained that past participation in Democratic primaries was a positive predictor for Democratic contact, with similar results for Republican contact. Education was only demographic variable included and it was only significant for Republican Party contact.

In their survey, Brady, et al. (1999) did move beyond mobilization for electoral activity alone. They included questions asking whether a person was contacted to work on a campaign, contact a governmental official, protest, and become involved in a community activity. Similar to findings in the electoral arena, the authors found higher levels of education, family income, political engagement and past political participation to be positive predictors of mobilization. However, these authors combined mobilization for all types of activity into an index. Thus, we do not know if all predictors affect mobilization for each type of activity in the same way. Interestingly, church attendance and working were significantly, but negatively associated with mobilization. Organizational membership was not significant, but the question used by Brady, et al. (1999, p, 158) was limited to membership in organizations that do not take a political stand). They thus excluded membership in organizations that are most likely to prospect for recruits. The authors further tested their recruitment model on contact to make a contribution and found family income to be the largest predictor of recruitment to make a contribution. They did not report the effects of any other variables (p. 161). In essence then, we are still limited to a one size fits all model for predicting mobilization. If recruiters are rational, they surely use different clues about who will respond, depending on the desired action. Not all actions require the same political skill or investment. Abramson and Claggett (2001) do address the idea that recruiters change their tactics based on the action requested, specifically voting, making a campaign contribution or any other campaign activity. As did others, they found past participation to be a strong, positive predictor of current recruitment, but the effect of past participation varied by the action requested. For recruitment to campaign activities, past campaign activity carried more weight than individual resources or group membership. In the case of requests for campaign contributions, age and individual resources had bigger effects than did past giving, and Blacks were less likely to be contacted than whites. Lastly, recruiters attempting to get individuals to support a particular candidate do appear to take into account past voting history, but here the effect of past participation is the smallest. In addition to age and education, strength of party ID was also a positive factor in recruitment. Goldstein (1996) focused on recruitment to lobbying efforts and in addition to the race and resources results mentioned earlier, he also found men and members of union households were more likely to be targeted. There is thus suggestive evidence of specific recruitment strategies for various types of action. However, we are limited in our understanding of the role accessibility plays in recruitment. For example, in Brady et al, (1999), the group membership variable was limited to non-political organizations, while Abramson and Claggett, (2001) only included groups with which an individual strongly identified. Group membership lists can cut the costs of recruitment for organizers, but targeting all groups may not be cost effective. More exploration is needed about the role played by group membership in the recruitment process, as well as other factors that might increase organizers' access to individuals. While we have a beginning understanding of the role played by an individual's social membership, we are thus far missing a consideration of the broader political and social context within which individuals live—their neighborhoods. Huckfeldt and Sprague (1992, p. 75) provide one of the few studies that examine the effect of the neighborhood on contact. For the gubernatorial and congressional races, the Republican Party was more likely to target those living in neighborhoods where there had been a high turnout in the Republican primary--neighborhoods also associated with higher educational levels. The authors used proportion of the neighborhood canvassed by the Democrats to predict individual contact. Not surprisingly, the likelihood of contact went up as the proportion in the neighborhood canvassed went up. When the authors added in controls for individual education and party ID, the neighborhood effect disappeared for Republican contact, but not for Democratic. Neither individual educational level nor party ID was significantly associated with Democratic contact. At least in this case, it appears Democrats may have targeted neighborhoods, while Republicans targeted individuals. This suggests that organizers look not only at the characteristics of individuals, but of neighborhoods as well. This particularly makes sense for non-electoral activities where aids such as voting records may not be available. If organizers don't have a lot of information about individuals likely to turn out for a meeting for example, it may be cost effective to target those neighborhoods perceived to have the resources necessary for participation or with a perceived stake in an issue. Conversely, some organizers might avoid resource poor neighborhoods or those perceived to be dangerous. Unfortunately, the individual and neighborhood variables utilized in Huckfeldt and Sprague's study were very limited. The political science literature on political mobilization is limited in terms of what actually guides the recruitment strategies of activists. However, literature in the field of community organizing (CO) is replete with guides on who and how to organize for political action. While much of the research in political recruitment has focused on national and electoral politics, but the CO literature focuses to a much greater extent on local communities and neighborhoods and their issues (See for example, (Alinsky, 1972; Fisher &Romanofsky, 1981; Piven&Cloward, 1979; Reitzes&Reitzes, 1987; Rubin & Rubin, 2008; Saegert, 2006)).

Some of the differences found in factors influencing recruitment to politics in general, may be that organizers use different strategies when recruiting for electoral politics versus politics at the local level where there is a greater concern with specific issues, such as schools, crime, the placement of toxic waste sites, access to city services, etc. According to the CO literature, the goal is to recruit individuals and organizations, particularly in poor communities who are directly impacted by the local community issues. If this is the case, we should see different profiles of the recruited based on the issue which political science has not been able to adequately address to date. Thus far, some evidence suggests that political recruiters are strategic with regard to the specific actions requested. However, the research in recent times are limited in four respects. There is little analysis of 1) non-electoral activities; 2) factors which might make one more visible or accessible to organizers; 3) neighborhood characteristics as a factor in mobilization strategies; and 4) the influence of specific issues on who is recruited.

First, given the race disparities in political participation, what role is played by race in the recruitment strategies of organizers? Does race enter as a factor for some forms of activity more than for others, if at all? Since mobilization strongly predicts political participation, the answer to this question not only has consequences for participation, but ultimately for which voices are heard in the defining of policy, particularly at the local level. Second, what role does accessibility play in recruitment strategies? Is it simple membership that matters, membership in specific kinds of groups, past participation or something as simple as having children? I argue that past participation and group membership make one visible, and thus accessible to recruiters. Given limited resources, organizers will probably choose to recruit those who are easiest to find. The use of voter registration lists is a prime example for electoral activities, but available lists are not limited to electoral activities. Many organizations keep lists of members and those who have participated in past activities. Often groups share their lists. As many people have experienced, once they are placed on a group's list, it is not uncommon to hear from other groups as well. People with children may be accessible as well, since schools in particular often use the children as a conduit of information to parents. To be sure, individuals might be notified of important education issues if they are a member of a school group, but non- school group members might also be notified of an action through their children. Third, how does neighborhood context influence the likelihood that residents will be contacted about political activities? Organizers in the electoral realm can use extensive voting lists to refine their recruitment strategies, but this resource is not available for many forms of political participation. If, as some have argued, organizers are rational and strategic, focusing their efforts on individuals with the skills and resources necessary for political action, might not the same be true for the targeting of neighborhoods? Cho et al (2006) found a negative effect on electoral turnout rates for neighborhoods with high poverty rates and percentage of Black and Hispanic residents, and a positive effect on turnout for neighborhoods with high levels of education. Possibly, some geographic areas are simply ignored by recruiters, while others are targeted. Indeed, if the information available to organizers at the individual level is limited, the search for potential activists might be akin to the search for a needle in a haystack. A focus on resource rich neighborhoods might be a far more cost-effective strategy than doing a broad sweep of the populace. On the other hand, organizers might ignore certain neighborhoods, possibly in the belief that there aren't enough individuals living in such areas who possess the needed political resources, or because of organizers' biases or fears.

Fourth, how does recruitment vary, if at all, by activity and issue? The final section will explore profiles of the mobilized based on the type of activity and issue for which individuals are recruited. My assumption is strategists use a different individual, social and neighborhood profile for when recruiting for attendance at a meeting than they do for pulling in people to attend a protest or searching for financial contributors, for example. The goal of the writer is to fill in some of the gaps within previous studies of political recruitment. One cannot fully understand the team of players already active in the political arena unless one first looks at who has been asked to play in the game, and specifically for which activities and issues.

Chapter 8

Intra Party Democracy and Decision Making

INTRAPARTY DEMOCRACY AND DECISION MAKING.

A study of the development political parties since independence, reveals a very high mortality rate. This can be attributed to the lack of proper intra-party governance. In other words, there is a very weak cohesion with the various parties that has ever been formed in Nigeria. Since independence in Nigeria, the concept of internal democracy has been relegated to the background through the activities of political parties from the First Republic and the germane issue has become contending in the present Fourth Republic. Research has shown that this lack of internal democracy in political parties led to crisis in the past civilian regimes, and a causal factor on which the military anchored its intervention in 1966. Conflicting interests and ramblings in the Nigerian present political parties is attributed to a lack of internal democracy in the political parties.

Political parties have existed and disappeared in different guises in the nation's political history (Adeleye, 2013). Herbert Macaulay, formed the first political party in Nigeria in 1923 known as The Nigerian National Democratic Party (NNDP). Its activities were restricted to contesting the election only in the Lagos City Council. UNDP hegemonic activities over the years led to the emergence of the Lagos Youth Movement (LYM), which became the Nigerian Youth Movement in 1934 and defeated the NNDP for the available three seats allocated for Lagos (Omotola, 2009).

There was a new turn of events by 1944 due to the agitations of Nationalists, which resulted in the formation of The National Council of Nigeria and Cameroon (CNCN) under the leadership of Herbert Macaulay and later Nnamdi Azikiwe. In the 1950s, most socio-cultural organizations transformed themselves into political parties.

The Yoruba Egbe Omo Oduduwa became The Action Group (AG) under the leadership of Chief Obafemi Awolowo and the Northern People's Congress emerged from the North in 1959. The emergence of the Northern Element Progressive Union (NEPU) was as a result of a breakaway faction of the NPC, the Radical Youth based in Kano, which later dominated the political landscape in their respective regions and spurred them on towards independence and the First Republic (Sklar, 1963). The First Republic political parties drew their strengths on a regional basis from the three regions. The aborted third Republic saw the activities of two major political parties, which were introduced by the then, Head of State General Gbadamoisi Babangida: Nigerian Republican Convention (NRC) and the Social Democratic Party (SDP). They contested until the annulment of the June 12 election, which the SDP was proposed to have won (Adeleye, 2013). According to Emordi et al, (2006) upon assumption of office by Abacha, the two existing political parties were dissolved, and five political parties were inaugurated: the United Nigeria Congress Party (UNCP), Grassroots Democratic Party of Nigeria (GDM), Democratic Party of Nigeria (DPN), National Centre Party of Nigeria (NCPN) and Congress for National Congress (CNC). These political parties were said to have conspired and adopted Abacha as their presidential candidates for his third term bid agenda. Upon transition to democracy, the candidate of the People's Democratic Party, General Olusegun Obasanjo, emerged as the winner of the 1999 election and became the manager of the Nigerian economy till the merger formed by CPC, ANPP and ACN – APC opposition party – emerged as the winner of the 2015 general election.

Internal democracy denotes various means of carrying along all party members in internal party decision making and other deliberations (Scarrow, 2004). Duverger (1963) emphasizes that internal democracy is the pillar behind a proper functioning of democratic system. In n different way, Sartori (1977) observed that the logic of party competition is what made a vibrant functioning democracy and not internal democracy. Internal democracy is an all-inclusive top to bottom approach to party decision making involving party primaries, representation, accountability and fair ground for all members to be carried on board by the party internally (Okhaide, 2012).

Internal democracy or intra-party democracy means parties have an agreement, laid down procedure and principles of mutual decision making and avoiding of conflict or managing it in order to prevent arbitrary decision or imposition of candidates as against the majority members wish. Internal democracy is vital for democratic consolidation and representation. It provides a room for proper recruitment of members, socialization, training, discipline, accountability and transparency. In other words, any party that lacks internal democracy is considered as undemocratic even though no political party can declare itself as undemocratic even if it is so. Some factors can undermine internal democracy by arbitrary leadership in the party and marginalization of some party members. The effects of absence of internal democracy create anti-party activities, conflicts, failure in election and deviation from the principles of democracy (Omilusi, 2016).

Internal democracy involves parties' selection of candidates, consultation, internal principles of party discipline and sanction, promotion of parties' ideology, accountability (Awofeso, Obah-Akpowaghaga & Ogunmilade, 2017). Hallberg (2008) identified two major methods of promoting internal democracy: the advocacy and legal/regulatory measures. The advocacy perspective includes selection of party leaders, party representative for election, collective decision making and peaceful negotiation. The second aspect is legal/regulatory means which should consist of party constitution, gentleman agreement on principles and regulations governing representation, minority consideration, negotiation and punishment for members.

The central purpose in this chapter is to review how the People Democratic Party (PDP) has fared in terms of internal Party Democracy and what lessons can be leant by political players in terms of consolidation intra party democracy and by implication deepening the democratic culture of the nation in general.

A CASE STUDY OF PEOPLES DEMOCRATIC PARTY (PDP) BRTWEEN 1999 AND 2013

INTRODUCTION
Party system is one of the essential tools for democracy but we must accept that conflict is inevitable in all democracies. This is true because democracy seeks the effective ways through which a society should be governed, borne not out of contest either internally or externally. Conflict results whenever two or more persons seek to possess the same object or occupy the same position and play incompatible means of achieving their purposes. What has the situation been like in the internal contest of the Peoples Democratic Party (PDP)? What are the factors responsible for intra-party conflict in the Peoples Democratic Party? How do these factors affect Nigeria as it moves towards democratic consolidation and sustainable development?

What is the way forward? From all indications, it is observed that the parochial idea of the party stalwarts in the Peoples Democratic Party is highly defective. Nigeria was until 1999, devastated with military rules. However, almost 14 years (1999-2013) into democratic rule and in spite of sustainable democratic government, peace and security have been threatened and difficult to achieve. To maintain peace and security, the role of political parties in the country is paramount. These among other roles include; democratic sustainability, maintenance of peace and security and serve as a unifying force in a divided polity. The general administration of election, despite sporadic minor setbacks, suggests that elections may not be a "fading shadow of democracy" or "without choice" (Schedler, 2002; Omotola, 2010). One may be persuaded to contemplate the celebration of Nigeria's democracy and doing that will amount to various misreading of the situation and an underestimation of the challenges of democratic consolidation by promoting democratic political culture and security, whatever push and pull, which are often much more daunting than the task of establishing it. Some core defies in Nigeria are difficult and tiring task of political conflict resolutions and internal democracy. This is because intra-party democracy is central to the maintenance of orderly society in any democracies. According to Scarrow (2000), democracy needs strong and sustainable political parties with the capacity to represent citizens and provide policy choices that demonstrate their ability to govern for the public good. With an increasing disconnect between citizens and their elected leaders, democratic political parties are continually challenged by a decline in political activism, and a growing sophistication of anti- democratic forces.

Political parties are crucial actors in representative democracies. Parties can help to articulate group aims, nurture political leadership, develop and promote policy alternatives, and present voters with coherent electoral alternatives. It has been observed in recent times that many political parties in Nigeria find it difficult to adopt an open system that will not only allow members of the party to participate in the decision making but also give them constrained opportunity to contest in elections under the party's platform. This kind of socio-political restriction is poisonous and has resulted in party wrangling, acrimony and cross-carpeting in many Nigerian political parties. One may ask the following questions: Is there intra-party democracy in Nigeria's political parties? Can Nigerian political parties stand the test of time in maintaining peace and security, and consolidating democracy when assessed against their roles? These and other related questions are engaged in this piece with a view not only to understanding the depth of the crisis and contradictions of 2011 primaries and general elections, but also to mapping a viable path towards maintaining peace and consolidating democracy in Nigeria.

Conflict and intra-party Democracy
The concept of conflict is the politics of power, a relationship between people in which some get others to obey them. One basic characteristic common to all human organization according to Dudley (1973, p. 8) is the interaction and interdependence among their members. Conflict in this study is structured around two main hypotheses. First, conflict is inevitable in any society where people are denied their basic human needs for identity, equality, recognition, security, dignity and participation. This was obvious during the PDP's last presidential primary election and convention. The second structure is that, conflict is likely wherever the performance of a government policy is biased in favour of a certain group. Political parties are one of the institutions that carryout and actualize the democratic principles in any organized democratic society. They have to perform a number of 'institutional guarantees' to effectively discharge what is expected of them in any democracies. Intra-party democracy is one of the institutional requirements. However, before a country can be sanitized and developed, there must be a number of internal sanitation and development in the prospective parties that look forward to form

government in such society. According to Scarrow (2004), internal democracy describes a wide range of methods for including party members in intra-party deliberation and decision-making. Intra-party democracy is a very broad term describing a wide range of methods for including party members in intra-party deliberation and decision making. Some advocates for intra-party democracy argue, on a pragmatic level, that parties using internally democratic procedures are likely to select more capable and appealing leaders, to have more responsive policies, and, as a result, to enjoy greater electoral success. Some, moreover, converge on the premise that parties that "practice what they preach," in the sense of using internally democratic procedures for their deliberation and decisions, strengthen democratic culture generally. On the contrary and more realistically, we would agree that intra-party democracy is not a panacea: some procedures are better suited to some circumstances than to others. Moreover, some procedures seem even to entail distinct costs, and there are stable democracies with parties that lack guarantee or regular processes of internal party democracy.

Nevertheless, the ideal of intra-party democracy has gained increasing attention in recent years because of its apparent potential to promote a "virtuous circle" linking ordinary citizens to government, benefiting the parties that adopt it, and more generally contributing to the stability and legitimacy of the democracies in which these parties compete for power. Unfortunately, the case of intra-party democracy in the People Democratic Party (PDP) cannot lay claim to democratic consolidation if it continues with the current mode of organizing her primaries most especially during the 2011 Presidential primary and the just concluded Party National Convention. Intra-party conflicts capture the reality of Nigeria's political parties because political parties had become useful for variety of tasks that required control or communication since political party was initially invented for more limited and self-serving purpose. Hardly a political system adjudged democratic without the central placement of political parties in its political process. This is because it is important and necessary for political parties to have intra-party democracy since political parties are the major vehicles for the expression of an essential feature of the democratic process. By extension, the fate of democracy and the nature of the political system itself lie in the health and resilience of the party system. The idea is that parties must be democratic not only externally in the operations, but also internally in the organizational functions. Those who emphasize the participatory aspects of democracy place the most value on intra-party democracy as an end in itself. They see parties not primarily as intermediaries, but rather as incubators that nurture citizens' political competence. To fulfill this role, party's decision-making structures and processes should provide opportunities for individual citizens to influence the choices that parties offer to voters (see Omotola, 2010, pp. 125-145). These opportunities will help citizens expand their civic skills, and inclusive processes can boost the legitimacy of the alternatives they produce. In this way, party institutions can perform useful educative functions while also transferring power to broader sector of society. The interplay and action existing between parties and democracies should show the parties' adherence to internal democratic structures. Intra-party democracy aims at developing more democratic, transparent and effective political parties. It also identifies specific challenges in the internal management and functioning of parties and party systems. These include; candidate selection, leadership selection, policy making, membership relations, gender discrimination, party funding among others. From this outcome-oriented perspective, parties' organizational structures should be judged above all in terms of how well they help the parties choose policies and personnel that reflect the preferences of their broader electorates. All these require critical attention on the issue-areas such as: is internal democracy a selling point for parties or does it pose important dangers for parties with regard to internal cohesion? If the above question is answered correctly, then we will be right to assert that internal democracy enhances a viable democratic culture within the party as well as society at large. It has positive effects on the representation of ideas of the electorate and may strengthen the organization by attracting new members and creating space for fresh ideas. Another important effect of intra-party democracy in line with the assertion of Gosnell (1968) is that it provides necessary vertical linkages between different deliberating spheres and horizontal linkage between competing issues. The elements which are instrumental to intra-party democracy cannot be over-emphasized in having effective and working internal democracy. First and foremost, it involves organizing free, fair and periodic elections of internal positions, as well as candidates for representative bodies. The second entails equal and open participation of all members and member groups in such a way that interests are equally represented.

THE BANE OF INTRA-PARTY CONFLICTS

IN PEOPLES DEMOCRATIC PARTY (P.D.P)

Party politics in Nigeria is associated with the pattern of colonial governance in the state. It could be recalled that decolonization as envisaged by the British in what later became the Nigerian State was viewed as a gradual process of constitutional transformations that would give greater freedom to the Nigerian people in form of participation in governance through *partyism* before the attainment of political independence. Thus, the nature and pattern of party politics during colonialism was to a great extent determined by the constitutional concessions permitted by the British Colonial System. For instance, while the 1922 Clifford Constitution gave birth to the first political party in Nigeria known as the Nigerian National Democratic Party (NNDP) in 1992, party politics in the State was restricted to just two cities; Lagos and Calabar. The implication is that party democracy during this era was restricted to two cities, and even in the cities, franchise was restricted because of property qualification coupled with the fact that the system was purely one-party system. However, shortly before the 1946 Richards Constitution, party democracy was widened with the birth of the Nigerian Youth Movement (NYM) in 1934. As a result, Nigerians in the two cities of Lagos and Calabar had the opportunity of choice between the NNDP and the NYM. With the operation of the 1951 Macperson Constitution, the Action Group (AG), the Northern People's Congress (NPC) was registered and they became a major player with the NCNC in the march towards Nigeria's independence (Adigwe, 1997).

At the dawn of Nigeria's political independence in October 1, 1960, several manners of political parties have emerged. In the First Republic, there were parties like National Council of Nigerian Citizens (NCNC), Northern People Congress (NPP) and Action Group (AG). The Nigerian Peoples Party (NPP), National Party of Nigeria (NPN), Great Nigerian People's Party (GNPP), Unity Party of Nigeria (UPN), People Redemption Party (PRP) and later the Nigerian Advance Party (NAP), which was later registered in 1982, were formed in the Second Republic (Oshaghae, 1998; Omotola, 2010). Nigeria had Social Democratic Party (SDP) and National Republican Convention (NRC) during the abortive Third Republic. In the present dispensation (Forth Republic), a lot of political parties have emerged with PDP standing out in the sense that for over one decade now, the PDP remains comfortably in charge of the government, while the opposition has continued to fragment into smaller parties with trifling electoral impact judging by the number of states they captured in 2007 and 2011 elections.

PDP came into being on the August 19, 1998. It was formed by a group called G.34 committee headed by Dr. Alex Ekwueme, the Second Republic Vice-President of Nigeria. According to Ojukwu and Olaifa (2011), PDP arose from three main sources. First, were the politicians who were denied registration by General SanniAbacha (a onetime Nigeria Head of State) during his self-succession project. They later changed to G.34 Men, a committee that petitioned against the self- succession project against Abacha. The second sources of PDP are those politicians who were not opposed to the self- succession of Abacha and not also part of his machine. The group was known as All Nigeria congress (ANC) which was led by Chief Sunday Awoniyi. The third were those who were followers of the late General Shehu Musa Yar'Adua under Peoples Democratic Movement (PDM). Chief Tony Anenih and AlhajiAtikuAbubakar (the former Vice-President of Nigeria) belonged to this group.

AN ILLUSION OF PARTY UNITY:

Since May 1999, PDP has been the ruling political party. Although part of the PDP's dominance is attributable to Nigeria's use of the first-past-the post electoral model, this electoral system is not the only factor that makes it difficult for opposition parties to make any headway in the polls. In addition, a lack of party funding and the external and internal regulatory framework equally affect the performance of parties. Despite these realities, the weak point of the opposition parties is their failure to cooperate and form coalitions. Had opposition parties done this in the past, they would have won more constituencies from the ruling party judging by intra-party conflict in PDP.

To further dwell on the intra-party conflict in PDP, it is crucial to ask how intra-party democracy can be implemented. What are some of the ways of expanding inclusiveness in party procedures, and what are some of the practical considerations associated with such techniques? It is impossible to give a complete inventory of the many ways in which parties have sought to incorporate supporters within their basic decision structures, but it is a bit easier to outline some of the primary choices that parties must make when implementing the more common forms of intra-party democracy. These choices fall under three main headings: selecting party candidates, selecting party leaders, and defining policy positions. The following causes are essential challenges. There is no doubt that internal democracy has some challenges and these are obvious in PDP. Poverty of Party Ideology Despite all pretenses to the contrary through their manifestoes, as much as the superficial classifications as the "left" and "right", "progressive" and "conservative", Nigerian parties seem to be bereft of clear ideological commitments. Whatever the case, it is important to note that at the very heart of the success or otherwise of political party is the important question of political ideology (Omotola, 2009). The issue of ideology has been so central to the activities of political parties across time and space that Morse (1896 ,p. 76) has argued that ideology, being the durable convictions held in common by party members in respect to the most desirable form, institutions, spirit and course of action of the state, determines the natural attitude of a party towards every public question (cf. Iyare, 2004, p. 81). Strickler and Davies (1996, p. 1025) similarly argue that "ideology functions as planks", that is, single issue statements within the platform, the exact ideological orientation of which is often used as a bargaining chip in seeking party unity. Here, the platform connotes a statement of the official party position on a variety of issues. Nnoli (2003, pp. 177-82) also concludes that ideology is a very crucial aspect of politics, not only by serving as a cognitive structure for looking at society generally and providing a prescriptive formula, that is, a guide to individual action and judgment, but also as a powerful instrument of conflict management, self-identification, popular mobilization and legitimization.

It may, therefore, be correct to assert that the first and most important vehicle of a political party, under an ideal situation, should be its ideological stance. In reality, however, this is seldom the case. Perhaps, due to the shallowness of democratic roots especially in Nigeria and the developing countries as a whole, other force of identity particularly ethnicity and religion would appear to have taken the place of ideology. The rising influence of money politics represents another crucial limiting dimension (Nugent, 1999; 2001; Omotola, 2004). What is the situation with Nigerian parties? Put differently, do

129

Nigerian parties have ideology? This conception has since changed and ideology has come to embody the ideas themselves. As a result of the changes, ideology has come to be presented as a subject representing two contradictory realities – the good and the bad, the former depicting ideology as "a system of thought that animates social or political action", and the latter as a "misleading, illusory or one-sided criticism or condemnation" (Nnoli, 2003, pp. 178-79). Ideology is like a superstructure upon which every other thing is built on. It consolidates political party. It precedes party structure, organization and manifesto. It is a set of ideas, beliefs and representations common to a specific social group. It consists of ethical interpretations and principles that set forth the purposes, organizations and boundaries of political life. One of the ways to assess the degree of internal democracy in a party is to ask who helps determine the content of the party's electoral promises which are in line with party ideology. In the most inclusive of parties, individual party members may be asked to vote on specific policy positions. More usually, parties do choose the less inclusive option of asking party conference delegates to endorse a set of commitments prepared by a platform committee. Often, the deliberation process may be more open than the actual vote. Party policy committees may take pains to show that they are listening to different viewpoints, for instance by holding consultation meetings around the country or soliciting comments via local (wards), State National Executives or Internet. Similarly, party leaders may permit an airing of viewpoints during debates at party conferences (Wayne, 2001). The point of such open consultation is to demonstrate that the party's policies have been developed in cooperation with the party's members, who are presumed to be representative of the party's most devoted supporters. Today, Peoples Democratic Party is functioning without an 'identified' ideology. The major question is what is the ideology of PDP? The PDP has capitalist and conservative dispositions without clear policy positions as a basis of popular mobilization and legitimacy of its (PDP) actions. Judging by their activities, it has been observed that "there is almost nothing to choose, between PDP and other parties in terms of ideological learning" (Iyare, 2004, p. 92). Until poverty of ideology is addressed, problem of intra-party democracy will continue lingering in PDP and other political parties in Nigeria.

As crucial to intra party democracy as ideology is, the same is also the issue of Party Funding. The crux of party funding and campaign financing against the background of the institutional designs guiding such activities in PDP is another fundamental reason for intra-party conflict in the party. Fisher and Eisenstadt (2004) argue that ironically, despite extensive studies on virtually all aspects of parties, financial issues seem to have eluded and escaped the attention of academic researchers. For any political party to function effectively, there is need for solid financial backing it enjoys from members. The importance of party funding is underscored by the contribution money can make in democracy and especially in developing economies where few elites control both the sources and distribution of money (Kura 2011). By implication, money more than anything, is a source of political power and political power in turn is a source of economic power. Little wonder, Karl Marx argued on the 'materialist conception of history', that it is the economy that serves as the foundation upon which is erected the superstructure of culture, law and government (Olaniyi, 2001, p. 28). The centrality of party funding is underlined by how it contributes to general crises affecting political party institutions. For example, Hopkin (2006) argues that the manner in which parties fund their activities has been quite embarrassing. The diversities of democracies as well as different typologies of parties suggest that party financing activities differ from one democracy to another and from one types of party to another. In contemporary clientele democracies, poverty, low level of education and general economic underdevelopment as well as the socio-cultural nature of such societies contribute to the "success" of clientelistic strategies of party funding. Perhaps, because of its complexities and susceptibility to corruption and absolute abuse, certain mechanisms are designed to regulate party funding. In 2002, the PDP campaign team organized a launching to boost the campaign for 2003 elections. In that event, over six billion naira was realized. At the end, the donors were compensated with contracts and political appointments. Looking at Anambra State chapter of PDP between 1999 and 2006, Chief Emeka Offor and Chris Uba made the state ungovernable because they were one of the outstanding PDP financiers. Chief Emeka Offor not only tormented Dr. Chinwoke Mbadinuju, the then governor of Anambra State, but also dominated the running of the affairs of the State. The pinnacle of the ugly situation was the abduction of Dr. Chris Ngige (former governor) in July 2003 because Ngige opposed to the move of Chris Uba (godfather) to colonize the State. Interestingly, PDP did not bother to carry out any investigation or disciplinary actions rather Ngige was made to leave the party with ignominy. It will be correct to infer that PDP has been inadvertently hijacked by plutocrats and kleptocrats.

Selection of Candidate Just like party funding, candidate selection and nomination procedures differ among democracies and among typologies of parties. The related question is: Who determines eligibility of party candidate(s) or leaders? This question seeks to infer who keeps the definitive membership records and how are the leaders and candidates selected as the party flag bearers in any general election? In any case, candidate nomination, which in broader terms is synonymous with recruitment, is one of the important functions of political parties across democracies. In fact, many party scholars define a political party in terms of this function (Sartori, 1976; Schlesinger, 1991). Generally, this is done by either locally or nationally. Katz (2001, p. 277) notes that candidate selection "is a vital activity in the life of any political party. It is the primary screening device in the process through which the party in office is reproduced. National party authorities may want to centralize this process, possibly fearing that local parties may be too lax in enforcing eligibility rules or that they may selectively enforce these rules in a way that will undermine the perceived fairness of the process. The method(s) which a party(s) employs in candidate selections and nominations has incontrovertible implications on those selected or elected and indeed how they behave in either party or public office (Gallagher and Marsh, 1988; Mainwaring and Shugart, 1997).

However, in some cases, particularly in Nigeria where there are "open" primaries, it may be civic authorities who are the de facto adjudicators of eligibility (in the sense that some selected or appointed party members across the country will be eligible to vote may participate). In fact, this may be one reason some parties find it attractive to use an open primary which PDP 'purported' to be using, because it avoids the potential difficulty of putting party authorities in a position to deny participation rights to those who might oppose them. With respect to inclusive candidate selection procedures, the main alternative to the primary election is selection at a party meeting. Recruiting candidates is a crucial task for parties. Parties' profiles during elections and while in office are largely determined by how candidates are chosen and where their loyalties lie. It is important to ask who selects the party members that desire to contest in an election? What are the laid down processes for selecting a candidate in a party? Whatever the way in which members or supporters are incorporated into the selection process, one important consideration is whether party rules limit their choices. For instance, some parties require that would-be candidates be approved by a party-selection board prior to being eligible to participate in party primaries or caucuses. In other parties, central party authorities reserve the right to withhold ex post facto, the nominations of individuals selected in intra-party contests (Ponguntke, 1998; Scarrow, 2005; Omotola, 2010). Such rules are intended to ensure that candidates are well qualified as both campaigners and representatives of party principles. They can also make it more difficult for those who do not support party policies somehow to "steal" nominations and embarrass the party. Whichever way, it is the responsibility of the party to decide who is eligible to contest in the election. Also, selection of party candidates should be devoid of prejudices. This is a serious problem in PDP, 2003 and 2007 elections, were characterized by long legal battles most of which were caused by intra-party squabbles over nomination of candidates at the primaries by the PDP. A notorious instance of what happened between Rotimi Amaechi and Celestine Omehia as well as the Ifeanyi Araraume examples in Rivers and Imo states respectively readily come to mind in this regard. In 2007, Musa Yar'Adua was single handedly imposed on the party by Obasanjo as his successor. The act caused a lot of party faithful cross-carpeting and defecting to other parties. Atiku was forced to leave the party for Action Congress (now defunct and forming a merger with other Parties to form the All Progressives Congress -APC). Another striking example was what happened in Anambra State chapter of the PDP where Professor Charles Soludo was imposed on the chapter as governorship candidate for the state by the National Executive of the party. The act triggered a spate of petition writing. The effect brought about factions in the party and last-minute cross-carpeting of some PDP members to other parties. The current imposition of Bamanga Tukura as the new PDP chairman is anti-core value of intra-party democracy. The imposition of Tukur was against the wish and consent of the people who had already voted Babayo ab initio as the representative from North East zone, where PDP had zoned it chairmanship seat to. Babayo won the zonal primaries but when it got to the PDP national convention his victory at the zonal level was put on the back burner and he was shortchanged.

ZONING ARRANGEMENT

Another reason for intra-party conflict is the PDP convention that permits zoning arrangement of its offices. The zoning formula for the office of the presidency in PDP has divided the Party particularly between the North and South. Some members of the party majorly from the North argued that it was still the turn of the Northern zone to produce the president in 2011 election, other members, some from the North and majority from the South claimed that the death of Yar'Adua marked the demise of zoning arrangement in PDP. Some groups in the party denied zoning formula in PDP. The first to brew the controversy was the former National Chairman of PDP, Prince Vincent Ogbulafor shortly after Jonathan was made Acting President that Jonathan was not eligible to contest the 2011 presidential elections. His position was based on Article 7(2c) of the PDP constitution, which defines how elective and party offices should be shared. Obasanjo who first benefitted in the zoning arrangement claimed ignorance of such arrangement in the party in an interview with the Voice of America. On the contrary, Alex Ekwueme, a founding member of the party and former Vice-President, debunked Obasanjo's claim. Although Obasanjo is the PDP Board of Trustees' Chairman and the first notable member to announce the eligibility of Jonathan to contest the 2011 presidential primaries of the party, but the zoning arrangement crisis was provoked when the former National Chairman Okwesilieze Nwodo declared the party's presidential primaries open to every qualified aspirants irrespective of their birth place because the party's zoning policy could be revisited and was non-existent. Dumping zoning policy was not only suicidal for PDP but also suggests that some politicians are using their advantaged positions in government to pervert democratic practice. The zoning arrangement in PDP according to Azazi (2012) is one of the reasons that hiking the level of insecurity in the entire country (The Punch April 28, 2012).

Party Executive Arrogance

According to Angelo (1988), Parties dominated by a single leader generally construct their appeal around the popularity, perceived integrity, and sometimes financial resources, of that individual. This leader articulates and embodies the party's programmatic aspirations. The Peoples Democratic Party in Nigeria democracy fit this description, either originating as or becoming (at least for a while) the vehicle for a single dominant leader (for example, the former president, Olusegun Obasanjo). In such parties, the leader may be self-selected (perhaps as the party founders e.g. the likes of Dr. Alex Ekwueme, Chief Tony Anenih, Late Gen. Shehu Musa Yar'Adua and Alhaji Atiku Abubakar), may be anointed by an outgoing leader, or may come to the fore as a result of demonstrated electoral appeal. He or she may gain the position with the formal endorsement of a party conference, but in practice, the leader can dominate party decisions while holding a variety of formal positions within the organization— or even while holding none at all. Such parties may use local branches and party assemblies to mobilize support, but their main characteristic is that the power to shape the party's political direction is tightly held at the center. In all, Intra-party crisis in PDP, without mincing words took its root in party executive since the birth of PDP in 1998. This affirms the saying that if the foundation of a building is faulty the building cannot stand well and if care and necessary action is not promptly taken, the building will collapse. The truth is that some PDP executives mostly at the National level believe that they can dictate the tune of the party at will. Between 1999 and 2007, Obasanjo took over the affairs of the National Assembly and feud with the major key actors of the party who were not ready to dance to his tune. Some of these personalities included; Audu Ogbeh, Atiku Abubakar, Ibikunle Amosun, Tony Anieh, Orji Uzor Kalu among others. This led to decamping of many founding fathers of the party such as Ibikunle Amosun and Orji UzorKalu among others.

Conduct of Primaries

The best way to test the tenacity and authenticity of any party's internal democracy is the conduct of primary elections. It has been proven from many studies that some primaries conducted in some political parties are sheer promotional agenda as they do not contribute positively to empowerment of the rank and file in those parties. Intra-party democracy can be questioned if party members are not aware about the choices they face. What happened in December 16, 2006 PDP's presidential primaries is fresh in memories. Researches reveal that Yar'Adua, the then Governor of Katsina State would emerge winner few days to the primaries. This was connected with the 'hide and seek' games played by the power that be which resulted not only to quick and unexpected withdrawal of some aspirants like Peter Odili, Donald Duke and Sam Egwu from the race but also forced to support Yar'Adua's candidacy. Little wonder, the party submitted that it only adopted 'consensus' approach at the eleventh hour. Consensus exists when people agree on something and not when forced to agree. In line with the above, President Jonathan sent a bill to the National Assembly seeking for the amendment of the 2010 Electoral Act. He demanded for an amendment of Section 87(8) of the Electoral Act to allow the political appointees of the president and states Governors as delegates at party conventions and primaries. Findings reveal that the section in question may not permit the President and Governors an important cheap figure of votes from political appointees. Interestingly, the House of Senate rejected the bill on the ground that it was laden with 'toxic provisions' (The Punch Editorial, 2010,).

CONCLUSION/SUGGESTION ON THE WAY FORWARD:

This paper should be deleted and write This book has been examined the political party governance These include, non-adherence to party ideology (if it has one), non-transparent method of candidates' selections in primary elections as well as in party leadership executive positions, the executive arrogance within the party which have not only torn PDP apart but also occasioned the decampment of many party stalwarts. To check the undemocratic attitudes in Nigeria's political parties the following way forward are important;

(a) There should be regular meetings of parties' National Executives. The regular meeting of the party stalwarts will help in checkmating the activities of the party in accordance with the party's constitution.

(b) Another way to ensure internal democracy in PDP and political parties generally, is to have party structure that is highly institutionalized. The notion of party institutionalization may be invoked to cover a wide range of features, including a party's autonomy from other actors or a self-acclaimed or anointed leader. This will democratize the extent of its internal organizational development, and the extent to which supporters identify with the party and view it as an important actor (Randall and Svasand, 2002). In a more narrowly organizational sense, two key features defining the level of party institutionalization are the degree to which internal decision procedures are formalized, and the extent to which the party has coordinated structures throughout its target constituency (Zabach, 2001). Low institutionalization tends to be a characteristic of newer parties (which PDP is not), primarily because it takes time to develop formal structures and develop a broad organizational network. But the obverse is not true; established parties are not necessarily highly institutionalized. Similarly, parties with high degrees of intra-party democracy are generally highly institutionalized because they need rules that define who is eligible to participate and what constitutes victory in internal contests.

(c)There should be ideological commitments and transparency in party financial administration. Ideology often plays some role in shaping parties' organizational decisions. This can be seen most clearly in parties whose organizational forms are closely linked to their ideological identities. All party members must be aware and observe the party financial guidelines. This will prevent kleptocrats from hijacking the party.

(d) The imposition of candidates into any elective position should be abolished. The right of every member must be respected and preserved. Consensus candidature and selection of candidates must be played down at all levels. Candidate emergence must be given constitutional backing instead of substituting such person for a candidate of selective approval.

(e) PDP should embrace the concept of reforms and review the zoning arrangement. Nigeria's Constitution of 1999 (as amended) is silent about any zoning formula. Therefore, the PDP should embark on genuine reform agenda majorly on the issue of zoning to allow improvement into the party and the entire country. The People Democratic Party should adopt a wide range of approaches to their internal organization, and they should constantly experiment with new structures and new procedures to cope with internal and external pressures.

(f) There is need to infuse a mechanism for social harmony and peace building. Any organization that lacks this mechanism may find it difficult to function effectively. This mechanism also represents the degree of social cohesion in communities and associational life, such as; social trust, tolerance, cooperation and mutual understanding, reciprocity and other networks of civic engagement that facilitate coordination and communication through which information about trustworthiness of other individuals and groups can flow, be tested and verified (Putnam, 1993).

Finally, building effective party structures for intra-party democracy is an endless task. Healthy organization can and will adapt to changing circumstances. Be that as it may, the Independent National Electoral Commission (INEC) must stick and attach much importance to the legal framework of election in Nigeria's constitution and the Electoral Act since it is a critical starting point for conducting credible, sustainable and effective elections in Nigeria. In a country like Nigeria, where there is widespread lack of expectation with politicians and parties full of detractions, and where there is growing interest in democratic self-determination; It will take responsive parties to rightly decide that they would be well advised to adopt more transparent and inclusive internal procedures. In such cases, the changes the parties make to benefit themselves may prove beneficial to the wider society and for the stability and legitimacy of democratic institutions. Also, without intra-party democracy, government pronouncements to conduct free and fair elections coupled with sustainable development will be a mirage. Conclusive respects for the will of the majority for free, fair and credible elections must be guaranteed in other to get intra-Party conflicts reduced. In all, there is need for a truly Independent Electoral Commission that would not only concentrate on electorate matters, but which will also monitor the structure and operation of parties in terms of membership recruitment, party financing and party discipline.

A PIP IN THE EAST AFRICAN EXPERIENCE

Leadership and candidate selection
One of the key processes of expanding inclusiveness in party procedures and decision making is in the recruitment and selection of party leaders and candidates. These processes allow parties excellent opportunities to demonstrate their inclusiveness by providing opportunities to incorporate party members and supporters in these processes. Leadership and candidate selection processes are some of the most crucial undertakings a party can make since the outcome determines not only the party's public profile and competitiveness during elections, but it also has consequences on "members and supporters" continued loyalty and support. It is therefore important that parties make choices that make such processes not only inclusive, but also free and fair and to be seen to be so. Considering the high stakes involved, parties have to contend with such questions as, who is eligible to stand as a candidate. What are the qualifications or limitations? Who may participate in the selection process and how can such a process be conducted? How can the process be guaranteed to be free and fair? Who, by and how are disputes adjudicated?

Leadership selection
The electoral systems in East Africa as in many African countries are single member parliamentary (constituency) and presidential systems.

This means that the selection of a party leader is equivalent to selecting the party's presidential candidate, should the party choose to field a candidate during elections. Whatever the case, the choice of a party leader determines the image as well as the course the party will take. This is more so in African party systems characterized by oligarchy instead of democracy. In most cases, overwhelming power and influence is concentrated in the party leader or a few of his cronies who hold significant sway over party policies, programmes and selection of other leaders and candidates.

Technically, almost all political parties surveyed select their national leadership through the delegates conference, a form of party caucus in which representatives from the lower branch or district levels of the party meet at the national level. According to most party rule books, these delegates are supposed to be elected by party members at the branch, district or constituency levels and are supposed to be widely representative of women, youth and other marginalized groups. It is important to note at this point that the delegates' conference or congress is generally described as the highest decision-making organ of the party whose decisions are binding to the party.

In practice however, these delegates are usually carefully handpicked by party operatives according to their loyalty to particular party elites from their own regions and calculated to give as much support as possible to the regional party stalwarts. In many cases, with the exception of a few, most parties do not have any real structures at the grassroots from where delegates should be democratically elected. The delegates' selection process is usually yet another demonstration of the politics of personality cults, sycophancy and patronage as opposed to genuine processes of intra-party democracy. Convening a national delegates' conference is usually huge logistical undertaking for most parties with limited financial means. Coupled with the acrimony, confrontation and friction that the exercise raises, many parties shy

away or totally avoid holding such conferences unless they absolutely
have to, usually in order to meet legal requirements for the party to
continue functioning as a legitimate body. In less institutionalized
political parties, party positions are usually divided between the
party elites, usually among its founders, chief financiers or regional
and ethnic chieftains in boardroom deals. Delegates" congresses are
subsequently mere pomp and ceremony meant to legitimise already
agreed upon leadership positions devoid of any real participation by
party members (Oloo 2007, Wanjohi 2003).

Highly centralised political parties such as CCM equally have less
inclusive leadership selection processes. The Central Committee
is the most powerful organ of the party with overwhelming power
over nomination and recommendation of party members for the
positions of chairperson and deputy chairperson of the party; the
president of the republic Tanzania; MPs and members of the House of
Representatives. Not only does the organ nominate members to contest
leadership positions, it also has the supervisory role of monitoring the
implementation of party elections as well as appointment of district
party leaders. Such a highly centralised system is characteristic of
ruling parties in one-dominant-party systems that have often retained
power since the era of jungle-party rule. This is the case with NRM in
Uganda where the influential National Executive Council nominates
candidates for top party positions such as president, chairperson
and deputy, secretary general and deputy as well as treasurer. Those
nominated are more often than not simply endorsed by the national
conference without any alterations.

The lack of inclusive and democratic leadership selection processes
with no clear mechanisms for neutral and independent dispute
arbitration often has negative consequences for party unity and
cohesiveness. Recent legislation of party law to create arbitration offices
within the offices of Registrar of Political Parties are yet to bear fruit

since they are still at infancy with little structures. There is also lack of trust and confidence in such external bodies which are perceived to be instruments of the appointing authority to adversely interfere with rival parties. Consequently, more often than not, intra-party rivalry spills out into open conflict and sometimes party splits.

Kenya has perhaps been the theatre of the most divisive party wrangles arising from undemocratic and non-inclusive leadership selection processes. In 2002 in Kenya for example, the then ruling party KANU disintegrated after incumbent President Daniel ArapMoi mismanaged his own succession by appointing a relatively untested Uhuru Kenyatta, son of his predecessor and first president Jomo Kenyatta as party leader. Senior party elites who had been waiting in the wings and looked to a democratic and inclusive succession process broke away from the party to form the Rainbow coalition and teamed with the opposition to dethrone KANU from power. Uhuru's leadership of KANU was ridiculed as a failed project. KANU lost massively in the ensuing election and has not recovered ever since. Subsequent wrangles over leadership elections in 2006 saw Uhuru's leadership of KANU annulled in court only to be reinstated later. This was followed by a split within KANU with the creation of a new faction, the New KANU.

In 2007, Similar leadership wrangles saw the split of no less than four leading parties in the run-up to that year's general election. Some of the parties affected were ODM, FORD-Kenya, KANU and NARC. Disagreements within ODM was over what process of leadership selection to adopt between a delegates (caucus) system or a consensus between the party elites. This eventually led to the split between the two contenders for the party leadership resulting in the creation of ODM-Kenya and ODM Party of Kenya. Disagreements within NARC led to the registration of the splinter NARC-Kenya party while FORD-Kenya split in two leading to the creation of New FORD-Kenya. The blow to FORD-Kenya which had once been the leading opposition party was such that in the ensuing 2007 general election, it managed to gain only one parliamentary seat with its party leader being defeated in his own constituency.

In Tanzania, leadership rifts in NCCR-Mageuzi led to the departure of charismatic party leader Augustin Mrema and his supporter to join TLP while in Uganda, the DP has had to grapple with intense internal leadership wrangles occasioned by undemocratic leadership selection processes pitting party leaders against John Kizito and Kampala city Mayor Nasser Sebaggala. The UPC has however come in for severe criticism both internally and externally for its undemocratic leadership selection. Former president Milton Obote remained party leader for life until his death in exile in Zambia on 10th October 2005. Thereafter, his wife, Maria Kalule Obote was elected party leader. This has sparked accusations of nepotism, gerontocracy and dynastic tendencies within the party. Party insiders fear that Obote's son and party MP Jimmy Akena, a member of the central committee is being groomed to take over the leadership of the party. They argue that his mother's elevation to party leader was a ploy to warm the seat while giving her politically inexperienced son ample time to learn the ropes before ascending to the party leadership, thus effectively handing it down from father, to wife to son. A critical party official confided that,

"...we have managed to transit from the single party movement system. But their [party leaders"] thinking and outlook as individuals, they have not moved and are still stuck in the old way of doing things. The leadership has not yet adapted to the new ways of doing politics in a modern global environment. Secondly, the kind of leadership we are having and their style of management tends to be centered or focused on other interests. They have their own personal interests which may be parallel from those of the party. That is why in the writer's view, once the district structures become empowered and the youth structures also get empowered, it will help to check that kind of thinking and cause certain readjustments in terms of management and focus." Such attitudes portray a party deeply divided within its ranks, not only among its membership and supporters but within the leadership as well. How these differences and conflicts are managed will determine the future cohesion and effectiveness of the party and the extent of membership loyalty.

Undemocratic and unrepresentative leadership selection processes therefore have significant and often negative consequences on party unity and cohesion, its effectiveness in contesting elections and where regionalism and ethnicity is the organising principle, wider considerations of national security and stability are at stake. Internal wrangles often lead to weakening of parties, splits, defections and formation of new or revival of moribund parties. This also creates a culture of political party speculation in which unscrupulous individual register 'briefcase" parties, waiting for disgruntled party leaders looking for ready-made outfits for sale to which they can defect and use as vehicles to mobilise their supporters and seek political power.

Candidate Selection

Candidate selection is a fundamental process of a political party's engagement with its membership and the wider electorate. The process by which candidates for elected positions are chosen is perhaps as important as the type of candidates selected. The result determines the party's competitive profile against its competitors during elections as well as determining the loyalty of its members and supporters. The degree to which party members and supporters are included in this process is therefore significant in determining a party's success in an election. The most open and inclusive form of candidate selection is the direct ballot or party primaries where eligible party members or supporters pre-select party candidates through direct elections. There are variations to this model depending on who is eligible to vote in the primaries. In most western democracies, participation is restricted to registered party members. This is however not the case with most African parties that do not have any real registered membership. The process is usually open to any registered voters that are eligible to vote during the general election itself.

However, before the electorate can participate in the primaries, there has to be a pre-selection procedure to determine eligibility and how candidates can put their names forward for consideration. The question here then is who determines eligibility for the candidates? All political parties studied have clear party rules and guidelines on candidate selection. In most cases, an election board is set up to vet interested candidates who must be approved by a party organ before they can be given the green light to contest. The more centralised the party structure, the tighter the control on vetting and clearance of candidates. This then limits the choices available for party supporters to choose from and this compromises intra-party democracy. On the other hand, a party needs to ensure that potential candidates are selected on specific criteria that will strengthen the party going into an election. Some considerations include a candidate's ability to finance their own campaigns, party loyalty, electability, adherence to party ideology, platform and ability to work with fellow party members.

Eligibility criteria for both parliamentary and presidential candidates closely mirror provisions contained in the various country's constitutions. These include guidelines on age and levels of education. Some parties stipulate certain requirements such as length of membership within the party although these are not strictly adhered to. In most cases, interested candidates collect application forms from the party's national secretariat and pay an application or nomination fee. In Kenya, this is usually a convenient fundraising strategy for the party from where funds for managing the party primaries and campaigns can be sourced. Applications are then vetted and approved by a mandated party organ such as an election board.

Not all parties however follow this pre-selection procedure. Due to the immense logistical and financial requirements for such a national exercise, some parties such as SAFINA in Kenya prefer to have a centralised candidate selection process in which applicants are vetted by the appropriate national party organs and given direct nominations to run as the party candidates in the parliamentary constituencies and civic seats. This is usually the practice with smaller parties with less capacity to mobilise and manage nationwide party primaries. It is therefore a compromise between openness and inclusivity versus efficiency. Though less acrimonious, such a process denies party members any role in the selection of its candidates.

In Kenya, party primaries ahead of the 2007 general elections have been described as being undemocratic and fraught with corruption, violence and outright rigging. In places where primary elections did take place, the process was marred by logistical and administrative shortcomings including lack of sufficient election materials such as ballot papers, untrained and inexperienced election officials and inaccurate reporting of results. The arising confusion was compounded by mistakes made at the national level in issuing of double nomination certificates to party candidates. In some cases, the national party secretariat handed out selective direct nominations to some preferred candidates. This led to protests and allegations of corruption, nepotism and cronyism leading to defections of potential candidates to rival political parties (Pinto 2007).

The need for inclusivity and openness in party primaries by opening the process to all potential voters regardless of party membership has potential costs to the party. This is often the case in situations where parties have no clear record of membership, or where parties fear alienating potential voters in the actual election by restricting candidate selection to registered members. In such a case as was witnessed in the Kenyan primaries, the use of national identity cards to vote in the nominations resulted in individuals voting in all the different party nominations. This exposed some political parties to infiltration and manipulation of the primary process where some politicians used their supporters to vote against strong candidates in the opposing political parties primaries as a strategy to face weaker candidates in the actual elections (Pinto 2007).

The logistical difficulties, limited financial resources and fear of ensuing wrangles and divisions are just but some of the factors that make party elites fail to carry out open, transparent and inclusive leadership and candidate selection processes. Poor institutional and organisational capacity, inherent structural weaknesses and pre-existing tensions between different camps and loyalties often impede the conduct of free and fair leadership and candidate selection processes. Consequently, these crucial party activities are often carried out by central national party organs and are characterised by careful regional, ethnic and personal power balancing and horse-trading that ensure the loyalty and contentment of leading and influential party figures who often command powerful influences over their regional and ethnic bases. Party leaders often prefer to keep such powerful kingpins in their camps as opposed to having them defect and either pose serious competition to their parties or carry with them a huge chunk of much needed votes during a general election.

Coalition building is also often merely a game of numbers as party leaders seek out partners that are likely to bring with them the largest voting blocs enough to win an election and form a government. Coalitions are therefore not based on any concurrence in ideology or policy positions, instead they are characterised by power sharing pacts and promises of government appointments for party technocrats, financiers and activists even before the first vote has been cast. All these processes add up to the emasculation of intra-party democracy by alienating party members and reducing then to mere pawns in a high stakes game between party elites. It is not surprising then that in such politics of personality cults, membership loyalty is not to particular parties, but allegiance is instead paid to particular party leaders usually commanding regional or ethnic bases. This was the case in Kenya where Raila Odinga, considered an undisputed leader of the Luo community since the early 1990"s has changed parties five times and each time, carrying with him the loyalty of an entire community. A similar scenario can be attributed to President Mwai Kibaki who since the creation of his own Democratic Party has changed parties five times as well and still commanding a sizeable following among the Kikuyu, the largest ethnic group in Kenya.

Chapter 9

Internal Party Democracy and Discipline

INTERNAL PARTY DEMOCRACY AND DISCIPLINE.

African political parties: From oligarchy to internal democracy

African political parties are products of distinct historical, socio-economic and political conditions that influence their character and functioning different from those prevailing in western democracies. The only somewhat parallel historical point with the European model was the immediate pre and post-independence period when African political parties were broad-based mass liberation movements embodying a single ideology of liberation from colonial rule. Independence political parties, formulated under the single ideology of majority African rule provided a unifying force among societies that were historically antagonistic along ethnic lines.

Unlike the majority of their western counterparts almost all African nation states (with the exception of countries such as Somalia) lack in distinctive cultural or ethno-linguistic homogeneity. They are highly heterogeneous along ethnic, regional, religious or clan cleavages. Although, western European polities such as the Netherlands may have had rifts encompassing Calvinists, Socialists, Catholics, western entrepreneurs, southern small farmers etc, they remained relatively stable and political competition was contained within established structures and traditions (NIMD 2008). African societies on the other hand lack in socially entrenched and institutionalized political, social and governance structures along which political competition can be channeled. They are therefore highly fractious and fragile. Political competition and organization tend to follow these pre-existing fault lines which in turn determine the structure of political parties. Manning (2005, P. 718) characterizes African parties as, not [being] organically linked to any particular organized social group, and so have often resorted to mobilizing people along the issues that are ready to hand – ethnicity, opposition to structural economic reform – without regard for the long-term consequences".

Modernization theory to this extent, therefore, falls short of capturing the essence of post third wave African political parties. Instead of providing stability and ordering the political system, reigning in divisive and potentially explosive social forces, African political parties and the elites that control them tend to play on these very social cleavages to gain power through inherently undemocratic means. This characterization seems to affirm Robert Michels' (1968) assertion that political parties have an inherent tendency towards oligarchy. According to this approach, not only do political parties develop undemocratic characteristics in the way they control and manipulate social cleavages, but also in their internal organization and decision-making processes. According to Michels,( ), the more parties become organized institutions, the less democratic they become. This structuralist approach contends that regardless of a political party's formal rules about internal checks and balances, organisation led to centralisation of power, oligarchy and the decline of internal democracy (Kavanagh 2003).

The paradox of the majority of African political parties is that most of them are poorly organised and lack institutional capacity, their decision-making processes are unstructured and power often lies in the hands of the party leader and a few of his cronies who are usually wealthy enough to bankroll the party (Wanjohi 2003). The role of the party membership is reduced to a bare minimum, usually to endorse decisions already made by the elite. Political mobilisation assumes the form of personality cults and loyalty is often to the party leader as opposed to the party as an institution. This encourages the politics of "party hopping" where leadership disagreements may lead to one leader jumping from one party to another and carrying his supporters with him/her. On the other extreme are the well organised, highly centralized and structured parties that have been in power since independence such as CCM in Tanzania. Centralisation then takes away decision making power from lower party organs and branches and concentrates it on a core group of party oligarchs such as the Central Committee of the CCM. Such parties are usually found in single-party regimes where the party and the state are so fused that they become indistinguishable from each other. Whatever the case may be, both categories of parties, either by default or design, are considerably lacking in internal democracy.

Other approaches advanced to explain the democratic deficit between African political parties and a truly representative democracy include developmental theory which argues that certain minimum socio-economic pre-conditions are necessary for democracy to thrive. It further argues that the low socio- economic condition of the African polity and the distinct lack of clear ideological foundations, allow for the development of clientelist and patronage based political structures through which access to, and distribution of state resources can be channeled. While describing the socio-economic basis for the lack of intra-party democracy in western societies, Otto Kirchheimer (1966) aptly captured a picture that is as much applicable to modern African political systems. In his view, contemporary political parties are characterised by the decreasing influence of individual party members, lack of specific class appeal in favour of other pre-existing social cleavages in order to appeal to voter support base, increasing autonomy of the leadership from internal checks and balances, and the complete lack of ideology in the parties" programmes.

In Africa especially, the continuing debate on the sequencing of democracy and development as well as the developmental prerequisites for democracy is more pertinent. Some African leaders such as Kenya"s former President Daniel ArapMoi have advanced similar arguments to explain their preference for single party rule (The Standard, July 22, 2008). Uganda"s President Yoweri Museveni imposed a total proscription of political party activity on the grounds that political parties breed conflict in fragile nation states; they are authoritarian, urban based groupings of small elites; they are corrupt; they have no clear policies; there is a lack of a middle class to support their existence; they are manipulated by external actors to achieve neo-colonial or imperial interests by proxy; or that other systems are more democratic than multiparty systems (Okuku 2002).

While some of these attributes may apply to some political parties in some African countries, it is certainly not the case that they are an accurate characterisation of political parties across the continent (McMahon 2004). It is arguable that political parties may not be the cause, but rather a reflection of pre- existing social cleavages and proscription or restriction of political party activity may not be the solution to these problems. Counter intuitively, effective and well-functioning political parties can serve as a pressure valve by which social tensions and frustrations can be channeled through peaceful means. The importance of well-functioning, effective and internally democratic political parties cannot therefore be overstated. Political parties that guarantee a degree of effective and transparent membership participation in deliberation of policy, leadership selection and overall decision making can instead provide avenues for social cohesion, minimise possibilities of open conflict and facilitate peaceful resolution of conflict.

Intra-party democracy in theoretical perspective

The primary democratic function of political parties is to link the citizenry with the government (Sartori 2005, P. 11). In order to play this role effectively, political parties have to provide opportunities for effective participation by party members, activists and leaders in the party's decision-making processes. Debate continues among scholars and theorists of comparative politics and democracy regarding the desirability and feasibility of intra-party democracy.

Definition

German scholar Robert Michels (1962) famously advanced his "iron law of oligarchy" which argues that political parties are inherently undemocratic and have a tendency towards oligarchy where the party elite and leadership assume control of the party at the expense of the party membership. According to this argument, intra-party democracy is therefore inconsistent with the elite preference for highly organised, structured and institutionalised party systems. Oligarchic political parties tend to have highly centralised and non-inclusive decision-making processes and are therefore not internally democratic. This view thus proposes that intra-party democracy is a prerequisite for a democratic state.

This thesis has been refuted by those who argue that intra-party democracy weakens political parties and is therefore undesirable. Proponents of this view argue that „in order to serve democratic ends, political parties themselves must be ruled by oligarchic principles" (Teorell 1999, P. 364). These two positions represent the deep divide and debate that surrounds the very normative and prescriptive approach to intra- party democracy. This section seeks to examine both arguments in detail and argues for the desirability and feasibility of intra-party democracy as a means to increase democracy in the wider society. Taking into account the nature of African party politics as discussed above, intra-party democracy would play a significant role in processes of consolidating and entrenching a democratic culture in African societies.

Intra-party democracy: A case for oligarchy?

Intra-party democracy is not a universally popular notion and several arguments have been advanced against it based on the assumption that democratic decision-making processes are prone to inefficiency. Too much internal democracy, it is argued, is likely to weaken the ability of a political party to compete against its opponents. Democratic principles demand that leadership at all levels be elective, that it be frequently renewed, collective in character, weak in authority. Organized in this fashion, a party is not well armed for the struggles of politics. (Durveger, 1954, P. 134)

Empirical research on political parties in countries such as Switzerland (Ladner and Brandle 1999), United Kingdom (Anstead 2008) and Australia (Gauja 2006) seems to generate similar conclusions with regard to the weakening effect of intra-party democracy on political parties albeit with some minor positive effects. According to AnikaGauja (2006), intra-party democracy impedes decision-making within parties, precludes parties from choosing candidates they regard as most appealing to the electorate and transfers key political decisions to a small group of activists at the expense of the broader party membership. Opposition to intra-party democracy is based on a key characteristic of western political parties faced with ever declining membership and the increasingly central role that party activists take as a result. The assumption is that party activists tend to take more extreme ideological positions than the party leadership or the electorate. Intra-party democracy is also seen as lessening party cohesion while increasing the risk of internal dissention. This impinges on party efficiency as more energy and time is spent on internal competition and conflict resolution as opposed to concentrating on the core priorities of electoral and governmental success. This may seem to make oligarchy a more appealing option for presenting a united front, both to the electorate and the opposing parties (Wright 1971, P. 446). This means that representative democrats are therefore likely to defend oligarchy as the best means to allow pragmatic party leadership to have direct access to and representation of the electorate thus by-passing party activists.

Proponents of the competitive model of democracy (Schumpeter 1942; Dahl 1956; Downs 1957 Miller 1983; Sartori 1987), argue that a system of competitive political party is necessary for effective interest aggregation and the channeling of those competing for government. Competitive democrats therefore view intra-party democracy as threatening the efficiency and compromising the competitiveness of political parties and thereby threatening democracy itself. Comparative political approaches to democracy such as competitive, representative or deliberative democracy seem to present compelling arguments against intra-party democracy in favour of oligarchy. The discourse hinges on the normative choice between direct (participatory) democracy and representative democracy. The questions posed are: what institutional safeguards can be built into representative democracy in order to guarantee acceptable levels of citizen participation in the absence of direct democracy? How can intra-party democracy fill this gap without compromising the effectiveness and efficiency of political parties? Proponents of direct democracy who favour direct citizens" participation in governance processes decry the failure of representative democracy conducted through the political party system as an ineffective alternative. Hence the preference, for example in Switzerland, centres on for direct democracy exercised through referendums (Ladner and Brandle 1999).

In the most part, African political parties are not characterised by the presence of an influential core of party activists. Consequently, such a theoretical basis for the arguments against intra-party democracy developed in the west does not apply. On the contrary, the fractious nature of African societies and the poor institutionalisation of political parties can be advanced as key arguments against intra-party democracy. The threat of internal discord, leadership wrangles; party splits and in some cases open violence present real challenges for intra-party democracy in Africa. These factors further weaken largely unstable African political parties, compromise their ability to select credible candidates, compete in elections and govern effectively and in some cases lead to the total collapse of political parties. The majority of African political parties are therefore more oligarchic than democratic in practice. Most do not have membership lists and when they do, these are not necessarily exclusive. Voters tend to have multiple party memberships and party loyalty fluctuates significantly. Allegiances are usually to the party leader as opposed the institution of the party. The lack of strong party affiliation and weak institutionalisation promotes a culture of political tourism and party hopping depending on the whims of the party leader or political expediencies. The foregoing arguments against intra-party democracy may seem plausible enough to warrant no further discussion on the matter. There are however compelling reasons to consider intra-party democracy desirable, not only for political parties but in the interest of democracy in the wider society as well. The next section will examine some of these arguments.

A case for intra-party democracy

Arguments in favour of intra-party democracy derive from the appeal of democracy in the wider sense as a system that "facilitates citizen-self-rule, permits the broadest deliberation in determining public policy and constitutionally guaranteeing all the freedoms necessary for open political competition" (Joseph 1997, P. 365). This approach combines perspectives of participatory and deliberative democracy that emphasise the central features of participation and contestation. The case for intra-party democracy depends on whether one adopts a liberal or participatory democracy perspective. Liberal democratic theory does not place a high premium on intra-party democracy since according to this approach, the political leadership plays the most important role while the citizens' participation during elections is merely to accept or reject their leaders (Sartori 1965). For the liberal democrat, democracy is not an end in itself, but is only important in so far as it safeguards liberty better than any other system (Katz 199746). In order to bolster the argument for intra-party democracy therefore, we have to look elsewhere.

The more compelling arguments for intra-party democracy can be found in participatory and deliberative democratic theories. Participatory democrats place a high premium on citizen participation in political processes and a sense of civic responsibility. According to van Biezen (2004) only then can a political system warrant the label of a „democracy". McPherson (1977) develops this argument further by proposing a pyramidal system of intra-party democracy "with direct democracy at the base and a delegate democracy at every level above that" supplemented by a system of competitive political parties (Teorell 1999:368). Since a truly participatory model of democracy in the form of direct democracy is not feasible in modern large and complex societies, political parties bridge the gap between citizens and government by providing avenues for citizens' participation through effective intra-party democracy.

The deliberative theory of democracy has of late gained ground by emphasising that democracy is a product of deliberation among free, equal and rational citizens (Elser 1998). This approach sees democracy as a process rather than an outcome. Dryzek (2000) concurs that democracy is thus a process of „deliberation as opposed to voting, interest aggregation, constitutional rights or even self-government.

This approach emphasises the process by which opinions are formed, policies formulated and programmes developed. It incorporates certain aspects of participatory and representative democracy as means to achieve its end. Participatory and representative aspects of democracy therefore provide the mechanisms, institutions and processes by which deliberative democracy can be realised.

All these models present various normative approaches to the concept of intra-party democracy. They are by no means conclusive or incontestable, but chart the broad parameters within which more refined and context specific structures and processes can be advanced in favour of intra-party democracy. These theoretical models can however be further problematised on the basis of practical feasibility and questions arise as to whether theorizing on democracy can sometimes be increasingly detached from political reality.

Away from normative prescriptive theorizing, empirical research on intra-party democracy tends to focus on a utilitarian perspective that seeks to establish ontological or causal relationships associated with processes and indicators of intra-party democracy. Previous research remains inconclusive on whether and to what extent parties need to be internally democratic in order to promote democracy within the wider society. According to Scarrow (2005 :) political parties that practice intra-party democracy... are likely to select more capable and appealing leaders, to have more responsive policies, and, as a result, to enjoy greater electoral success... (and) strengthen democratic culture generally (Scarrow 2005, p.3) Other arguments in favour of intra-party democracy suggest that it encourages political equality by creating a level playing field in candidate selection and policy development within the party; ensures popular control of government by extending democratic norms to party organisations such as transparency and accountability; and it improves the quality of public debate by fostering inclusive and deliberative practices within parties (Gauja 2006, p. 6).

In Africa, political parties are perceived more as vehicles for contesting and attaining public office as opposed to institutions of democratic consolidation. The desirability of intra-party democracy is therefore more likely to be viewed in terms of its usefulness in improving the overall effectiveness of the party against its competitors. This denotes an outcome-oriented approach, but as the discussion above suggest, this liberal view of democracy is incompatible with intra-party democracy viewed from a participatory perspective (Wanjohi 2003, Salih 2003, Oloo 2007).

The success of intra-party democracy in Africa therefore lies in a normative approach that seeks to change attitudes towards a process-oriented approach. This is the more pertinent in light of the weak social base on which democracy is founded in most of the continent's polities. Attention should thus be paid to processes that entrench a democratic culture by increasing citizens " participation or what Scarrow (2005) terms as incubators that nurture citizens political competence. In such polities where levels of civic awareness are extremely low, intra-party democracy provides opportunities to expand civic education and awareness through participation while at the same time devolving power and decision making processes to broader sections of society.

CONCLUSIONS AND RECOMENDATIONS

Political parties are essential institutions for the proper functioning of a democratic society. As social organisations designed for contesting and attaining political power, political parties serve several functions including determining the content of the political order, selecting authoritative leaders, resolving disputes, maintaining order and promoting the various interests of the community among diverse and contending social forces. In order to achieve these objectives, Political parties have to offer genuine avenues for effective membership participation in shaping the content, character and output of political parties. Intra- party democracy is therefore essential for the creation and growth of well-functioning and sustainable democratic institutions hence fostering and deepening a democratic culture within the wider society.

Intra-party democracy, as an element of participatory democracy, encourages a culture of democratic debate and deliberation of critical issues and therefore collective ownership of decisions; promotes party unity through reduced factionalism and/or fragmentation; creates legitimate internal conflict management systems and reduces opportunistic and arbitrary use of delegated authority. The attainment of these democratic ideals can only be realised depending on the extent to which processes of effective membership participation are formally stipulated and practically implemented in the party's organisational rules and procedures. While debate continues on how much democracy is good for political party effectiveness, the general consensus is that intra-party democracy is desirable for its role in increasing the levels of participatory democracy in the wider society.

Institutional arrangements are essential for the attainment of intra-party democracy. Although the status in most of the political parties studied suggests that institutional arrangements do exist, they do not satisfactorily influence intra-party democracy. The first sub-hypothesis is thus partially supported in the empirical findings though there is a significant variance between the form and substance of democracy largely owing to the personalised and informal conduct of party-political activity in the region due to low levels of institutionalisation. As Wanjohi (2005) explains, there is a gap between the character and attitudes of the political elite on the one hand, and the needs and aspirations of the majority of the people on the other. The situation is as such because the institutional arrangements are either not adhered to, are weakly enforced or simply disregarded by the party elites.

Although African political parties are products of distinct historical, socio-economic and political conditions, they do share certain organisational similarities with their western counterparts in their tendency towards oligarchy and authoritarianism and declining membership. The difference is that while in the west the danger lies in the increasing role of party activists that risks alienating the larger party membership, African political parties are held captive by the personalised nature of political organisation where the political elite and business class have virtual control of parties. Participatory democracy in African political parties is thus compromised as the general membership is rendered ineffectual (Oloo, 2003). The lack of intra-party democracy in most African political parties has been correlated with such characteristics as internal discord, leadership wrangles, party splits and in some cases open violence. These factors further weaken largely unstable political parties, compromise their ability to select credible candidates, compete in elections and govern effectively and in some cases lead to the total collapse of political parties.

The prevailing political party systems and the external regulatory and governance environments do significantly influence the internal functioning of political parties and vice versa. In East Africa, both Uganda and Tanzania have a one-dominant party system that tends to disadvantage the opposition parties" capacity to function as effectiveness in the wider political environment. The reverse is also the case in that the weakness of the opposition parties and the resulting inability to challenge the status quo ensures the survival of the existing party systems to the detriment of a truly participatory democracy taking root within the wider society.

Ethnicity and regionalism are significant factors in political mobilization and hence the content and structure of internal political party organisation in the region, especially in Kenya and Uganda. In

Kenya and to some extent in Uganda, the party-political environment is characterized by. The resulting coalition building in Kenya is not institutionally structured and is not based on clear ideological and programmatic considerations. They are simply power-sharing deals between the political elites who use the party members as bargaining chips for personal political gains. This was evident in the coalition arrangements which were nothing but power-sharing agreements in Kenya after the divisive 2005 constitutional referendum and the 2007 general elections. In both cases, the substantive socio-economic and political issues behind the constitutional referendum and the post-election violence respectively were not addressed. Empirical research findings show a varied pattern with regard to the presence of indicators of intra-party democracy among the sample of political parties studied in East Africa. The key indicators of intra-party as outlined in the definition as institutionalisation, decentralization and inclusiveness were measured according to their presence in such aspects as party institutions, policy formulation, candidate and leadership selection and membership participation. The empirical findings show a mixed pattern in terms of the extent of institutionalisation and adherence among the twelve political parties that were investigated. Several conclusions regarding the four sub-hypotheses can therefore be deduced in relation to the main hypothesis.

Adequate institutionalisation of party structures and processes are necessary in securing and enforcing the principle-agent relationship between party members and the elected party representatives. The deliberative model of democracy advocates that intra-party democracy can only be realised when party decision- making and operational procedures are debated freely and collectively agreed upon among all members as equals. This necessitates institutionalised decentralisation in which lower party organs and members in lower levels of leadership are included in the party's deliberative decision-making processes. This means that the representational capacity of political parties should be institutionalised in such a way that it is geared towards the articulation, realisation and protection of the interests of the membership as opposed to the prevailing situation where elite interests supersede or tramp the interests of wider society altogether.

In order to address some of the systemic, institutional and structural weaknesses of the party-political environment, all three East African countries have enacted various legal and constitutional laws most of which take the form of political party laws. Other than reforming the entire party political and electoral systems, these laws are only targeted at the regulation of political parties, laying down guidelines for their registration, funding and conduct. Legal regulation of political parties is therefore becoming a standard norm in the region and is widely seen as a positive development especially where public funding of political parties is concerned. This strengthens the competitive capacity of opposition parties against the ruling parties which often have undue advantage owing to their access to state resources. With regard to intra-party democracy, party laws however contain significant short comings as they do not go far enough in specifically setting out guidelines, requirements, reporting and oversight or supervisory provisions to ensure higher standards of adherence by political parties. The issue of party law and political party regulation is contestable since political parties lie in the border between civil society and the state. It remains debatable whether indeed aspects of intra-party democracy should be externally legislated by the state or be left to self-regulation within political party structures and institutions. This research also reveals that intra-party democracy is significantly influenced by unwritten informal institutional arrangements, which are value driven. These values are internalised by individuals through the socialisation process and may include political culture and political legacy, clientelism and patrimony. Not all informal institutional arrangements are necessarily negative and detrimental to intra-party democracy. To the contrary, some informal institutional arrangements can be complimentary, functional and may serve to solve the principle-agent conflicts arising from competing interests of social interaction. This may in turn serve to promote the efficient performance of formal institutional arrangements (Helmke and Levitsky, 2004). Indeed, some informal institutional arrangements may enhance participatory democracy by promoting a culture of debate and consultations within the party thereby promoting intra- party democracy. It is therefore necessary to identify and encourage those informal institutional arrangements that are critical to the enhancement of intra-party democracy while guarding against those that may impede the promotion of intra-party democracy.

The lack of inclusiveness in ideology and policy formulation processes support the second sub- hypothesis and represents the most significant failing in all three indicators of institutionalisation, inclusiveness and decentralization among all political parties in the region on the . This is one of the most centralised and non-inclusive aspects of most political parties both institutionally and structurally. Party formation and ideological orientation is usually the preserve of a few individuals who characteristically become the party "owners". These founders then centralize power and decision-making prerogatives among themselves. More often than not, the process of policy and campaign platform formulation is outsourced to expert consultants more often than not close associates of the party founders or party leadership. The process thus severely compromises intra-party democracy by disenfranchising party members, diminishing the sense of ownership and compromising party loyalty. Such practices only serve to entrench personality politics where loyalty to the party is substituted with personal loyalty to the party leader hence further diminishing prospects for party institutionalisation and overall democracy.

The main hypothesis and third sub-hypothesis are partly supported regarding participation in leadership and candidate selection processes. This conclusion derives from the fact that most parties fail to hold internal leadership elections and although most parties conduct primary elections for the nomination of parliamentary candidates, there are critical deficits. In terms of internal leadership elections, a large number of parties have never held credible elections since their formation and are perpetually led by interim officials. For those that do hold elections, there are significant delays and when held, they are usually marred with corruption, intimidation, bribery, threats and in some cases open violence. Conflicts arising from the undemocratic nature of these processes are so intense that it often leads to party splits or the exit of some leaders along with their supporters to join other parties. Some examples include splits in NCCR-Mageuzi in Tanzania, FORD, FORD-Kenya, KANU, ODM and NARC in Kenya. Newly enacted party law in Kenya and Uganda and a review of enforcement mechanisms in Uganda are intended to rectify these anomalies.

In terms of candidate selection, there are strong tendencies towards centralisation, imposition of unpopular candidates, automatic nomination by the national secretariat, outright rigging and manipulation rules of procedure. This is despite the fact that although most parties have clearly stipulated internal rules regulating the selection of party candidates in the party law but these are hardly adhered to. The scenario is compounded by the fact that there are no clear, impartial and credible conflict resolution mechanisms. At the same time, there are not external candidate selection rules in the national constitution and where conflict arises, the courts are hesitant to arbitrate preferring to leave such disputes to be resolved through internal party machinery. Only recently have arbitration powers been granted to the registrar of political parties, but these bodies too seem hesitant to interfere. As such, while institutional arrangements theoretically enhance intra-party democracy, in practice, both the absence and, where they exist, weak internal and external enforcement of these institutional arrangements undermine free and popular participation in candidate selection processes. It can therefore be argued that the sub-hypothesis is only partly supported in empirical findings.

Finally, concerning membership participation in party decision making processes such as conventions, the main and sub-hypothesis are only partially supported. Existing institutional arrangements among almost all political parties do not fully comply with internal constitutional provisions and hence fail to fully enhance intra-party democracy. Party conventions are hardly conducted and when they are done, its usually close to general elections where party leaders use them to endorse already pre-selected presidential or parliamentary candidates. In some cases, delegates' attendance only serves to legitimise undemocratic pre-election power sharing pacts packaged as coalitions. Party conventions are largely held contrary to the timeframes and procedures set in party constitutions. The findings show that in some cases, these conventions have been legally contested in court for being un-procedural such as one that preceded the split of KANU and the creation of New- KANU in 2005 as well as the split of FORD-Kenya and creation of New FORD-Kenya in 2007. Neither the national constitution nor the party law defines clear and enforceable procedures for conventions. Due to these limitations, both the main and sub hypotheses are only partially supported.

With regard to membership participation in the formation and dissolution of inter-party coalitions, there has been a glaring absence of any form of regulation in existing institutional arrangements. This has served to adversely undermine intra-party democracy. Although there are new stipulations in the newly enacted party law in Kenya, this only serves to institutionalize and regulate the instruments of the coalition with the electoral commission and parliament but does not ensure and safeguard the interests of party members in the process.

It therefore only serves to further legitimise undemocratic decisions made by party leaders to the further exclusion of citizens. Similarly, provisions in existing party laws in Tanzania and Uganda prohibits the formation of coalitions hence denying party members and political parties the free will to decide what form of political organisation best suits their interests.

Chapter 10

Party Administration

DEMOCRATIC POLITICAL PARTY ADMINISTRATION:
MANAGING THE DAY TO DAY ACTIVITIES OF A POLITICAL
PARTY.

The importance of daily administration of a political party can not be overstretched. This is because political parties face a lot of challenges in their daily administration. There must certainly arise a whole lot of issues and crucial questions such as: how do political parties react to social changes? What are the advantages, disadvantages and challenges parties face with regard to new and social media? How and to what extent can party members be included in intra- party decision-making? In what way do parties deal with internal conflicts? How can corruption be dealt with and prevented within a party? These and many other questions arise in relation to political party management, the overall organizational aspect of political parties.

In recent times, political parties are part of different political, economic and social systems and accordingly face different challenges, but when it comes to management, they all have one thing in common: management is closely connected with the perception of the political system they are part of. Consequently, forms of mismanagement and the abuse of power within political parties have a strong negative impact on citizens' consent towards the political system they live in and on the legitimacy of the political party itself. It is therefore, a serious task for all parties to continuously improve their party management, to adapt it to the latest changes and challenges within the societies they represent and to search for institutionalized forms of party management that guarantee good governance.

In this chapter, attention will focus on Party Administration in ANC, South Africa; National Congress Party, India; The Democratic Party, USA; and CPC, China

The African National Congress of South Africa: Experiences of Party Management.
The African National Congress (ANC) describes itself as a "liberation movement" with a long- range project of racial and class emancipation (ANC 1969, 2000, 2002, 2007), but it is also a political party in a constitutional, representative democracy. It commands the support of almost two-thirds of those who vote in South Africa's competitive elections. Through its mass membership and long-standing alliances with the Congress of South African Trade Unions (COSATU) and the South African Communist Party (SACP), the ANC dominates the political terrain in this country and seems set to do so for many years to come. The movement, however, faces major governance and organisational challenges.

The ANC emerged relatively recently as the pre-eminent force in South African politics. Founded in 1912 by black elites in response to a political settlement that favoured whites but the movement was elitist and politically conservative. In the 1920s and 1930s, these weaknesses lead to the marginalisation of the ANC. Faced with the National Party's intensified "apartheid" (racial separation) doctrines after 1948, the ANC launched a series of defiance campaigns that brought it to a

170

position of national leadership for the first time. The ANC joined with other anti- segregation forces in the 1950s to propagate the "Freedom Charter", a quasi-socialist and non-racialist agenda. Concealing the divisions between "Africanists" and "non-racialists", the Charter did not, however, prevent the breakaway in 1959 of the Pan Africanist Congress (PAC) with its more activist Black nationalist agenda (Butler 2013a, pp. 16–32).

The political turmoil of the 1940s and 1950s culminated in the suppression of black opposition The African National Congress of South Africa: Experiences of Party Management in 1960 after the Sharpeville Massacre (Lodge 2011, pp. 74–108). Subsequently, the ANC was banned and launched an armed struggle. The joint military wing of the ANC and the SACP, the "spear of the nation" (Umkhonto we Sizwe, or simply MK), embarked on a long and mostly fruitless campaign of sabotage against a state with overwhelming military and intelligence superiority. Key ANC leaders, including Nelson Mandela, were jailed for treason in the 1963 Rivonia trial, and other ANC leaders went into extended exile and did not return to the country until shortly before the first non-racial elections in 1994 (Butler 2013a, pp. 45–7).

The ANC has exhibited marked ideological diversity. Religious activists have worked alongside communists and traditionalists (Erlank 2012). Communism was especially influential in the development of the ANC – but not straightforwardly so (Cronin 2003; Netshitenzhe 2003, Slovo 1988). Note well that the ANC was to remain a black African movement at leadership level until 1985. Multiracial anti-apartheid struggle was largely the product of an increasingly deep partnership between the African ANC and the non-racial SACP. Black Africans, unlike their white, Coloured, and Indian peers, were able to hold dual leadership positions in both entities.The SACP adopted a resolutely pro-Moscow profile, but it was always primarily an organisational rather than an ideological vehicle: members of the SACP, many of whom were white or Indian, considered themselves to be a vanguard within the ANC. The SACP was greatly weakened by the collapse of communism in the USSR, and this epochal event led to mass resignations as well as too many doctrinal and political changes. Also, economic policy conservatism, meanwhile, led to growing tensions between the ANC and both the SACP and the ANC-aligned union federation COSATU, which was formed in 1985.

The memberships of the three movements overlap substantially. Almost all SACP cadres are also ANC members but the sharply eroded prestige and power of the communist party after 1989 has turned it into just one of many major factions in the ANC. The SACP does not stand for election but rather lobbies to place its candidates on ANC electoral lists. This strategy gives opportunity to have the leadership of COSATU strong links with both parties, and it is both a major funder of the SACP and an important mobilising force for the ANC.

Thus, the ANC embraced labour and civil society allies in the "transition to democracy" period of the early 1990s, and it was widely acknowledged as the natural party of government. Over its first decade of rule, it also became an impressive electoral machine. The liberation movement's uneven democratic tendencies coexist with democratic centralist and hierarchical conceptions of legitimate authority. The struggle between these elements are unlikely to be decisively resolved in the foreseeable future. This is because the country's constitution, however, entrenches representative democracy and liberal political rights.

Achievements since 1994
The ANC has successfully managed many political and economic challenges associated with profound inequality and social division.

1 These racial classifications were a cornerstone of the system of apartheid. They remain very much in use today.

Five achievements stand out. First, the ANC has secured political stability. Despite its strong electoral performance – the ANC has secured between 63 and 70 per cent of the vote in national elections since 1994 – it has mostly avoided the use of non-democratic means to achieve its goals. Its carefully constructed programmes have helped to structure citizens' electoral choices; filtered, prioritised, and reconciled demands; and neutralised potentially divisive ideological conflict (Butler 2007, p. 36).

Second, the movement's continuing electoral popularity has allowed it to enforce an unpopular but necessary programme of economic stabilisation (Maphai & Gottschalk 2003). Third, the ANC has created a new system of government out of the chaos of the apartheid state (Picard 2005). Fourth, it has retained a degree of trust among the poorest citizens, for whom the first decade-and-a-half of democracy brought a deepening of poverty rather than a relief from it (Simkins 2004).

Finally, the ANC has discouraged racial and ethnic conflict. Despite three centuries of white supremacy, segregation, and apartheid, the ANC has relentlessly promoted non-racialism as an ideology and as a guide to practice, regulating internal discussion of ethnicity and averting overt tribalism in competition for office. Ethnic balance has (until recently, at least) been a cornerstone of ANC party lists and National Executive Committee (NEC) elections, and key ANC institutions and the cabinet itself have a carefully managed diversity (Butler 2005).

The movement has evolved from a party of exile (and prison) to a mass movement. It combines the hierarchy and democratic centralism of an

exile movement with the mass organisational politics that characterised the domestic anti- apartheid struggle. Members continue to voice their demands for participation, and committed activists bewail any dilution of the party's ideological character in the pursuit of wider electoral support. As an electoral party, however, the ANC has become "catch-all" in character (Lodge 2004).

The complex interests and voices in the movement dictate that both central discipline and wide deliberation are necessary to maintain political unity. A large activist base remains essential for the ANC to mobilise electors at registration and voting time, and to enhance the legitimacy and understanding of the movement's programme of government. The ANC's system of alliances allows diverse class and ideological interests to be represented, but the movement's own policies to build a black business and middle class have created internal class tensions that threaten its own unity. The ANC leadership now contains a very significant "black bourgeoisie" as a result of Black Economic Empowerment policies and the politicisation of some state procurement processes (Butler 2011). The movement has also fostered the growth of a black middle class, particularly in the public sector but most ANC activists at the grass roots level remain poor (Butler 2013a, Jordan 2011). This has resulted in significant tensions based on the different class positions and economic interests of activists and leaders.

Challenges

The ANC has been confronted by four major challenges in recent years. First, a growing proportion of the ANC's active membership has little respect for conventions of authority in the movement. The ANC's membership has grown by over 300 per cent since 2002 – from 416,846 members to more than a million today (ANC 2012). Most of the new members know little or none of the party's history and values.

Second, the ANC has been suffering from "money-politics" and "careerism" – i.e., the use of the movement by its members as a stepping stone to political office or public positions that can be abused for personal gain, and the use of private resources to win internal party elections. In the 2012 elective conference at Mangaung, for example, the deputy presidency of the ANC was contested by political leaders who had also become extremely wealthy business people. At the lower levels of the movement, the leadership has not been able to stamp out corruption, in part because it is itself implicated in it (Butler 2010).

Third, the internal politics of the ANC has been marked by factional conflict such that at the national level, former president Thabo Mbeki's faction tried to suppress competition for senior ANC offices. Mbeki's intention in 2007 was to retain the ANC presidency and to control the state presidency from ANC headquarters. This effort backfired dramatically when Mbeki's competitor, Jacob Zuma, swept to the ANC presidency.

Finally, there has been ongoing organisational disarray. Manipulation of internal elections and the abuse of access to resources have resulted in paralysing political turmoil, in particular at the local and provincial levels.

Party Organizational Structures
The ANC operates at four levels. 1. The National Conference, which is held every five years, elects the NEC. 2. ANC conferences in South Africa's nine provinces elect Provincial Executive Committees (PECs). Regional Executive Committees are elected at the sub-provincial level, and ANC branches exist in almost every community (ANC 2007).

There are also three "leagues". The ANC Women's League (ANCWL) is open to women who are members of the ANC, and it has national, provincial, and branch structures. It functions "as an autonomous body", but its constitution, rules, and regulations must comply with the ANC's own constitution (ANC 2007, p. 73). The ANC Youth League (ANCYL) is open to people between the ages of 14 and 35, and it also operates on national, provincial, and branch levels. The ANCYL has been a major force in the internal politics of the ANC since the 1950s. It was recently involved in attempts to remove ANC president Jacob Zuma – whom it had previously helped to elect – and as a consequence, its leadership was suspended in the run-up to the 2012 Mangaung Conference.3 The ANC recently launched an ANC Veterans' League open to long- standing ANC members aged 60 years or above.

The ANC's "tripartite alliance" with the COSATU and the SACP also operates at the provincial and local levels, although it is highly inconsistent in its operations except at election time.

With 80 members, the NEC is the executive body of the ANC between conferences. This is the latest of the five annual ANC conferences at which policy positions are endorsed and national leaders elected by branch delegates and others.

National Level
The National Conference is the supreme body of the ANC; and 90 per cent of its delegates come from the branches the community-level structures that overlap with municipal boundaries and are meant to be elected at "properly constituted branch general meetings" (ANC 2007, p.10). The number of delegates is intended to be proportional to paid-up membership, and each branch "in good standing" – i.e., deemed to have fulfilled necessary procedural and membership regulations – is entitled to at least one delegate. The remainder of the voting delegates at the Conference are allocated by the NEC "from among members of the Provincial Executive Committees, the ANC Veterans' League, the ANC Youth League, and the ANC Women's League" (ANC 2007, p. 11).

The formal responsibilities of the National Conference are as follows: to determine the policies and programmes of the ANC; to deliberate upon reports by the ANC President, Treasurer-General, and Secretary

General; to deliberate on the activities of the various Leagues; and to elect the "top 6" office holders and the remaining 80 "additional members" of the NEC (ANC 2007, p. 11).

The NEC is the highest organ of the ANC between National Conferences. It is elected by secret ballot at national conference, and 50 per cent of its members must be women. The NEC elects a National Working Committee (NWC) to serve as the secretariat and "engine room" of the movement (ANC 2007, p. 11). The NEC's responsibilities include overseeing provincial, regional, and branch structures; overseeing the ANC Veterans' League, the ANC Women's League, and the ANC Youth League; and managing candidate selection processes. Candidate selection for national elections is controlled by a National List Committee appointed by the NEC. The NEC subcommittees cover areas such as: communication and media; education and health; economic transformation; international relations; legislature and governance; organisation building and campaigns; political education; and fundraising. The members of these committees are primarily drawn from the NEC; many of them are cabinet or deputy ministers in the national government (ANC 2013b). In some areas of policy for example, economic policy and international relations – there are strong (but concealed) conflicts between party committees and government departments.

The national headquarters in Luthuli House, Johannesburg provides institutional support. However, its key areas of activity include organisation and mobilisation, political education, information and publicity, and finance. The three full-time office holders – the President, the Secretary General (SG), and the Treasurer-General have significant permanent staff. The national headquarters is managed by the SG, but a secure President, such as Thabo Mbeki, can dominate its operations (Butler 2005, 2007).

Just as relations within ANC headquarters have fluctuated, so has the balance of power between state and party (Lodge 2004, Butler 2007). In the 1990s, a relatively small coterie of former political exiles dominated key positions in the movement. During Mbeki's ANC presidency (1997–2007), government ministers increasingly dominated the NEC and government departments dominated policymaking. Since 2007, however, there has been a resurgence of NEC committees. This has resulted in the ANC serving as a veto point in government decisions. It has also resulted in slow and cumbersome decision-making within the state.

The ANC President, Cyril Ramaphosa is the political head of the ANC. He is elected to a five- year term at the National Conference. There are no limits on how many terms can be served. The ANC President, by recent convention, is the ANC's candidate for the state presidency, a position that is filled by the National Assembly after parliamentary elections (Republic of South Africa 1996). There is an ANC policy commitment to avoiding "two centres of power" - a division between the leadership of the ANC and of the state. The Deputy President, performs a primarily supportive role. Nonetheless, there is arguably a convention that the ANC Deputy President should become ANC President.

The National Chairperson formally presides over the National Conference, the NEC, and the National Working Committee (NWC), but in practice this office confers few real powers. The Secretary General is the chief administrative officer of the ANC. The Treasurer-General is "the chief custodian of the funds and property of the ANC" and should (in theory at least) "receive and bank all monies on behalf of the NEC" (ANC 2007, p. 16.10). In reality, the control of party finances within the ANC is deeply contested.

Provinces, Regions, and Branches

The Provincial Conference is the highest organ of the ANC in each of the country's nine provinces. Branch delegates have 90 per cent of the votes (ANC 2007, p. 17.1). Provincial conferences elect a 20-member Provincial Executive Committee (PEC) by secret ballot, as well as senior office holders. These elections have been volatile and factionalised in recent years.

PECs dominate provincial decision-making and usually possess veto powers over provincial government decisions, including government contracts and tenders. The regions and branches – and their Executive Committees – are partially overseen by the provinces. PECs appoint Provincial List and Candidates Committees to regulate candidate lists for provincial and local government elections, but they are subject to oversight by the NEC (ANC 2007. P.19.9) Provincial Regions are demarcated to overlap district and metropolitan municipal boundaries in each province (ANC 2007, p. 21). Regional Executive Committees supervise and direct the work of the ANC and all its organs in the region, including the ANC local government caucuses. The ANC describes itself as a mass organisation and branches are ostensibly the "basic unit of the organisation" (ANC 2007, p. 23.1). It does indeed possess a mass membership and there are various institutional mechanisms for branch delegates to influence policy and elect leaders, but only a branch in "good standing" is entitled to participate in elective and policy conferences. Moreover, national leaders and regional powerbrokers both try to manipulate and control branch opinion. This results from administrative and organisational weaknesses, from a hierarchical ideology, and from the manipulation of electoral and other processes. Regional offices control paper-based membership systems and are able to control branch accreditation. Mbeki succeeded Nelson Mandela, Zuma succeeded Mbeki, and Ramaphoza succeeded Zuma in just this way.

3. Intra-Party Democracy and Decision- Making Processes

Although branch delegates comprise 90 per cent of the voting delegates at ANC conferences, where policy positions are deliberated and endorsed, conference resolutions are drafted by national committees. Candidate and leadership selection processes are more highly contested. In a statement in early 2012, Zuma observed that the ANC should review its election systems "in order to enhance internal democracy, credibility of the process as well as the integrity and suitability of candidates" (ANC 2012a). This would "protect the ANC from the tyranny of slates, factions and money". The proposals that are being considered include the establishment of a permanent electoral commission.

The ANC's "broad church" character combines histories and practices associated with exile, military organisation, domestic struggle, trade unionism, communism, and imprisonment, which together help explain its complex behaviour. It displays both democratic and hierarchical aspects, and its style of conflict resolution is sometimes described as consensual. This conventional assessment of the movement has been undermined by escalating conflict and attempted centralisation in recent years, and by the increasing role of procedural manipulation and money-politics in internal elections.

In 2012, conference delegates endorsed a new focus on organisational issues. The next decade will be a "decade of the cadre" in which members will allegedly enjoy ideological, academic, and moral training in a "comprehensive political school system". Cadres will be subjected to "performance monitoring", "firm and consistent action" will instill discipline, and "integrity commissions" will purportedly blossom (ANC 2013a, p. 4–6).

Inside Luthuli House, an information technology revolution will apparently sweep aside antiquated membership and communications systems. Political funding transparency will oblige wealthy loyalists to donate openly and generously to the Treasurer-General's office, and fundraising will be restricted to mandated officials. The idea of banning simultaneous membership in more than one constitutional structure, ANC leaders hope to exclude provincial power brokers from the political centre (ANC 2013a, p. 5–6). The dangers posed by unwieldy and technologically backward internal systems came into sharp focus before the Mangaung Conference. Members of the "change faction" spoke darkly about the paralysis into which they would plunge the movement if they were defeated by unfair procedural means.

Few such challenges to auditing, accreditation, and delegate selection processes actually materialised. Despite complaints that many branches included "ghost" members, that delegates were not properly elected, and that money and other inducements were used in internal power struggles, the margin of victory enjoyed by the Jacob Zuma slate made it credibly impossible to reject the outcome. In future elections, the lack of credibility of internal electoral and campaigning processes could generate significant tensions. In particular, the ANC has recently passed through a period of more than 30 years – spanning exile and democratisation – in which the key leaders at the national level were drawn from families from one region (the Eastern Cape), belonging to one language group (isiXhosa), and drawn from closely related ethnic groups (amaXhosa and abaThembu). The recent transition to a more balanced leadership, but one increasing dominated by amaZulu leaders from KwaZulu-Natal, has generated significant political tensions. Contested internal elections that possess an ethnic or regional dimension could in future pose a threat to party survival (Butler 2013b).

Current elective processes cannot confer such legitimacy upon leaders in a closely fought internal election because money-fueled lobbying plays a prominent role in every province. Cycles of money and power connect public offices to ANC positions. Auditing, accreditation, and record- keeping systems of all kinds are largely paper- based, where they exist at all. Political actors at all levels have learned the art of manipulating membership numbers. Three times every five years, the movement is paralysed by elective or candidate list processes. The weaknesses of internal systems also prevent the ANC from successfully performing the broader functions of a political party. It cannot serve as a strong bridge between activist citizens and the national political elite, because it can neither communicate the discontent of ordinary people to the leadership, nor serve as an instrument for the political education and mobilisation of the poor (Butler 2013b).

Major obstacles confront those who wish to "modernise" the ANC. Party modernisation is time consuming and painful, and it could well be deferred once again to a future that somehow never arrives. Furthermore, if new organisational systems are brought in to end the manipulation of paper records by the regions, a computer- enhanced Luthuli House might then use its technological power to impose stricter discipline on recalcitrant activists, or even to engage surreptitiously in membership and list rigging escapades of its own. For these reasons, many activists are deeply suspicious of information technologies.

Settlement of Intra-Party Conflicts/ Disputes and Intra-Party Ideological Differences

The 2012 conference adopted new policies on lobbying, the use of resources in internal elections, and improper conduct in political meetings (ANC 2013a). Despite much talk about renewed discipline and the political education of cadres, the party is increasingly unruly at the provincial, regional, and local levels. In some provinces (notably KwaZulu-Natal), there has been an upsurge in political assassinations.

The ANC strongly discourages the use of the courts to resolve organisational issues. Instead, members are obliged to take their complaints about breaches of the ANC Code of Conduct through internal disciplinary processes, which are set out at every level of the movement. Unfortunately, those who should enforce the rules are often those who also break them. At the local level, branches have been subjected to destabilising factionalism. Regional power brokers are often responsible for manipulating branch politics, and those who lose out in elections routinely turn to street-level protest. Also, factions can crystallise around the Youth League, local SACP organisers, civic activists, trade unionists, or a range of other actors.

Provinces also exhibit factionalism and similar motivations appear to be key drivers in the less wealthy provinces. Ethnic and racial mobilisation has played an alarming role in intra-party conflicts in the Western Cape, and to some extent elsewhere. On the contrary, disciplinary processes are themselves controversial and often result in fresh waves of disputation and violence. The most effective purges of allegedly corrupt or violent activists have been managed by national officials, and they have been interpreted (mostly accurately) as factional power plays rather than as genuine efforts to resolve conflict.

At the national level, the NEC operates two disciplinary committees with the power to sanction, suspend, or expel members: the National Disciplinary Committee and the National Disciplinary Committee of Appeal (ANC 2007, p. 25). This machinery has not been used often – with the exception of the closing down of the ANCYL in 2012, when it was spearheading a campaign to remove Zuma from the ANC presidency. As a result of controversies over centralisation in the Mbeki era (ANC 1997a, 2001), it is widely believed by activists that disciplinary sanctions are primarily designed to favour incumbents and to suppress opposing factions.

Measures for Preventing and Controlling Corruption

The transition from authoritarian rule created vulnerability to corruption and criminality. This is because, the local state, the legal system, and the police were compromised by the history of apartheid. "Bantustan" (racial enclave) bureaucrats brought with them traditions of bribery, money laundering, and nepotism. The ANC acted carefully to create an institutional framework to improve governance and limit the abuse of public authority by officials. Unfortunately, it has not been energetically applied (Camerer 2011).

Given the ANC's political predominance, the securing of political office is often a first step towards public office and potential private gain. ANC Secretary General Kgalema Motlanthe (2005) used an ANC National General Council to lament memorably: "[T]he central challenge facing the ANC is to address the problems that arise from our cadres' susceptibility to moral decay occasioned by the struggle for the control of and access to resources. All the paralysis in our programmes, all the divisions in our structures, are in one way or another, a consequence of this cancer in our midst."

International indices suggest that corruption is not strikingly high for a middle-income developing country (Transparency International 2013). The ANC deals with political corruption allegations primarily within party structures. However, sustained attempts to bring some political leaders and officials to trial have been rejected because such efforts have been viewed as power plays in factional conflicts. Thus, they have succeeded only in destroying anti-corruption institutions. Similarly, parliament's non- partisan public accounts committee tried to investigate corruption in a major arms procurement programme (Holden and Van Vuuren 2011); the result was that the ANC deployed new senior members to the committee with apparent instructions to disable it. In the mid-2000s, one effective national investigation and prosecution unit, the "Scorpions", pursued then Deputy President Jacob Zuma on fraud and corruption charges; it was dissolved when Zuma secured the ANC presidency. There is, however, some renewed willingness to subject lower ranking public sector officials to the law, and new legislation may soon result in prosecutions of such officials (DPSA 2013).

The ANC has debated internal controls on members' business activities for almost a decade – without reaching any conclusions. Proposed measures to end "revolving doors" between state, party, and business do not appear to enjoy significant support (Butler 2011, p. 67–8). Indeed, the ANC has used its cadre deployment powers to transfer significant funds from state-owned enterprises into party coffers via party-linked businesses. The recent introduction of "integrity committees" at all levels of the ANC is not likely to change current abuses of office for financial gain, and money-politics is likely to continue eroding public trust in ANC and state institutions (Butler 2010, p. 237–50).

Congress Party: Ideology, Organization and Finance. India Example
The Indian National Congress (hereafter, the Congress) surprised everyone when it defeated the Bhartiya Janata Party (BJP)–led National Democratic Alliance (NDA) and returned to power in the 2004 parliamentary elections at the head of a coalition, the United Progressive Alliance (UPA). It has won two consecutive elections, winning again in 2009, something it had not done since 1984. The elections resulted in both the BJP and the Communist Party of India (CPI (M)) becoming politically weaker but paradoxically the Congress appears weaker, too. It has not made any significant gains in states that it has lost to the opposition in the past decade, notably Bihar, Uttar Pradesh, West Bengal and Tamil Nadu. The overdependence on the Nehru-Gandhi dynasty remains an enduring fault line in the party. The excessive reliance on the family's charisma is not enough in an India defined by the mobilization of a plethora of identities and aspirations, and the diffusion of political power from New Delhi to the states.

The point of departure for this research is the 2004 parliamentary elections that brought the Congress back to power at the centre (central government in New Delhi), helping the party to assert its national presence. This is a fascinating moment in the history of India, which is at once a rising power with an expanding middle class and a poor, unequal and misgoverned country. This process of change started in 1989 when the leadership, constituencies and electoral strategies of political parties – including that of the Congress – underwent significant changes. From this point, the Congress ceased to be the fulcrum of the political system and increasingly had to respond to shifts in politics – the rise of the BJP and of various regional parties which doubled their share of the votes and seats at the expense of national parties – as well as economic changes, many of which were in turn brought about by its own policies in its previous stint in power in the first half of the 1990s. This period is also particularly interesting because in some ways the Congress had to reinvent itself in these changed circumstances.

Four key elements are essential to an examination of political parties, especially the Congress party: (i) ideology and programmes as embodied in policies; (ii) leadership; (iii) organization; and (iv) party finance. This paper aims to capture the structure of the Congress, as well as the transformation within the party, both in its policy and strategy and in its organization and leadership. It also investigates the structure and direction of change within the party and its governance agenda in response to these changing conditions, as well as its own internal dynamics.

Origin and Development of the Congress.

This brief historical background sets the context for understanding the political development of the Congress. The political history of modern India is intimately intertwined with the history of the Congress - India's largest and oldest party. It is unique not only for its longevity but also for its role in the building of the Indian nation. It played a crucial role in shaping modern India and establishing a democratic system. Globally, the Congress is one of the most important, durable and influential political parties in the world. No party, at least in the developing world outside Western democracies, can claim such a long innings in power.

Established in 1885, the 125-year old party was born out of India's struggle for freedom from British rule. As the vanguard of the national movement, it was the natural party of governance from Independence in 1947. Out of the past 66 years the congress has run the central government in New Delhi for all but 11. In most general elections held prior to 1989, with the exception of that in 1977, it commanded an outright majority or emerged as the party with the highest number of seats in parliament. As a movement that became a party, it encompassed virtually every shade of political opinion and social constituency of the nation.

Led by Jawaharlal Nehru, the Congress reaped the rewards of its role during the anti-colonial movement against the British. Although dominated by upper-caste/class leaders, there were various castes, communities, regional and linguistic groups represented in its higher echelons. Its early hegemony was based on a concrete set of achievements: an independent model of industrial growth; considerable reduction in large-scale feudal landholdings, which benefited the upper peasantry; growth in infrastructure; expansion in educational facilities and technical personnel. It did deliver some tangible benefits to the broad mass of the population through various development projects, the initiation and construction of the public sector and the provision of public services, such as health, education and transport.

This political system worked until the split in the Congress in 1969 when Indira Gandhi acted against the old guard, accusing them of being reactionaries and against progressive policies, such as the nationalization of banks and abolition of privy purses of princes. The consequence was a radicalization of the Congress in the short term and centralization of power, and Indira Gandhi's complete control over the cabinet and the party. This ensured that the once robust Congress roots withered and governance became less institutionalized, more personalized and highly centralized. She discarded the intra-party democracy of the old decentralized structure and placed individuals who were personally loyal to her at the head of Pradesh Congress Committees. It was clear that her lurch towards authoritarianism had cost the party heavily in terms of its popular credibility in north India which had to suffer the worst excesses of the Emergency – a watershed in Indian politics since popular opposition to it break the political monopoly of the Congress. Its three-decades-long rule at the Centre was broken when the 1977 general elections brought the Janata Party, a conglomerate of four parties (the Jana Sangh, BhartiyaLok Dal, Congress (O), and the Socialist Party), to power.

Much of the responsibility for the decline of the Congress and the weakened governmental and administrative institutions was attributed to Indira Gandhi's personal ambition and dynastic proclivities as she went about refashioning the party to suit her political interests. However, neither the need to reshape the Congress nor her capacity to do so would have been conceivable had the party not already been in serious and growing disarray. In all, the decline itself was not due to factors that were altogether internal to the Congress or because of the top leadership's centralizing drive but essentially the result of paradigmatic changes in the polity, economy and society. The Congress was both shaping and being shaped by societal changes. As the Congress was changing, so was India.

It is pertinent to note that "Privy purse" was a payment made to the royal families of erstwhile princely states as part of their agreements to first integrate with India in 1947, and later to merge their states in 1949, whereby they lost all ruling rights. The Privy Purse continued to be paid to the royal families until the 26th Constitutional Amendment of 1971 – by which all their privileges and allowances from the central government would cease to exist. This however was implemented after a two-year legal battle.

On the request of Prime Minister Indira Gandhi, President of India Fakhruddin Ali Ahmed declared a state of Emergency under Article 352 of the Constitution, effectively bestowing on her the power to rule by decree, suspending elections and civil liberties. It was one of the most controversial decisions times in the history of independent India. The Emergency lasted for 21 months, from 26 June 1975 to 21 March 1977. (Perry Anderson, The Indian Ideology, Three Essays, New Delhi, 2012, p. 145).

All these trends were indicative of a great ferment in Indian society. Social and political change was aided by affirmative action and reservation policy, which created a lower-caste elite of substantial size that had acquired education and joined non- traditional occupations and professions. This section formed the nucleus of a small but highly vocal political leadership which began to alter the public discourse. This process came to a head in the course of the Mandal Commission's proposal to extend reservations in central government jobs and education to the "Other Backward Classes" (OBCs) in 1990, a course that was vehemently opposed by the upper-caste middle classes. The backward castes were questioning the way the country had been governed and, above all, their exclusion from bureaucratic and political power. These trends point to a social revolution that had given voice to previously marginalized groups and enabled them to gain access to the political system. In consequence, political power moved downwards from the old established elites to new groups who pushed for a politics of parity and equality of opportunity. The Congress gradually lost the support of the backward castes, scheduled castes and even Muslims who had constituted its most loyal supporters, as they began drifting away in several states. The latter two groups had constituted the very foundation of the Congress's political power, and once they began shifting their loyalties to different regional parties, the Congress's political dominance was truly shaken.

Prior to the early 1980s, the political impact of religion was limited and communal parties won few seats. Ethnic and secessionist troubles in Punjab, Kashmir and Assam allowed room for such tendencies. Its greatest failure was in the way it approached the growing Hindu assertiveness spearheaded by the BJP and Rashtriya Swayamsevak Sangh (RSS) combine. As the Congress resorted to ethnic appeals and flirted with religious politics to shore up its dwindling support, it was eventually to become the principal victim of these actions. It committed strategic errors in its approach to the politics of organized religion taking shape outside the party system. Above all, this created conditions conducive to the rise of the BJP, which formed a government at the Centre in 1998, ending decades of erstwhile political isolation. With the emergence of a clear right-wing alternative at the Centre and regional parties in the states, the Congress found it difficult to occupy and define the middle ground as political competition was increasingly along communal and caste lines. These developments were undermining it in two ways: directly, by challenging secular pluralist foundation of the political system, and indirectly, by shifting the political discourse away from development to ethnic identity issues. In all, the Congress sought to remain broadly centrist, but the centre ground got squeezed. Since then, secularism/communalism has remained an important ideological divide in Indian politics. The Gujarat violence of 2002, in which over 1,000 Muslims were killed, was a turning point in compelling the Congress to confront the BJP's divisive politics.

Ideology and Strategy.
The central pillar of Congress ideology was the legacy of Nehru's leadership in the freedom struggle and the first decades of the nascent

state which he steered with great distinction. The legitimating ideology of the Congress since independence had been secular nationalism and developmentalism. It was in the name of these ideals that it claimed to speak for the nation, regardless of creed or class. Thus, India's Constitution, with its focus on secularity, political democracy, social justice and quasi-federalism, is a representation of the ideology of the Congress as a nationalist organization.

However, major ideological shifts took place in the overall framework of development in the early 1990s, from a state-regulated economy to a market-centred one and to a greater role for religious politics. Post-1991 the Congress committed itself to economic reform and freedom for markets. The basics of this policy were put in place in the early 1980s during the period when Indira Gandhi (1980–84) was prime minister and later during Rajiv Gandhi's prime-ministership (1984–2009). It is worthy of note that this economic transition had actually begun during Indira Gandhi's last term in office (1980–84), when she moved away from garibihatao (remove poverty) to creating an environment in which the industrial sector would take the lead in economic development strategy. Indira Gandhi's government began to change the traditional anti-capitalist approach of the Congress to embrace a pro-business orientation. Increasing growth and enhancing production were to become the hallmark of policy from 1980 onwards.

The pace of economic liberalization has been subtle shaded by the need to avoid conflict and confrontation. Hence, changes have occurred in a piecemeal manner as the Congress did not altogether abandon its commitment to the dirigiste regime while pursuing its commitment to economic liberalization. From time to time it has sought to continue what many see as the social democratic strand in the party's political tradition. Indeed, the Congress Party's distinctiveness lies in the fact that, even though its current policies are conditioned by global economic forces, at the same time, in order to dominate national politics, it is sensitive to the compulsions of democracy and development in a poor country. Post-2004 the Congress government began to shape a new form of welfare politics through the introduction of rights-based legislation, such as the right to employment (2005), the right to education (2009) and the right to food (2013) and larger allocations for the social sector. Articulating the party's philosophy, Finance Minister Pranab Mukherjee claimed that the Congress's development strategy had changed radically with the right to information act, employment, education and food for a large section of its people.6 »I don't know [of] any [other] country in the world which has given the legal right to food to its people, Pranab Mukherjee said, referring to the right-to-food legislation. These legally mandated rights went counter to the global consensus on market- led growth which overrides political and ethical concerns about inequality. Thanks to the revenue- rich state, the United Progressive Alliance was able to unveil the biggest ever post-independence expansion of public expenditure.

The repertoire of social policies built up by the Congress was a sign that mass perceptions do matter in democratic politics. The UPA's experience shows that there was room for government policies to provide direct benefits to people who were unable to meet their basic needs. Greater political participation has led to a sharper sense of inequity and an attempt to use politics to rectify it. The need for the Congress to change course and accommodate the broader social interests of the poor to secure their political support was the strongest indication yet of these pressures.

Note well that numbers matter in electoral politics yet the Congress is currently going all out to woo the upwardly-mobile middle classes at a time when the economy has witnessed a loss of economic momentum, causing both a political crisis and policy paralysis. The Congress has had to reconcile the contradiction between economic reforms, which benefit the elite and upper-middle classes, and its mass support among

POLITICAL PARTY GOVERNANCE

the poor, who have been the losers in this process. This contradiction results from the change in India's social structure from an elite/ mass structure to one with a substantial middle class sandwiched in-between. For some time now, the Congress has been wondering how to reconcile attempts at appealing to the newly powerful middle class, with its focus on its traditional support base, India's poor. Rahul Gandhi, vice-president of the Congress has been, in some ways, a lightning rod for that conflict. His political sympathies may privately lean towards a pro-poor platform but fear of middle-class antagonism to social welfare policies has meant that he remains non-committal in public. He has acknowledged the need to take on board the aspirations of the middle classes, who are not finding their concerns reflected by the political process.

Organization and Leadership.

The Congress is a party for the masses, that is to say, it attempts to base itself on an appeal to the masses. Congress has no cadres: it recruits anyone who is willing to join. Formally, the organization developed by Mohandas Karamchand Gandhi's reorganization of the Congress in the years 1918 to 1920 has been retained. However, before Independence, the Congress organization extended down to the village level. Each district had a committee that reported to a provincial committee. India's division into provincial committees was based on regional languages. The provincial committees reported to the All India Congress Committee (AICC), a body of about 350 people. The Congress Working Committee (CWC) was responsible for policy decisions and daily administration.

After independence, the Pradesh Congress Committee (PCC) became the centre of power in each state. District units of Congress corresponded to administrative boundaries of districts. Each PCC has a Working Committee of 10–15 key members and the state president is the leader of the state unit. The PCC is responsible for directing political campaigns at local and state levels and assisting the campaigns for parliamentary constituencies. The AICC is formed of delegates sent from the PCCs around the country. The delegates elect various Congress committees, including the CWC, which consists of senior party leaders and office bearers, and takes all important executive and political decisions. The CWC and the president remain at the top of the national party structure, which runs the party at the national level on a day-to- day basis and take all the key decisions. Control of the presidency is critical for the control of CWC, the Congress Parliamentary Board (CPB) and the Central Election Committee.

For much of its history the Congress had strong state units and dedicated workers. Because of this, its influence penetrated downwards quite effectively, at least to the sub-district level and sometimes further down to the taluka level (an administrative division at the local level, also known as tehsil). This influence had, however, been seriously eroded since the late 1979s as the party machinery began to break down. Until the early 1970s, the Congress used to have regular elections, even if they were sometimes stage-managed. No elections were held after Indira Gandhi felt let down by the Congress organization leaders. Elections which had been promised early in Prime Minister Rajiv Gandhi's tenure were never conducted during his term as party president. Since then, elections have been repeatedly postponed on one pretext or another. Sonia Gandhi joined the Congress in 1998 and was immediately elected as the president and has remained in the post ever since. She was elected unopposed as the president of the Congress for the fourth time in September 2010.

There is no reliable information on party management and how the Congress deals with different voices and clashes of interests within the party. There are no objective answers to the question of party management and internal conflict resolution because there are no rules and regulations for the same. However, it is clear that the Congress, despite several changes of leadership and personnel at various levels, operates with a centralised top-down structure. Decision-making is the preserve of the high command, headed by the Congress president – a post which for the most part has been occupied by a member of the Nehru-Gandhi family.

Most parties in India are controlled by influential political families but none more famous than the Nehru-Gandhi family. The top leadership has remained within the family, with Jawaharlal Nehru, Indira Gandhi, Rajiv Gandhi and Sonia Gandhi all heading the Congress. As a party, the Congress has never been quite the same without a member of the Nehru-Gandhi family at the helm as it is believed that only a member of this family could capture votes across the many divisions of caste, creed and class. The reliance on the family has failed time and again but this has not lessened the party's dependence on them. This dependence is confirmed by the elevation of Sonia Gandhi's son, Rahul Gandhi, as the vice-president of the party in January 2013, despite the disastrous performance of the Congress under his leadership in the north Indian state of Uttar Pradesh legislative assembly elections a year earlier.

This family-centric arrangement and the ready acceptance of the »natural order« within the Congress is surely a sign of its limitations. The dynasty has become the organizing principle of the party, a substitute for ideology. The dynasty's primacy and pre-eminence are justified by its role as an arbiter and keeps the party united, which is generally prone to factionalism and indiscipline. The Nehru-Gandhi family has been able to play this role because of the perception that it is fair and just in its judgments in adjudicating factional disputes. Groupism and infighting are rampant, which needs a neutral arbiter to keep the peace. It could be argued that Sonia Gandhi's presence at the top has prevented the fragmentation of the party. Conflicts are settled by Sonia

Gandhi who takes the final decision and the squabbling leaders accept her decision. This is not true when a non-Gandhi is at the helm. For instance, during the presidency of NarasimhaRao and Sitaram Kesri, every decision was hotly contested, with leading dissidents coming from the ranks of the top leadership. Under Sonia Gandhi, on the other hand, the Congress negotiates unity among contending factions by leaving conflict management to her. This approach works in states where the Congress has a semblance of organisation; it does not work in states where the organization is defunct, as in Uttar Pradesh, Bihar and West Bengal, or where vicious factional struggles persist, where her writ does not run. In these states, disputes have to be settled locally, often without a reference to the conflict- resolution mechanism of the AICC.

More than one-third of all Congress MPs inherit their seats by family connection (twice the figure for the BJP), and most of them are young MPs. In Germany, for example, parties are required to meet certain conditions in nominating their candidates. They have to be chosen by a direct secret vote at both constituency and federal levels. Likewise in America laws were enacted that required the use of secret ballots in intraparty elections.

The lack of internal democracy is incontrovertible, even after the party's new importance under the UPA government (2004–2014) following Sonia Gandhi's decision not to take up the prime-ministerial post which altered the party/government equation in favour of the former. There are institutional and systemic obstacles to democratic accountability within the Congress, most conspicuously the lack of credible elections and the failure to nurture state leadership. Most of the coveted party posts are distributed through nomination and not election. The Congress has also shied away from holding internal elections to the AICC or CWC or PCCs. AICC and CWC members have not come from the election process for decades.

Comparative evidence from other democracies show that the general trend is toward greater internal democracy, decentralization and transparency within parties. The British Labour Party, the Spanish Socialist Party and the Progressive Conservative Party in Canada have seen movements by party activists and by the rank and file to reduce the power of entrenched party elites. Likewise, there are strong shifts within parties to democratize nomination and leadership selection processes and make them open to broader and more inclusive electorates.13 There is no discernible trend in this direction in India. One consequence of the lack of internal democracy is that it has clogged the conduits for political mobilization. The lack of intraparty democracy reduces the quality of deliberation and representation and thereby the quality of democracy. As a result, institutions like parliament are rapidly declining in terms of deliberative capacities and oversight functions. It is no surprise that the LokSabha now debates and deliberates for just one-third of the time it used to spend on them.

Party democracy requires that all parties exercise greater transparency and account-ability and open up specific areas to public scrutiny. This requires that parties have regular elections (based on secret ballots) and term limits for office bearers and that their finances and other activities come under public scrutiny and regulation. In a petition filed with the Central Information Commission (CIC) the Association of Democratic Reforms (ADR) argued that political parties must be treated as public authorities because they receive substantial government support in the form of free air time on Doordarshan and All India Radio during elections, discounted rents for party offices and large income-tax exemptions. The CIC in a landmark ruling (June 2013) mandated parties to provide requisite information in regard to the funding of political parties and their expenditure, membership registers and the constitution under the provision of the Right to Information Act (RTI). The CIC ruling has visibly shaken political parties which keep secret the information on their donors and managed not to reveal the source for a large part of their incomes by showing them as small voluntary donations without disclosure. Even as activists argue it will go a long way in ensuring transparency in finances, parties are united in their resolve not to reveal donors. The result of lack of scrutiny had led to parties being able to accumulate unexplained wealth running into hundreds of crores of rupees and so far, political parties have managed to stay out of any kind of financial accountability, which they evade by reporting most donations to be under 20,000 rupees. This allows even the mainstream parties, which receive corporate funding, to altogether escape scrutiny.

Members of Parliament cutting across party lines had closed ranks to override the CIC decision bringing political parties under the purview of the information law. This only goes to show that when political parties themselves are subject to the transparency law, they are willing to go to the length of amending this landmark legislation to ensure that they are not open to public scrutiny under the Act.16 Without even waiting to legally challenge the order of the CIC bringing parties under the ambit of the RTI Act, the government decided to amend the Act to nullify the effect of the aforementioned order. Ironically, the Congress-led UPA which birthed the RTI Act is itself debunking a law that is its own creation because it is being harnessed for unearthing scams and corrupt practices.

The government was all set to bring legislation in the monsoon session of Parliament (August– September 2013) for amending the RTI to keep political parties out of the ambit of the transparency law. However, in the face of sustained public pressure and civil society campaigning against amending the RTI, the UPA government referred the RTI amendment bill to a parliamentary standing committee for elaborate study. Instead of negating the effect of the CIC's order by exempting political parties from mandatory public disclosures, the government can use this as an opportunity to find ways to make political parties more financially accountable and less corrupt.

Party Finance.
Indian elections are entirely privately funded, which makes illicit election finance pervasive. This stands in contrast to most other countries, which have partial or full public funding or transparent regulation and financial accountability of election finance. Contributions were provided in several ways, through companies, individuals, industry groups, party membership fees, contributions of candidates and their friends and a levy on parliamentary income provided a small part of the funds needed. But as elections became more competitive and progressively more costly, financial support and funds assumed a new importance. Electioneering is labour- intensive and expensive in India's sprawling urban and rural constituencies. Parties and candidates need large sums of money for advertising, polling, consulting, travel, vehicles, fuel, and the printing of campaign materials that have to reach voters in constituencies.

There are laws to limit campaign finances and restrict expenditure in elections but they are ineffective because it is easy to circumvent them. At present, parties are required to declare to the Election Commission donations in excess of 20,000 rupees. However, non-reporting and under-reporting are common and the Election Commission does not have the power or the capacity to verify declarations. The huge gap between statements submitted and real expenditure during elections is an open secret. Indeed, the low expenditure ceilings induce circumvention and evasion. The main source of funding comes from donations of under 20,000 rupees. To evade disclosure most contributions of less than 20,000 rupees are given to individual candidates and political parties anonymously, which means it is possible for a donor to give any amount of money if it is less than the stipulated amount.

Elections are an expensive business in India and the Congress party leans heavily on this business for election expenditure. Congress is the biggest beneficiary of corporate largesse based on a quid pro quo between the party and business groups. Donations by business groups have been the major source of funding for the party since India liberalized its economy in 1991. In addition, a great deal of money comes through illegal channels. The trend of underhand funding also intensified after liberalization. The richest party, raising and spending more money than all other parties. Its income went up from Rs 222 crores in 2004–2005 to Rs 307.08 crores in 2010–2011. Its total assets in 2011–2012 stood at 2471.45 crores.

The flawed system of campaign finance and limited requirements with regard to reporting and disclosure of expenditure drive parties and politicians to misuse their powers to raise funds for election expenditure. Donations from corporate and private interests heavily influence government decisions, policy and legislation. Since the party receives huge amounts of money from business groups to win elections it will inevitably favour them in terms of policies and concessions. Thus, the revelations of corruption and crony capitalism which have dominated the headlines mostly refer to the period 2004–2009, when the party was celebrating its role in presiding over an unprecedented boom. Transparency in the funding of parties and the monitoring of their expenses is essential in any functioning party-based democracy. In India, the gap between acknowledged and actual party expenses is huge. Also, lack of transparency and accountability within parties reinforces corrupt fund-raising and parties spend much more than campaign laws allow them. Most of these problems arise from complete dependence on private funding and the absence of state funding. Opening up the accounts of political parties to public scrutiny could be the first step in making them more accountable.

Conclusion.

The Congress has not fared well since UPA-2 came to power in 2009. From 2004 to 2008, India experienced heady growth averaging 8 per cent. The overall achievements of UPA-1 are considerable: the right to information, the employment guarantee and larger allocations for the social sector. By comparison, under UPA- 2 there has been a rapid decline of economic growth, high inflation, stagnation in industry, infrastructure bottlenecks and a middle class– inspired civil society revolt against corruption and the political class. Growth has slowed down as the economic strategy of the past few years is showing signs of losing steam. Giving up on its strategy of reform by stealth, for the first time in eight years the CWC declared clear support for a growth-first perspective and the government's reform agenda in the belief that it would generate dynamism in the economy and provide funds for UPA's pro-poor programmes. Sonia Gandhi's endorsement of the prime minister's economic roadmap towards the end of 2012 suggests that neoliberals have been able to convince the top leadership that reform measures, such as foreign direct investment (FDI) in retail and liberalization of insurance and pension funds, are the only way out of the economic slowdown and to deliver a new round of prosperity. Such a business-driven development model is a recipe for exacerbating inequality. Indeed, the pattern of corrupt state– business relations in sectors such as mining, infrastructure and land has worsened inequality.

The Congress's political recovery and revival, which began in 2004, depended on its ability to sharpen the focus on economic and political inclusion, which helped to renew its relevance. Since then, it has been keen to demonstrate that its policies stress both growth and equity, mediating and arbitrating between various interests, which included the middle classes and the poor. The extent to which this approach will endure and help the party to meet the new challenges of a rapidly changing society depends on its capacity to rebuild its organization, ensuring substantive representation for marginalized groups and defining an overarching vision for a country focused on promoting high growth, even though it is divided by rising inequalities.

A Case Study of the Democratic Party of the United States

The Democratic Party of the United States is the nation's oldest political party. Formed by the country's first politicians, who opposed the spirit of faction but founded a political party in order to elect legislators who would support their view of the direction the country would take, the Democratic Party was programmatic at its inception but exists largely for electoral purposes today. The political system in the United States has been characterized as a competitive two-party system (Maisel and Brewer 2012, p, Chapter 2). Certainly, the description as a two-party system is accurate, as only the Democrats and the Republicans compete for most offices. But in truth, whether the system is competitive or not depends on context of what election one is describing in what locale. For the vast majority of offices, American politicians run in single- member districts with plurality winners. Only the President is elected nationally, but the winner of the presidential election is actually the individual who accumulates most Electoral Votes from 51 separate elections (50 states plus the District of Columbia); all save two of these elections are contested under plurality winner-take-all rules. United States Senators are elected in plurality winner statewide elections; members of the House of Representatives are elected by plurality winner in geographically determined districts within the fifty states. Many states and many districts within the states heavily favor one party or the other. While the two parties are closely competitive nationally, winners in many states and districts are easily predictable well in advance and elections in those are not hotly contested.

How the Democrats and Republicans – the two parties that have vied for power in the United States since the mid-nineteenth century – are distinguished from one another has varied throughout their long histories. In the late nineteenth century, the key distinction reflected partisan differences during the Civil War. The Republicans were the party of Lincoln, who had freed the slaves and preserved the Union by military force; the Democrats were viewed as the party that resisted government action to bring on the end of slavery. In the first years of the twentieth century, the Republicans were the party favouring the gold standard; the Democrats favoured softer money and a silver standard. After the Great Depression, the Democrats were viewed as the party of Franklin Delano Roosevelt, who led the country out of the Depression and through World War II, favouring an activist government willing to serve as the employer of last resort, to aid those unable to provide for themselves. The Republicans resisted the New Deal and favoured less government.

For most of the last half of the twentieth century, the Democratic Party was considered a center- left party; the Republicans, center-right. The Democrats favored a government that was more active in economic affairs, more permissive on social issues, and less interventionist in international affairs. Though the differences were often nuanced, the Republicans were for market- based economic policies, more conservative social policies, and a more interventionist foreign policy. Both parties were umbrella organizations; it was not at all unusual for individuals to agree with one party on some issues and the other on different issues.

In the past two or three election cycles, however, the Republicans have become a more doctrinaire and programmatic party. While the Democrats have remained a center-left party, accepting individual variation from the party norm, the Republicans have moved far to the right, considered by many (including many establishment Republicans who feel deserted by their party) as an outlier party (see Mann and Ornstein 2012; Edsall 2013). The Republican lurch to the right has been particularly evident in the first two years of President Obama's second term. On issue after issue, successful bipartisan negotiations have eluded leaders, as Republicans, who hold the majority in the House of Representatives, have refused to compromise.

In a federal system, with electoral as well as governing separation of the executive and legislative branches of government, party is a complex term. The late V. O. Key provided the useful analytical distinction among three aspects of party – the party in the electorate, the party in government, and the party organization (Key 1964). The party in the electorate is comprised of those voters who normally cast their vote for a particular party. They are not members of the party in any formal sense, but many identify with the party and, barring unusual circumstances, usually cast their ballots for candidates of that party (Campbell, Converse, Miller, and Stokes 1960). This is because each state's internal politics are often based on issues different from those dominating national politics, voters who constitute the party in the electorate for a party in a state with regard to elections for offices within that it – for example, state governor or state legislature – may well be part of the party in the electorate for the other party in national elections. However, one defines the party in the electorate, it is a fluid concept, with party coalitions and allegiances changing as the issues confronting the government and the two parties' responses change (Brewer 2010).

The party in government comprises elected officials who won office under a party's label. The President is the leader of the Democratic Party in government. The Senate Majority Leader, Senator Harry Reid of Nevada, and the House Minority Leader, Congresswoman Nancy Pelosi of California, are also leaders of the Democrats in government. The most important aspect of the party in government to note, however, is that, while leadership positions exist, the leaders' powers are mostly persuasive, not formal. Each elected officeholder has his or her own independent power base. However, the leaders can seek legislators' support for policies, but in the final analysis, each Senator or Representative decides whether to support the party position or not, depending on whether he or she thinks it is in his or her best interest. What is good for a national party candidate may not be good for a state or local party candidate. Party leaders in government cannot whip legislators to support a position. Party leaders in government have only limited powers to discipline legislators who do not follow the party policy line.

If the party in the electorate is a fluid concept, and if the party in government comprises literally hundreds of individuals with independent and autonomous bases of support, the party organization is a structure in search of a function. The Democratic Party organization, the formal structure of the party, is what is most often meant when one says »the Democratic Party. That organization has a hierarchical structure, formal rules, and institutional component parts with detailed responsibilities. Yet the Democratic Party organization has no power over those who run for office under its label and no control over the actions of the party in the electorate.

Fifty years ago, Cornelius Cotter and Bernard Hennessey wrote a book about the two national party committees, entitled Politics without Power (Cotter and Hennessey 1964). The description was apt at the time. In the ensuing half century, under the leadership of a succession of strong party leaders, in a series of independent but parallel steps – each party reacting to the successes of the other – both the Democratic National Committee and the Republican National Committee have increased their power, not in a formal sense, but in a practical, political sense. That aspect of the Democratic Party in the United States will be discussed in the remainder of this research work.

Democratic Party Organization and Structure.
The Democratic Party is hierarchical and decentralized. The party is organized at the most local level – wards or precincts in urban areas,

towns in rural areas. Each of these local units has a party committee and a party leader. In the vast majority of localities throughout the country, these slots are either self-recruited and essentially self-appointed or vacant. In only the rarest of circumstances are these committees active – and then only in the majority party in one-party areas.

Local committees elect or recruit individuals to serve on county committees. Also, counties, or their functional equivalent in a few states are a local unit of government with responsibilities assigned by state governments. There are over 3,000 counties in the United States, with state totals ranging from three in Delaware to over 250 in Texas. County political committees have traditionally had practical importance because, before the advent of the civil service system, county government controlled many patronage jobs, which are given to the supporters of the party in power. While patronage positions are largely a relic of a bygone era, the county committee as a political unit remains intact.

County committees elect their own leaders because in the past, county political leaders, particularly those in urban centers, have been among the most important (and at times corrupt) power brokers in a state (Royko 1971, on the power of the legendary boss, Richard J. Daley of Chicago and Ackerman 2005, on Boss Tweed of Tammany Hall in New York). Many retain considerable power today, though none has the near dictatorial power alleged to have been held by bosses of the past, and rampant corruption is mostly a thing of the past. However, county committees and their leaders are responsible for politics at the local level. In the past, they often selected candidates. Since the advent of the direct primary election – an election in which the party in the electorate selects candidates to run under the party label, party leaders have had a role in recruiting candidates for office, especially when the office does not hold much prestige, but they cannot guarantee that a recruited candidate will win a contest nomination or an election.

At times, the role becomes to de-recruit another candidate, perhaps by suggesting that they run for another position, so that the chosen candidate can be nominated. County committees and bosses lost much of their power when they lost the ability to guarantee nominations, a loss that occurred at different times (and with different processes) in different states (Key 1956; La Raja 2010, in Maisel and Berry 2010).

County committees in turn elect members of Democratic state committees, which have functions parallel to the county committees at the state level. Whereas county committee members are often self-recruited and in certain cases need convincing that their service is worthwhile, state committee members, particularly in the majority party in a state, frequently face competition to gain their seats. State committee members in turn elect their chair and other officers. These officials, paid for full-time service in most states, run a professional organization that has significant campaign responsibilities on behalf of party candidates.

At the pinnacle of the party organization committee hierarchy is the Democratic National Committee (DNC). The DNC comprises the state party chair and the highest ranking official of the opposite gender from each state, 200 additional committee members apportioned among the states according to population and party strength in recent elections are elected by either the state committee or delegates to a state convention, representatives of various Democratic elected officials and party groups (for example, College Democrats, Democrats Abroad, Democratic State Attorneys General), plus up to 75 additional members chosen to ensure gender equity and representation of groups important to the party coalition, for example, organized labor. The DNC elects its own chair, who need not otherwise have been a member of the committee, five vice chairs, and other officers, all of whom become voting members of the DNC.

The DNC by party bylaws must meet at least once a year. However, between meetings, work is done by an Executive Committee, elected by and serving at the pleasure of the DNC. The Executive Committee must meet at least four times a year. Its actions are subject to the rules set forth in the Charter of the party and the actions of the National Committee and the quadrennial Democratic National Convention (Charter and Bylaws 2012).

The responsibilities of the Democratic National Committee, again as specified in the Charter and Bylaws, include: issuing the Call to the National Convention; running the presidential campaign; filling any vacancies that occur for Presidential or Vice-Presidential candidate between the convention and the election; and formulating and presenting party policy statements.

The change in the role of the Democratic National Committee (and of its Republican counterpart) since Cotter and Hennessey's (1964) characterization of these bodies and comprising powerless political hangers-on has been the institutionalization of national party organization. The two national party committees are now aptly described as financially secure, institutionally stable, and highly influential in election campaigns (Herrnson, 2010, Maisel and Berry 2010: 245). The work of the national party that Herrnson describes is largely done by the full-time, year-round professional staff that works under the direction of the party chair, often in the name of the DNC. The party structure has adapted to a changing political environment, characterized as more democratic, candidate-centered, and largely dependent on the expenditure of large sums of money to run highly technical modern campaigns. Had the party not adapted to perform a function needed by candidates for office (Aldrich, 1995), the party would have become largely obsolete, as many predicted some years ago (Broder, 1972).

The institutional role of the party organization in assisting candidates and assuming important electoral functions is further highlighted in the roles of two committees, vitally important to the party but outside the formal hierarchy, the Democratic Senatorial Campaign Committee (DSCC) and the Democratic Congressional Campaign Committee (DCCC). The two so- called Hill committees (the Congress is located on Capitol Hill in Washington), and their Republican counterparts, began as efforts by incumbents to help fellow legislators win re-election. They have evolved into significant institutions that raise substantial sums of money to support not only incumbents (but only those who are electorally endangered) but also challengers to vulnerable incumbents in the opposite party. The legislators who lead these committees are considered among the most important members of the congressional party leadership, that is, the party in government. They work hard to recruit good challengers and candidates in seats without an incumbent running. They also work to discourage poor candidates (or candidates thought to be less strong in a general election) from challenging their recruited candidates. They raise money for these candidates, train their staff, do research on their opponents, and generally play a key role in winning seats for the party in the House and Senate.

The most important role that the Democratic Party plays in the United States is to nominate a candidate for President. This role is played by the quadrennial Democratic National Convention. The Convention is, in fact, the ultimate decision maker for the party. However, for more than half a century, the Convention has played a pro forma role, ratifying a candidate for President who was selected by the party in the electorate in a series of state contests (mostly primary elections, but in some states local caucuses and statewide conventions of delegates elected at those caucuses). The Presidential candidate, in turn, selects his or her Vice-Presidential running mate, who is ratified, without controversy, by the delegates to the National Convention. What is most important, then, is not what the National Convention does, but rather how delegates to that National Convention are chosen.

Delegate Selection Rules and Party Decision Making.
If a careful observer of Democratic politics and the Democratic National Conventions that nominated Harry S. Truman for President in 1948, or Adlai E. Stevenson in 1952 and 1956, or John F. Kennedy in 1960 described the process to someone visiting the United States to watch a Presidential nominating contest in the twenty-first century, their descriptions of how a nomination is won would be absolutely useless. Everything has changed radically, largely because of two critical episodes of American history: the Civil Rights Movement and the Vietnam War.

Prior to 1964, African Americans were excluded from all state politics throughout the South, the region in which most Blacks lived. The Democratic Party in the South, which dominated regional politics, was a virtually all-White, pro- segregationist party that fought for individual states' rights to pass laws on issues related to race as they wished. That changed with the Civil Rights Movement, with the Presidency of Lyndon B. Johnson (a pro-Civil Rights Southerner), with the passage of important Civil Rights Act of 1964 and the Voting Rights Act of 1965, and with a successful challenge to White domination of the Democratic Party in the South, led by the Mississippi Freedom Democrats who gained, at the insistence of President Johnson, symbolic seating and important rule changes at the Democratic National Convention in 1964. Blacks from then on became an important part of the Democratic coalition, in the South and in the North (White 1965). In 1968, the American public was divided over national policy in Vietnam. President Johnson decided not to seek re-election after he was challenged by anti-Vietnam War candidates in his own party. At that time the delegations to the Democratic National Convention in many states were chosen well in advance of the gathering, often by party leaders without consulting the public. While primary elections were held in some states, in many more the majority of delegates were chosen and closely controlled by party leaders. In a tumultuous Convention, Johnson's Vice President, Hubert Humphrey, was nominated for President, despite the fact that he had entered no primaries and that anti-War candidates had prevailed in contest after contest (White 1965).

As a result of this selection, viewed by most as secretive and undemocratic, party leaders convened a series of reform commissions whose goal was to make the party more democratic and its processes more open, timely, and accountable to Democratic voters. The Democratic National Committee adopted the suggestions of the first reform commission and applied the rule changes to the 1972 Call to the National Convention. While subsequent reform commissions tweaked those rules, the basic principles behind these commissioning govern delegate selection and party governance today.

Those basic principles, as laid out in the Article 2, Section 4 of the Democratic Party Charter, states that the National Convention shall be composed of delegates equally divided between men and women. The delegates shall be chosen through processes which:

(a) assure all Democratic voters full, timely and equal opportunity to participate and include affirmative action programs toward that end;
(b) assure that delegations fairly reflect the division of preferences expressed by those who participate in the Presidential nominating process;
(c) exclude the use of the unit rule 2 at any level;
(d) do not deny participation for failure to pay a cost, fee or poll tax;
(e) allow participation in good faith by all voters who are Democrats and, to the extent determined by a State Party to be in the interests

of the Democratic Party in that State, by voters who are not registered or affiliated with any party.

In short, the process is designed to be open, timely, non-discriminatory, and representative of the Presidential preferences of those who choose to participate in the process. States are given leeway as to how they implement these principles. Most states hold Presidential Primaries and choose delegates whose Presidential preferences reflect those of the voters in those primaries. Other states hold well-publicized and open meetings (caucuses) of any voters who choose to associate with the party (formally in some states; less so in others), record the Presidential preferences of those who attend the meeting, and elect delegates, frequently after statewide conventions, who reflect those preferences.

The adoption of these principles has not been without controversy and conflict. The first Presidential nominee under the new rules, Senator George McGovern of South Dakota, lost very badly in the general election; President Richard Nixon was re-elected with the highest electoral vote total ever recorded. Old-school political leaders, who lost much of their influence under the new rules, blamed the rules for McGovern's defeat, and some scholarly analysts viewed the reforms with skepticism (Polsby, 1983). It is pertinent to note that over a series of elections, rules were altered to permit so-called Superdelegates, party leaders and elected officials who were delegates to the Convention by virtue of their office and without having to pledge to support a particular candidate. The goal was to allow some peer-review of the potential nominees, by those who had or would have to work with them. But, as the proportion of Superdelegates at the Convention grew, those less likely to gain support from the political establishment objected. This criticism reached a peak in 2008, because many of the Superdelegates favored Senator Hilary Clinton, despite the fact that those voting in the early primaries and caucuses favored Senator Barack Obama. Most of the 2008 Superdelegates eventually favored Obama, reflecting the party in the electorate, but the number of Convention attendees given automatic status was reduced nonetheless.

Rule Violation and Political Corruption.
The Democratic Party has an elaborate series of mechanisms at every level to deal with rule violations. The most important potential violation of party rules would involve state rules for electing delegates to the National Convention. A state could try to structure its rules, in violation of national party principles, to aid one candidate or another. Two examples suffice to demonstrate the conflict resolution principles in play. In 1972, when the reform principles were first implemented, a number of state delegations were challenged, as some party leaders tried to avoid the new rules and proceed as they always had. The Illinois delegation, headed by the powerful leader of the Cook County Democratic Committee, Chicago Mayor Richard Daley, was challenged by a reform slate that claimed that the Daley delegation was elected under a closed and undemocratic process that violated the new rules. The California delegation, pledged entirely to …

Senator McGovern as a result of a winner-takes it - all primary, was challenged because its election violated the prohibition of a unit rule (which functioned to eliminate any representation from those who did not finish first in a plurality winner election). The Credentials Committee and the Convention, in accepting its report, ruled in favor of the challenge to Illinois' delegation, seating the reform delegation instead, and against the challenge to California's delegation, retaining the McGovern delegates. While the legal reasons were complex, the political reality was clear; McGovern had a majority of the delegates, and his supporters would do nothing that might jeopardize his nomination – regardless of the principles involved (White 1973).

In 2008, Florida and Michigan delegations were elected through processes that started before the first date permitted under the Call to the Convention. The specified penalty was a loss of delegates to the Convention. However, after Obama won enough delegates to secure the nomination, the party reached a compromise with the offending states. Once again, pragmatism ruled over principle. The party did not want to alienate voters in states that would be important for the general election. Once the basic principles have been adopted and accepted, rule violations become less important than pragmatic politics. This 'non-principled' approach is accepted by all involved. Parties can, however, be involved in political corruption. Much of what the party does in politics today involves campaign finance – and the laws are complex. On one hand, policing is done through disclosure and media exposure; on the other, the offended party seek legal redress through either the courts or the Federal Election Commission. The Democratic Party Charter's reference to the unit rule is to a rule, once mandated in some states and permitted as an option until 1972, that awarded all of the delegates allotted to state or district at the National Convention to a plurality winner in that state's or district's contest for delegates. That is, the state or district voted as a unit.

Again, the researcher would argue that pragmatism rules, for two reasons. First, the laws are written and have been interpreted so imprecisely that parties have a great deal of leeway in how they act. The Federal Election Commission, which is composed of an equal number of Democrats and Republicans, is a weak agency that takes very little action. Secondly, even though parties spend a great deal of money on campaigns, as a percentage of total campaign spending the amount is negligible. Parties help to coordinate others' spending and donations, but the money they actually spend themselves amounts to less than 10 percent of that spent in almost any campaign. Corruption is not a major problem when the stakes are so low.

Conclusion.

Political parties in the United States are unlike parties in other nations. This is because the party organization is so loosely linked to either the party in the electorate or, more importantly, the party in government, also, American parties, in the post-reform era, have influence but not real power.

Democratic Party rules and the structure of the party guarantee that certain fundamental principles of participation, representation, and democracy are followed in the Presidential nomination process. Beyond that, however, the party's importance and power are derived from its ability to serve the candidates who run under its label. The party does this through raising money, coordinating candidate efforts to raise more money, and providing technical and political assistance and expertise to candidates, but it does not do so by providing any guarantees that their assistance will result in nomination, much less in election. This has been most evident recently in the Republican Party in the United States, when insurgent Tea Party candidates have defeated establishment Republicans, including incumbents. The Democratic Party could easily be susceptible to a movement with equal appeal from the left.

As a result, officeholders owe very little to party leaders. They are free to vote and act as they choose, knowing that the party does not control their electoral fate. In many nations, that would define a weak party. In the United States, it defines a party as strong as the context of the electoral process will allow.

The Communist Party of China since the Initiation of Reform and Opening Up: Continuation and Transformation.

In the 1980s, a school of thought represented by Peter B. Evans, ThedaSkocpol and Eric Nordlinger etc. advocated "bringing the state back in" in the research of politics. In view of the close relationships

215

between the Communist Party of China (CPC) and the state, many scholars concede that "bringing the CPC back in" is a prerequisite for analyzing Chinese politics. In this way, the CPC as well as the country's politics can be better understood.

The official narrative of the CPC's transformation can be found in Jiang Zemin's speech at the meeting celebrating the eightieth anniversary of the founding of the party. He said: "The CPC has evolved from a party that led the people in the fight to seize power nationwide to one that has led the people, for a long time, in exercising state power. It has developed from an organization that managed the nation's reconstruction under external blockade to one implementing all-round reform and opening up". In other words, the CPC has transformed itself from a revolutionary party to a ruling party along a process from seclusion to opening. The Report of the 18th CPC National Congress (2012) reads, "We should enhance our capacity for self-purity, self-improvement, self- innovation and self-development and build the party into a learning-, service- and innovation- oriented Marxist governing party." This represents the first official statement on the transformation of the CPC since the initiation of reform and opening up in 1978 and was followed by the publication of a dozen articles on this issue in the People's (Tribune, August 2013, p.)

Party Structure and Membership.
The structure of the CPC is determined by the rules set out in the party's constitution. The most recent amendments to it were made at the 18th CPC National Congress. In general, the CPC consists of central, local (provincial, municipal, and sub-district), and primary (grassroots) organizations. In addition, there are representative organs under the Central Committee and local party committees and organizations established under central and local state organs and mass and economic organizations, cultural institutions, and other non-party entities as well as the army and its party apparatus. Local party

organizations operate administratively at the provincial, municipal, and county levels. The structure of the CPC has basically remained the same since the initiation of reform and opening up except for the existence of the Consultative Commission from 1982 to 1992.

Central Organizations of the CPC.

The central organizations of the CPC include its National Congress, Central Committee, Political Bureau of the Central Committee, Standing Committee of the Political Bureau, General Secretary of the Central Committee, Secretariat of the Central Committee, Central Commission for Discipline Inspection, and Central Military Commission. The central organizations' structure has been stabilized since the 14th CPC National Congress, in 1992. Amendments to the CPC constitution in 1992, 1997, 2002, 2007, and 2012 did not make changes to the central organizations or authorities.

Primary Organizations: Exploring a Setup Based on Local Areas.

The past few years have witnessed some fundamental changes in the structure of CPC primary organizations. The report to the 4th Plenary Session of the 17th CPC National Congress, held in 2007, declared the following:

"We shall devote efforts to developing primary organizations in all sectors and covering party organizations and work everywhere. Where there are masses, there is party work. Where there are party members, there are party organizations. Where there are party organizations, there is an entire organizational life, and party organizations shall play a full role. Besides setting up party organizations in local areas and employment organizations, we shall improve the structure of primary organizations to help members take part in party events and help party organizations play a role."

The following are among our efforts in party building in local areas over the past decade:

First was setting up party organizations based on employment and local areas. This change is due to the gradual breakup of many employment organizations and improvement of communities. In other words, with the de-politicization of the society, there is a trend toward de-politicization in terms of the structure of primary organizations. Given this context, primary organizations will gradually lose administrative support. Also, party organizations based on residential and business locations are a case in point. They are developed on the basis of local areas or "local areas + employment." In terms of participation, party members belong to "one organization" and therefore can take part in the events of numerous party organizations. These are new experiments in the action and management model of party members in the new era.

Second was practicing larger regional party building based on administrative divisions, mainly at the sub-district level. The framework is as follows: Party work committees of sub-districts were revamped as party work committees of communities (sub-districts level). One Organization and Two Committees – i.e., party organizations of administrative sections, comprehensive party committees of economic and social organizations, and party committees of neighborhoods – were established in what is known as the "1+3 mode".

Their characteristics include the following:
a) Altering organizational structure and exercising full coverage: A network of full coverage, without gaps, is established by party organizations. By linking, dispatching, and joining various party organizations, the network paves the way for developing primary organizations on the basis of full coverage, strong appeal, and openness.

b) Adjusting the current party-building framework based on the division of administrative structures and management functions:

Larger party committees i.e. regional committees are put in place, based generally on big communities. Party committees' members include leaders of communities, two new (economic and social) organizations, and local employers.

c) Devoting more effort to developing member service centers (or Sunshine Stations): These serve as a work platform for party building in local areas.

d) Third was setting up temporary party organizations based on local areas. The coexistence of official structures and their unofficial counterparts is manifested in temporary party organizations. Whether members are migrants or locals, they have dual identities as participants in official, primary organizations and temporary, primary organizations, partaking in the events of both.

Scale of Party Organizations: Expanding as Ever.

The last decade has witnessed an expansion of the CPC in absolute and comparative terms. Another criterion of change in party membership is comparative scale-the ratio of party membership to population. After the initiation of reform and opening up, the ratio increased from 3.96 percent in 1981 to 4.60 percent in 1992. In 1997, 2002, 2007, and 2012, the ratios were 5.00, 5.21, 5.61, and 6.28 percent, respectively. The party is expanding slowly by this measure. Yet another aspect is the number of primary organizations were expanding rapidly. There were 3,451,000 of them in 2003 and 42,010,000 by the end of 2012. In view of the three criteria here, the CPC has obviously become more powerful since the beginning of reform and opening up.

Party Members: from Relatively Fixed to Growing Diversified Sources.

Concerning the composition of party members, the emergence of new social strata is the most remarkable change, debunking the stereotype of "two classes, one stratum." Opinions of Reinforcing and Expanding the United Front at the New Stage in the 21st Century by the Central Committee, published in November 2006, defined the new social strata as including entrepreneurs and technical workers employed by scientific and technical enterprises in the non-public sector, managerial and technical staff employed by foreign-financed firms, self-employed and private entrepreneurs, employees in intermediary enterprises, and freelance professionals. The phrase new social strata first appeared in Jiang Zemin's speech at the meeting celebrating the 80th anniversary of the founding of the CPC on 1 July 2001: "Most of these people in the new social strata have contributed to the development of productive forces and other undertakings in the socialist society through honest labor and work or lawful business operations. They join workers, farmers, intellectuals, cadres, and PLA officers and men in an effort to build socialism with Chinese characteristics. They, too, have made contributions to this cause."

According to statistics, there were 1.49 million party members in the non-public sector in 2002. In 2003, China conducted a pilot program to attract party members from among entrepreneurs and technical workers in non-public sector enterprises. In all, 226 private entrepreneurs joined the party. Afterward, party members from the non-public sector increased rapidly. In 2006 and 2008, they numbered 2,863,000 and 3,582,000, respectively. By the end of 2009, party members from economic and social organizations in the non-public sector increased to 3,841,000, accounting for 4.9 percent of the total membership of the party. Also, party members from among workers and farmers account for the majority, but their overall proportion is decreasing while government cadres and managers and technicians from enterprises and institutions are steadily increasing. Young party members, as represented by students, increased dramatically for a while, but the rate of increase has slowed in the past two years (Table 2).

Intra-Party Democracy and Decision Making.
The CPC has made proposals and elaborated on intra-party democracy in implementing the theories of Marxism-Leninism and in this regard, has gradually deepened its ideological awareness in its theory and its practice. Intra- party democracy covers the party's congress system (including elections and nominations) and the safeguarding of party members' rights at the primary level, collective leadership, and so on.

In terms of process, after the sabotage of the Cultural Revolution and economic stagnation, intra-party democracy made only sluggish progress, such as in the tenure and safeguard systems of party members' rights at the primary and collective leadership levels. Since the beginning of the reform and opening up era, more remarkable achievements have been made in theory and practice. Currently, there is an urgent need to advance intra-party democracy because not doing so can to some extent hamper the people's democracy. On the other hand, the framework for five aspects of party building could be a breakthrough for intra-party democracy.

Therefore, intra-party democracy should be highly valued. This is because according to the 16th CPC National Congress, held in 2002, "Intra-party democracy is the lifeline of the party, which plays a promoting and demonstrative role for people's democracy." At the same time, the party represents the equal status of democracy and centralism. The report of the 4th Plenary Session of the 17th Party Central Committee reads, "Intra-party democracy is the lifeline of the party. Centralism and unity are the foundations of the party. We shall adhere to the combination of centralism based on democracy and democracy under the guidance of centralism. Through safeguarding the democratic rights of party members, we shall enhance primary democratic building within the party, promote intra-party democracy, widely consider the will and propositions of the entire party, and respect the enthusiasm, initiative, and creativity of party members and party organizations at all levels. All efforts are to safeguard the centralism and unity of the party." Secondly, China's principle of democratic development is based on the unity of the party's leadership, the people being the master, and rule by law. We shall adhere to promoting people's democracy through intra- party democracy. The solid unity of the party is a guarantee to the great unity of the people of all ethnic groups across the country.

The development of party representatives at all levels is manifested by political arrangement, that is, a combination of democratic procedure with consultation and elections. With such a big party, this approach is conducive to ensuring "real" democracy within the party. Since the reform and opening up, the development of party representatives at all levels has become more and more democratic. Many improvements have been made in nominating procedures, including increasing multicandidate elections and scope and proportion. A system of directly electing party representatives has been implemented in some local areas. That is, primary party representatives are elected directly while party representatives in local areas and nationwide are indirectly elected.

Another issue is that of "open recommendation and open elections," which combines intra-party democracy and people's democracy. Candidates are publicly nominated by party members or voters, and then party members (or representatives) and voters elect major leaders of the party organs and the government. The significance lies in the public opinions being considered in the nomination process. Party members, and to some extent voters, are entitled to certain voting rights. Currently, differences exist in this regard due to variations in the mode of determining candidates and electoral modes.

The Principle of Decision Making: Democratic Centralism.
Democratic centralism is practiced when major decisions are to be made. From the perspective of the party's nature and positioning,

democratic centralism is the fundamental system of organization and leadership, the most important organizational and political discipline forms the organizational essence of the party. Democratic centralism is an application of the party's mass nature and an important, enduring system. In decision making, adherence to and improvement of democratic centralism receive the most attention, because it is the oldest applied democratic principle, the most workable, and most widely applied. In some sense, the principle is applicable to all aspects of decision making within the party. In 1999, Jiang Zemin proposed principles of internal consultation and decision-making collective leadership, democratic centralism, case-specific consultations, and decision through meetings. Afterward, he reiterated the principles on many occasions. In his view, these principles reflect the very essence and basic requirements of democratic centralism. They manifest the implementation of democratic centralism and function as an important guarantee for collective leadership and promotion of solidarity. Democratic centralism must be practiced earnestly as the basic system of internal consultation and decision making by party committees.

Reconciling Inter-Party Differences.

Differences and conflicts within the CPC stem from tendency rather than faction. As noted, the CPC is based on democratic centralism, which has a well-defined organization and discipline. How to establish a reasonable internal balance for dealing with relations between higher and lower party organizations and among peers is of vital importance. Such a balance can help to reconcile internal conflicts and prevent organizational splits. Approaches to reconciling conflicts and differences are as follows.

First is democratic centralism itself, in two respects. Rigorous centralism involves the lower party organizations being subordinate to higher party organizations. There is also a vertical leadership relationship between party members and party organizations and between higher party organizations and lower party organizations. All the constituent organizations and members of the party are subordinate to the Central Committee.

The collective leadership system, with the minority being subordinate to the majority, is the norm in all the party's leading bodies at every level. As Mao wrote, "The collective leadership system is the highest principle of the party organization of our kind." Jiang Zemin later noted, "Deng Xiaoping made a remark on the importance of democratic centralism when he summed up the lessons of the upheavals in Eastern Europe and the disintegration of the Soviet Union. He pointed out that we shall have an open debate on the principles of democratic centralism under the current context. After the Communist Party of the Soviet Union eliminated democratic centralism from the party constitution, their party became fragmented." The top leaders of the CPC are in agreement on the cause of the party's demise in the Soviet Union.

The second approach involves intra-party discipline, which is built to enhance, maintain, and safeguard solidarity and unity. That every party member abides by democratic centralism is the most important aspect of it. Those who violate party discipline will be punished justifiably. As Jiang Zemin notes, "Every party member is equal before discipline.

The third approach consists of criticism and self-criticism. Mao Tse-tung, in "On Coalition Government", remarked that one should "fear neither criticism nor self-criticism. . . [for] this is the only effective way to prevent all kinds of political dusts and germs contaminating the minds of our comrades and the body of the party."11 Deng Xiaoping reminded that criticism and self-criticism within the party can "maintain party solidarity and unity on the basis of Marxism-Leninism and help comrades overcome their shortcomings and correct their mistakes in time.

The fourth approach consists of intensive education. In recent years, the Central Committee has conducted a series of education and study programs conducive to maintaining the solidarity and unity of the party. Among these are Three Emphases Education (which stresses theoretical study, political awareness, and integrity), Retrospectives on Three Emphases Education, the Education Campaign to Preserve the Advanced Nature of Party Members, Learning and Practicing Scientific Outlook on Development, Contending for Excellence, and the Mass Line Campaign.

Combating Corruption.
With soaring economic development since the beginning of the introduction of reform and opening up, corruption became rampant in China. According to Transparency International, in 2002 China ranked 59th in Corruption Perceptions Index among 102 countries and regions, and in 2012, it placed 80th among 176 countries and regions.

The CPC attaches great importance to battling corruption. The Report of the 17th CPC National Congress stated that resolutely punishing and effectively preventing corruption affects popular support for the party and bears on its very survival. Combating it is therefore a major task at which the party must remain diligent. The Report of the 18th CPC National Congress asserted that fighting corruption and promoting political integrity – an issue of great concern to the people – is a clear-cut and long-term political commitment of the party. If it fails to handle this issue appropriately, it could prove fatal, possibly even leading to its collapse and the fall of the state. The report held the following:

"We should keep to the Chinese-style path of combating corruption and promoting integrity. We should persist in combating corruption in an integrated way, addressing both its symptoms and root causes and combining punishment and prevention, with emphasis on the latter. We should advance in an all-around way the establishment of a system of combating corruption through both punishment and prevention and see to it that officials are honest, the government is clean, and political integrity is upheld. We should strengthen education about combating corruption and promoting clean government and improve the culture of clean government. Leading officials at all levels, especially high-ranking officials, must readily observe the code of conduct on clean governance and report all-important facts concerned. They should both exercise strict self-discipline and strengthen education and supervision over their family and staff, and they should never seek any privilege. We should ensure that strict procedures are followed in the exercise of power, and tighten oversight over the exercise of power by leading officials, especially principal leading officials. We should deepen reform of key areas and crucial links, improve the system of anti-corruption laws, prevent and manage risks to clean government, avoid conflict of interests, prevent and fight corruption more effectively and in a more scientific way, and increase international anti- corruption cooperation. We should rigorously implement the system of accountability for improving party conduct and upholding integrity. We should improve the system of discipline supervision and inspection, improve the unified management of representative offices of party commissions for discipline inspection, and enable discipline inspectors to better play their supervisory role. We must maintain a tough position on cracking down on corruption at all times [and] conduct (thorough investigations into major corruption cases) and work hard to resolve problems of corruption that directly affect the people. All those who violate party discipline and state laws, whoever they are and whatever power or official positions they have, must be brought to justice without mercy."

The CPC has attempted to combat corruption in a number of ways during the past year.

First, emphasis was placed on weeding out corruption by applying institutional checks to power, party operations, and personnel management. The 3rd Plenary Session of the 18th CPC National Congress was the one to propose the policy of restraining power by means of institutional checks, upholding people's right to oversee power, and exercising power in the open. At the 2nd Plenary Session of the 18th Congress of the Central Commission for Discipline Inspection, which convened 21–22 January 2013, General Secretary Xi Jinping agreed that the party should enhance restraint and oversight of power, constraining it by means of institutions. A punishment mechanism should be established to deter officials from involvement in corruption and a prevention mechanism instated to help them avoid corrupt activities. A safeguard mechanism should be developed to make it difficult to commit corruption. When examined more closely, combating corruption will, first of all, be a long-term task. The party must always remain alert against corruption. The key lies in sustained efforts over the long term. Second, so-called tigers and flies – corruptive powerful leaders and lowly officials – must be brought to justice. Third, combating corruption necessarily involves addressing its symptoms and causes. Currently, the focus is on the symptoms, buying time for tackling causes. Fourth, privilege should be protested. Deng Xiaoping once said that granting privileges to cadres is a main cause of isolation from the people. Indeed, if comrades pay undue attention to their personal and family interests, they will have little concern and energy for the people.

Second, an effective power constraint and coordination mechanism should be set up, and a system of combating corruption through punishment and prevention put in place. The 3rd Plenary Session of the 18th CPC National Congress held that the party should establish an operating institution featuring scientific decisions, resolute implementation, and forceful supervision. We must have in place a system of combating corruption through both punishment and prevention and see to it that officials are honest, the government is clean, and political integrity is upheld.

Third, we improved party conduct by introducing the Eight Stipulations. Improving party conduct is an arduous task. However, the Eight Stipulations are a stepping-stone and call to mobilize. The meeting of the Political Bureau of the Central Committee on 4 December 2012 passed the Eight Stipulations on Improving Party Conduct and Having Close Link with the People. Emphasis is placed on the issue of putting the stipulations into practice. Every stipulation is specific and workable, not mere hallow words. Do's and don'ts are clear, easing the burden on people's oversight.

Fourth, combating corruption on the Internet was promoted. The web site of the Central Commission for Discipline Inspection and the Ministry of Supervision was launched to assist whistle-blowing. The basic duties of the commission and Ministry of Supervision are as follows:

- recording whistle-blowing and accusations against party organizations and dealing with party members and persons subject to administrative supervision for discipline and administrative violations;
- receiving complaints from party organizations, members, and persons subject to administrative supervision about their punishment due to violations of party discipline and administrative or other treatment;
- proposing advice and suggestions on construction of the party, conduct, honest and clean government, discipline, supervision, and inspection work.

Fifth, inspection tours from the central level of the CPC were conducted. Inspections and handling cases are different in regard to participants, procedure, approach, and legal bases. The duties of every organ and department are clear- cut. The responsibility of groups on inspection tours is to find and report problems. This is a stipulation of the Work Rules of Inspection Tours. Take, for example, the Central Committee. The Leading Group of Inspection Tours of the Central Committee is responsible for examining organizations at the central level. It guides and promotes nationwide inspection tours and reports to the different central organs. It reports evidence of violations of laws and discipline to the Central Commission for Discipline Inspection of the Central Committee. For problems related to official nominations and promotion, the Leading Group defers to the Organization Department of the Central Committee. After handing over evidence, the above-mentioned departments shall handle the reported problems and evidence according to precedence. Within the stipulated period of time, the two provide feedback to the office of the Leading Group of Inspection Tours.

In another measure, newly appointed cadres are being encouraged to make their property public to an extent. That is a "silent anti-corruption revolution."

Conclusion: What is the CPC?

The Communist Party of China is undergoing changes. Some are dramatic and others are gradual. No party remains unchanged forever. The ideology of the CPC is both abstract and pragmatic. The latter includes Mao Tse- tung's Thought, Deng Xiaoping's Theory, Three Represents, the Scientific Outlook on Development, and the theoretical system of Socialism with Chinese Characteristics. The pragmatic, after 1949, was manifested through the planned economy period (1949–1979), based on the ideas of egalitarianism; the pursuit for economic growth, safety, abundance, and stability (1979–2004); shared beliefs and values (2004–2012) and the Chinese Dream (2012–present). The CPC harbors idealism as well as pragmatism. Based on Austin

Ranney's classification of parties as being missionary or broker, the CPC is a missionary party with a strong sense of responsibility.

There are flexible forms of organization for the CPC. It is undergoing a transformation from a Leninist party based on building party organizations through employment associations to one by location. Meanwhile, it still adheres to democratic centralism. The CPC is no longer a purely Leninist party. It has 85,127,000 members and is growing. It is a mass party that will strive to represent the interests of the overwhelming majority of the people, including all new social strata. It is something of a catch-all party. From the perspective of political decision making, the CPC stands as an elite party. Viewing the CPC from its various perspectives helps in better understanding of the party as well as politics in China.

Chapter 11

Building and Developing Party Platform: The Nigerian Experience

A CAPACITY ASSESSMENT OF NIGERIAN POLITICAL PARTIES.

Deepening democracy requires going beyond elections to building strong institutional foundations including the rule of law, constitutionalism, strong media and civil society, and, perhaps most importantly, political parties. Prima facie, political parties provide a vital channel by which citizens can aggregate their interests, make policies, and hold government accountable. Although many observers frequently and justly criticise political parties for their many failings, it is difficult to imagine a robust democracy without functional political parties.

Political parties are undoubtedly a key ingredient of building a robust democracy, the character of the parties and their *modus operandi* have a significant impact on democracy, with political parties often having glaring gaps that block the exercise of participatory democracy. Many political parties, especially in transitional and semi-authoritarian states, lack proper internal democracy. They also frequently fall under the sway of powerful economic and political elites, sometimes called "godfathers," who use their resources to control the party at the expense of its members. Parties frequently conduct their business in a secretive way, demonstrating a lack of transparency. In many cases, they only appear around election time to capture votes but fail to account to their supporters once the elections are over. Some parties also fail to develop their appeal to citizens beyond ethno-regional appeals or the patronage available to incumbents. Parties in many developing countries lack adequate capacity in areas ranging from membership recruitment and retention to policy development and resource mobilisation. A particular weakness demonstrated by most political parties is the failure to include women in leadership, decision-making and policy-making processes. Yet, women belong at the heart of democratic politics. Due to these weaknesses, parties often do not meet the criteria of "robust, transparent, internally democratic and accountable" that characterize strong democratic parties.

Given their status as an essential component of a "deepened democracy" and their frequent inability to constitute themselves as robust and democratic parties, there is a strong case that parties should receive assistance and support to realize their full potential as essential pillars of a stable and vibrant democracy. That is why the Democratic Governance for Development (DGD) Project, a joint donor-funded project managed by UNDP in support of deepening democracy in Nigeria, which is funded with contributions from the EU, the UK Department for International Development (DFID), the Canadian International Development Agency (CIDA), and the UNDP, provides technical support to political parties as a means of strengthening accountable and responsive governance institutions, and consolidating democratic governance in line with international best practices.

The DGD recognises that any assistance to political parties should be firmly based on a thorough and rigorous assessment of the parties' capacity and their position in the existing party system. Through

POLITICAL PARTY GOVERNANCE

this assessment, DGD has mapped out a clear picture of where the parties are now, what their capacity gaps are, and how the DGD can best engage with them to enhance their capacity to serve as robust and internally democratic institutions. The results of the assessment represent the first step to supporting Nigeria's parties to meet their remaining challenges as they seek to institutionalise themselves as the vanguard of Nigeria's struggle for democracy. To meet DGD's goal of "Improving the Democratic Quality of Political Engagement," parties in Nigeria must strive for a positive role in deepening democracy in Nigeria.

Nigeria's parties have a history of formation, dissolution and re-formation due to the many transitions in Nigeria's post-independence political history. Parties have frequently mobilized supporters based on ethno-regional, religious, and personality politics, while various regimes have sought to constrain them to have a "national character" or adhere to particular ideological frameworks. Party development over time also witnessed the dominance of party elites at the expense of members and the use of undemocratic methods by these elites to struggle for control over the parties. For these reasons, Nigeria's parties have faced particular challenges in building stable identities over time and attracting consisting membership through appeal to particular ideological values.

The key findings of the assessment are disaggregated into the party system and the party capacity components. To establish the strengths and weaknesses of Nigerian parties, the party system in which they operate is the first key determinant of their capacity. The research establishes that there are a number of key gaps in Nigeria's political party system. The most important include

(1) An unclear legal framework
(2) Poor relationship between parties and INEC

(3) Lack of civility and insufficient inter-party dialogue

(4) Lack of cohesion in political parties leading to frequent "cross carpeting" between parties

(5) a lack of ideological and policy orientation in the contest for power between parties; and

(6) A limited ability of opposition parties to compete with the ruling party.

At the level of individual party capacity, a number of challenges also stand out. These vary considerably by party, with the ruling party much stronger on many dimensions due to its depth of leadership and access to resources. The next three or four largest parties in the National Assembly also have considerable strength throughout the country, while the capacity of the next level of parliamentary parties is much lower, and the capacity of the non-parliamentary parties is extremely limited. Key among the challenges across the largest parties include: 1) human resource capacity at the state and local level; 2) lack of effective internal communication between their national and sub-national branches; 3) parties' limited abilities in use and application of technology; 4) lack of national, data-rich, and computerized membership databases; 5) lack of a uniform, consistent and accessible way of recruiting, admitting, and managing members; 6) limited competence in research and analysis that looks at their own performance and supports clear plans and strategies for building the party; 7) lack of an inclusive and research-based policy and manifesto development process that provides a clear policy framework for them to govern; 8) lack of ideological or institutional identities outside their ethno-regional or religious affiliations, or the personalities of their leading figures. Parties also face considerable challenges in the area of internal democracy with party elites frequently manipulating party rules to subvert internal party democracy for their personal political interests. Women and youth are particularly disenfranchised within party leadership, occupying a minimal percentage of party leadership positions and having very limited influence on party decision-making.

To address some of the challenges above, the UNDP and DGD have a number of options for interventions that can have an impact in making the parties more effective channels for democratic participation in politics. At the level of the party system, the DGD should consider:

1) Supporting an inter-party dialogue forum that consists of the parliamentary parties;
2) Supporting regular liaison meetings to address mutual concerns of the parties and INEC;
3) Supporting legal or administrative reforms that limit the ability of political leaders to switch allegiances frequently between political parties;
4) supporting the establishment of mechanisms that ensure that state resources are not used to the advantage of the incumbent in elections, and that all candidates get mechanisms for equal access to the media; and
5) sponsoring and publicising widely a series of debates and town-hall meetings that engage parties and candidates in issue-based debate, as well as providing support as needed for parties to develop policy positions and ideological orientations.

DGD can also have an impact by increasing the democratic engagement of political parties through working directly with political parties on individual political party capacity issues. Some proposed areas for intervention, based on the findings of this assessment, include the following:

1) Carry out a comprehensive evaluation to generate baseline data on a set of key indicators against which political party development can be measured;

2) Support the parties to carry out participatory SWOT self-analyses and develop an action plan or strategic plan mapping out their priority areas for party development in the short- and medium-term;

3) Establish a Political Parties' Leadership and Governance Institute that provides professional training and guidance for party leaders at national and state level;

4) Engage parties on key dimensions of party building such as: holding regular meetings with members and carrying out community outreach programmes targeting members and supporters; compiling a national, computerised membership database; formulating a party policy platform, engaging party members to contribute to the platform, and publicising the party's platform through debates and meetings; supporting parties to develop resource mobilisation strategies that can help them source funds from members and well-wishers; facilitating the internal communication of political parties through the creation of communication platforms; and other similar initiatives.

Nigeria's Political Party System.

Nigeria operates as a one party dominant political system in which the dominant party controls enormous resources compared to the others. At the beginning of the Fourth Republic, only three political parties were registered, but the Supreme Court decision allowed for the liberalisation of the regime and many more parties were registered. There are three categories of political parties – the dominant party on its own, parties with parliamentary representation and the other small parties most of which were established as possible platforms for important politicians that lose out in the bigger parties or to access resources from the electoral management body. Parties with executive seats are tightly controlled by the President and State Governors, and party leadership is at the beck and call of these executives who can change them at will. The President is the leader of the dominant party although a party chairman exists and state governors are the leaders of their party at that level.

Overall, the liberalisation of the party regime did not significantly change the nature of political parties. Parties are run by godfathers and barons rather than members, and they have clientelist networks that are used by the party barons to "deliver" crowds for rallies and party congresses. Indeed, parties tend to treat their members with disdain and utter disrespect. Consequently, the political relationship within the parties is essentially one between patrons and clients and the clients are mobilised on pecuniary, ethnic or regional basis.

Legal and Institutional Framework including relationship with INEC.

Nigeria has an illiberal regulatory regime for the registration and operations of political parties. Section 222 of the Constitution specifically restricts the qualification of a political party to organisations registered by the Independent National Electoral Commission under the stringent conditions stipulated by Sections 221 – 229 of the Constitution. Section 229 of the 1999 Constitution defines political party thus: "Political party includes any association whose activities include canvassing for votes in support of a candidate for election to the office of President, Vice – President, Governor, Deputy Governor or membership of a legislative house or of a local government council. It is therefore a very narrow definition that reduces the essence of political parties to canvassing for votes.

Section 222 of the 1999 Constitution specifies the conditions under which an association can function as a political party. It states that "No association by whatever name called shall function as a political party, unless:

a) The names and addresses of its national officers are registered with the Independent National Electoral Commission;

b) The membership of the association is open to every citizen of Nigeria irrespective of his place of origin, circumstance of birth, sex, religion or ethnic grouping;

c) A copy of its constitution is registered in the principal office of the Independent National Electoral Commission in such form as may be prescribed by the Independent National Electoral Commission;

d) Any alteration in its registered constitution is also registered in the principal office of the Independent National Electoral Commission within thirty days of the making of such alteration;

e) the name of the association, its symbol or logo does not contain any ethnic or religious connotation or give the appearance that the activities of the association are confined to a part only of the geographical area of Nigeria;

f) The headquarters of the association is situated in the Federal Capital Territory, Abuja.

g) The names and addresses of its national officers are registered with the Independent National Electoral Commission;

h) The membership of the association is open to every citizen of Nigeria irrespective of his place of origin, circumstance of birth, sex, religion or ethnic grouping;

i) A copy of its constitution is registered in the principal office of the Independent National Electoral Commission in such form as may be prescribed by the Independent National Electoral Commission;

j) Any alteration in its registered constitution is also registered in the principal office of the Independent National Electoral Commission within thirty days of the making of such alteration;

k) The name of the association, its symbol or logo does not contain any ethnic or religious connotation or give the appearance that the activities of the association are confined to a part only of the geographical area of Nigeria;

The effects of all these is that parties that emerged during the Second Republic and the first phase of the Fourth Republic needed to be very big and capable of controlling a significant region at least.

The Independent National Electoral Commission (INEC) and the State Independent Electoral Commissions have powers under the Electoral Act 2010 to be present at conventions, congresses, conferences or meetings of political parties as monitors to ensure that the parties respect their procedures. In the 2011 elections, however, parties were able to disregard the role of INEC and do as they please, by marginalising INEC under a barrage of court injunctions. At the party congresses, leaders were elected and candidates were nominated for elective positions. The elections were however pre- determined at most times and party bosses tended to have the final say in the selection of leaders. This is the underlying logic that has led to the process of continuous internal party crisis in the country. INEC has been empowered by the 2010 Electoral Act to deregister parties that fail to win seats, and it has used this power to deregister seven parties so far. Following the termination of various cases in the electoral tribunals, INEC has resumed the process of deregistering political parties and it is expected that about thirty more parties will be deregistered.

Competitiveness.
Competition in Nigeria's party system is very intense within the ruling party and less so between the political parties. This is due to the fact that since 1979, Nigeria has developed the tradition of major blocs of the political elite coalescing into a single political party conceived as a hegemonic party. In elections that are relatively free and fair, namely, the 1959, 1979 and 1999 elections, the parties that had the highest votes, the Northern Peoples' Congress, the National Party of Nigeria and the Peoples' Democratic Party failed in their desire to be hegemonic or dominant through the polls. In the subsequent elections of 1964, 1983 and 2003, they all abused their incumbency powers to transform

themselves into dominant parties. In essence, they used electoral fraud to boast their control of the political process and weaken opposition parties. Competitive party politics is thus weak as the ruling parties have often falsified the electoral game while the parties in opposition have too narrow a political base and insufficient resources to effectively compete for power.

In the 2011 general elections, the competition for the presidency of Nigeria was between three major candidates and political parties. They are:

- Goodluck Jonathan - People Democratic Party (PDP);
- Muhammad Buhari – Congress for Political Change (CPC); and
- Nuhu Ribadu – Action Congress of Nigeria (ACN)

At the polls, the PDP polled 22,495,187 after winning from 24 out of the 36 states and FCT. This was followed by the CPC who polled 12,214,853. The ACN came third with 2,079,151. In terms of the National Assembly, the PDP won over 60% of elected representative and senators in the National Assembly leaving the other political parties to share the remaining seats among themselves. The important thing about the 2011 elections was the marked improvement in the integrity of the elections and the significant reduction of electoral fraud. The Attahiru Jega led INEC has shown a capacity to continuously improve the conduct of elections in the country and move towards free, fair and credible elections. If this tendency is sustained, the competitiveness of political parties will receive a boost and the political class will begin to believe that it is possible to get to power without being the candidate of the ruling party. In other words, party competition will gradually become real.

Fluidity.

We have mentioned above that party membership is ephemeral as people engage the political process as patrons or as clients. This means the attachment of people is not really to political parties but to patrons or godfathers who pay for their engagement. The implication of this is that participation in political party activities is mediated by political bosses to whom people owe allegiance. Party life is most active around election time and patrons and godfathers engage in party activity to obtain nomination and elections for themselves or their surrogates. When they fail to obtain the position, they tend to move out with their clients to other parties in search of new opportunities. In Nigeria therefore, both for the patrons and their clients, adherence to political parties is very fluid and opportunistic. It is also true that many people own multiple party cards as they seek to be invited to as many party congresses as possible where the tradition is to pay participants for their votes. Such people therefore move from party to party in search of opportunity.

Ideology and Issue Based Politics.

The ideology question and the left/right divide have largely disappeared from Nigerian political parties so much that conflicts are focused on the issue of personalities, ethnic groups, geopolitical zones and the control of power. And yet, ideology matters in Nigeria. Nigerians are profoundly opposed to the liberal economic policy articulated and imposed on the country by the Bretton Woods institutions. Political parties can therefore articulate this vision but have refused to do so. The Constitution requires that all political parties draw their manifestoes from Chapter Two of the Constitution on Directive Principles of State Policy. That section of the Constitution places a lot of obligation on the state to provide for the welfare of citizens. It is virtually a social democratic manifesto. Party manifestos however elicit little interest or debate because the parties simply provide them to satisfy a constitutional obligation. The key challenge for political party development is therefore to bring issue-based politics back to the agenda. During the Second Republic for example, the UPN was known for its commitment to free education, the NPN for its housing policy and the PRP for its opposition to taxing the peasantry. It is difficult today to associate any issue with any political party. The motivation for engagement in party activities in Nigeria today is simple – power and money. The motivation for political contest is dominance and control not ideology of issues.

Lack of Civility and Exclusionary Politics.

Civility is one quality that is largely absent in political party life. The most important aspect of the internal functioning of political parties in Nigeria since 1978 is that they have a persistent tendency to factionalise and fractionalise. As people go into politics to seek power and money, the battle for access is very intense and destructive. Thugs, violence and betrayal are often the currency for political party engagement. Indeed, the period leading to each election is marked by the assassination of party leaders and contestants for various offices. The reality in the political field is that many political parties are essentially operated by political 'godfathers' who use money and violence to control the political process. They decide on party nominations and campaign outcomes and when candidates try to steer an independent course, violence becomes an instrument to deal with them. The result is that they raise the level of electoral violence and make free and fair elections difficult. Although parties have formal procedures for the election of their leaders, these procedures are often disregarded; when they are adhered to, the godfathers have means of determining the outcomes. The level of violence, thuggery, and monetization of Nigerian politics provides a significant disincentive for women to take part as candidates, and the monetization aspect also makes young people less likely to influence politics in an effective way due to their lower level of access to resources (Ezeilo, 2012).

Lack of Civility and the Female Politician.

The female politician is the major victim of the lack of civility in the political process. She suffers from various modes of marginalisation

242

many of which are hurtful and full of invectives. In general, party officials refused to take the candidature of female aspirants seriously. Ironically, one of their main reasons was the affirmative action policy adopted by some of the parties waiving nomination fees for female aspirants. Party executives in most constituencies set out to label women as aspirants with less than the required commitment to the party. Party barons at the local level repeatedly argue that by convincing the national executives to remove nominations fees for them, women have demonstrated a lack of commitment to the development of the party. This argument was used to make declarations that male candidates are more committed to the party because they make their financial contributions willingly and that commitment should be recognised and rewarded. Such officials therefore succeeded in labeling women aspirants as "anti-party" people and thereby created the basis for their exclusion. It is worthwhile recalling the analysis of Geof Wood on the role of labelling in elimination competition: "The authors of labels, of designations, have determined the rules of access to particular resources and privileges. They are setting the rules of inclusion and exclusion, determining eligibility, defining qualifications... The authors of labels successfully imposed on others are powerful. Once a negative label has been successfully imposed on an aspirant, it is easy to exclude the labelled person irrespective of the formal rules and procedures established, because the person's legitimacy has been eroded.

A second negative labelling strategy used to exclude women aspirants has to do with the cultural deviant label. The way the argument is presented is that Nigerian culture does not accept assertive, or public, or leadership roles for women. Concerted allegations and campaigns portraying women aspirants as people acting in ways that contradict their culture were systematically used as part of the strategy of marginalisation – see Ibrahim and Salihu, 2004. Many party officials made open or covert assertions that some female aspirants are too assertive and independent and therefore cannot be team players.

Closely associated with negative labelling is the direct use of invective, that is, the use of abusive language to demoralise and delegitimise female aspirants. Indeed, it is well known in the sociology of elite competition that the use of invective and insults is an effective strategy of eliminating political rivals. Many of the female aspirants profiled in Ibrahim and Salihu, 2004, were subjected to whisper campaigns and innuendos about their alleged loose sexual and moral standing and some were directly insulted with the use of invectives like prostitute and harlot. Campaigns were organised around the "true marital status" of female aspirants as a means of questioning their moral standing.

As the case of Onyeka Onwenu, the golden voice of Nigerian music shows, women have had to face simultaneous attacks on their marital status from different angles. While some men questioned her legitimacy to contest for the Chair of a Local Government in Igboland because she was married to a Yoruba man, other men were spreading the rumours that because she was using her maiden name, rather than a "marital name", she must be unmarried and therefore did not have the moral standing to contest for the post. The moral standards Nigerians set for women politicians are higher than those for male politicians. It is generally known, for example, that many male politicians go on the campaign trail with girlfriends and/or sex workers. Male supporters see such behaviour as a normal sign of the virility of leaders. For women however, even when they are not sexually promiscuous, indeed, even if they are saints, the burden of proof is placed on them to show that they are morally upright.

The 1979 Constitution introduced the concept of indigeneity into Nigerian public law as an equity principle to guaranty fair regional distribution of power. Over the years, the principle has been subverted and used to discriminate against Nigerian citizens who are not indigenes of the places where they live and work. Women who are married to men who are non-indigenes of their local governments suffer systematic discrimination. In their own constituencies, they are told that by marrying out, they have lost their indigeneity. In their husband's constituency, they are told they do not really belong because indigeneity is based on the consanguinity (blood relation), principle. It is particularly insidious for women because many of them who actually married people from their indigenous areas lost their indigeneity when their home areas were carved out in subsequent state creation exercises as Nigeria moved from three regions to four regions, to twelve states, to nineteen states, to twenty-one states, to thirty states and finally to thirty-six states. The indigeneity ploy is usually used only when women seek for political office. Jadesola Akande shows for example in her profile of Chief Titilayo Ajanaku, that when the aspirant successfully campaigned for the top candidates of the Unity Party of Nigeria – Obafemi Awolowo and Bola Ige, the party was happy. When however, the proposal to offer her a political post in the state arose, they remembered she was "an Egba married to an Ijesha man" and was not therefore an indigene of Oyo state (Ibrahim and Salihu, 2004.)

While women suffer greatly from the large repertoire of techniques used to eliminate people from political party primaries, less powerful men also suffer. The lack of civility within party politics has therefore translated into the following elimination tactics:

1) Declaration by powerful "party owners", party barons, state governors, "godfathers" etc that people must support one candidate and others must withdraw based on "consensus" which means the decision of the boss. As these people are very powerful and feared in their communities, their declarations carry a lot of weight.

2) Zoning is another technique, which is usually used by party officials. Zoning and other forms of administrative fiat are used to exclude aspirants by simply making the party zone out the seat in question to an area where the aspirant being excluded is not an indigene.

3) Violence and the use of thugs and sometimes security operatives are often used by "powerful" candidates opposing challenge from other candidates.

4) Money is of course a major factor in party primaries and is used both to bribe officials and encourage voters support particular candidates. Since in general, aspirants supported by part barons have more money than other aspirants, the playing field is not even as poorer candidates get eliminated because they simply cannot match their opponents – Naira for Naira.

5) One of the most disturbing techniques used to eliminate aspirants and candidates is what Nigerians call "results by declaration". This means that a candidate would win a nomination or election and returning officers who had been bribed or compromised would simply disregard the results and declare the loser to be the winner.

Given the general lack of civility in party politics and the prevailing culture of violence and invective, the Babalakin Commission of Inquiry into the 1983 elections stated in clear terms that:

"The nature of politics and political parties in the country is such that many men and women of ability and character simply keep out of national politics. For the most part, political parties are dominated by men of influence who see funding of political parties as an investment that must yield rich dividends." (FRN, 1986, p. 348)

The fundamental objective of political party development should be to reverse this trend and get more people with ideas and vision to integrate the leadership of political parties. As Nigeria moves towards the 2015 elections, it is imperative that political parties imbibe the culture of internal democracy as a means of creating harmonious conditions that would not only enhance their performance but also be of help when they eventually win elections.

Although the 2011 elections were deemed to be the best organized and most credible in the country's chequered electoral history, they were far from flawless. International observers described the votes as a 'significant improvement' over previous ones, which we believe is a correct characterisation. Pre-election violence, including bomb attacks (which killed dozens of people) as well as the cumbersome new voting system (modified open ballot system) used – in which registered voters had to be certified at designated polling units in the morning and then vote in the afternoon negatively impacted on the turnout for these elections.

Capacity of Nigeria's Political Parties

Political parties in Nigeria demonstrate significant strengths but contain a number of features that make them less than ideal vehicles for the representation of the political demands and aspirations of Nigerians. The largest parties have demonstrated a considerable amount of capacity in mobilising the vote but are weakened by a number of technical limitations and a lack of internal democracy.

Most of the parties assessed in depth for this survey have a fairly strong foundation in terms of their party constitutions. These constitutions provide for the establishment of a clear and coherent party structure and for the conduct of internal democracy within the party. All of the parliamentary party constitutions also prohibit discrimination on the basis of gender (Ezeilo 2012). Some parties go further to include commitments like "ensuring gender balance in governance" (Labour Party) and mainstreaming women's concerns in all policies and programmes (PDP). It is less clear the extent to which the parties have rules and policies governing both elections and the day-to-day functioning of party offices and activities.

What seems evident is that many of these party laws and rules are not followed or are manipulated to support the interests of powerful individuals and groups in each party, especially on the dimension of internal democracy. As Ibrahim (2011, p.101), writes, "Parties have formal processes of the election of leaders but these processes are not followed, and when they are, the godfathers have developed ways of determining the outcomes." Therefore, while the legal framework guiding party activities is reasonable, adherence to these frameworks is often problematic.

Regarding the presence of national and local party structures, there is considerable variance across the parties assessed for this study. Parties tend to have local party structures in areas where they have candidates and elected representatives, but only the PDP can claim structures and branches throughout the country, whereas several of its closest competitors, including CAN & CPC (now APC) APGA, and ANPP have widely established structures at sub-national levels, even if these are not uniformly established across the country. The rest of the parties have a sporadic presence throughout the country depending on where they have strongholds, their level of resources to invest, and their types of alliances. Parties generally rely on access to public resources and manifest themselves most strongly where they are in control of a state governorship or a large number of elected representatives.

The party secretariats also vary considerably in their level of existence and functionality depending on the party, with the largest parties having larger and more functional secretariats including zonal, state and local offices, and the smaller parties having much more limited presence. Even in places where secretariats are established, secretariats tend to cater for individual party leaders rather than concentrate on establishing an effective and unified party bureaucracy. With the ending of INEC funding to political parties in 2012, smaller parties face particular difficulties in getting access to resources to maintain their offices.

One of the more challenging areas for parties is the existence and engagement of party members. Although parties obviously have supporters during elections that vote for them, and 49% of Nigerians claimed a party affiliation in the 2008 Afrobarometer survey [this is between 12-20% lower than the levels of affiliation in Kenya, Ghana and Uganda for the same survey], most parties do not rely on regular members. Few parties at the national level have consistent or reliable membership registers, although ACN seems to be updating theirs, while other parties maintain registers at the branch level. It is unclear whether parties hold regular meetings with membership at various levels. Ibrahim, (2011, p. 103) argues that, "In terms of membership, it is clear that party members are active only during elections." This lack of activity between elections may not be so unusual compared to other countries, but it is clear that the extremely elite-dominated nature of Nigeria's parties and their reliance on godfatherism make members particularly disempowered. As one-party leader put it, party members need to be "enlightened" to avoid being "victimised" by unscrupulous party leadership.

Two groups of party supporters that remain particularly marginalised from membership and leadership are women and youth. Parties have few women within their leadership structures and run few female candidates. According to research conducted by Joy Ezeilo (2012), women comprise less than 15% of political party leadership structures and less than 6% of all political party candidates. There are few, if any, clear provisions for encouraging women leaders and candidates, or making special provisions to promote gender equality within party manifestos and other party policy documents. At the membership level, only 44% of women feel close to political party, compared to 59% of men, according to the 2008 Afrobarometer survey. Several reasons stand out in terms of explaining the marginalisation of women within parties in Nigeria, including the domination of parties by rich "godfathers" (who are almost exclusively men), the lack of leadership by the state in promoting gender equality in parties, the lack of gender sensitivity among party leadership, the lack of a critical mass of organised women within party leadership circles, the cost of participating in political leadership, and certain values and norms that discourage women's participation in political leadership.

Youth face similar challenges to women in accessing political party leadership, as the combination of the domination of party finances by an elder elite and age-based discrimination severely restrict the opportunities of aspiring young political leaders at the national level. Persons with disabilities (PWD) also face similar challenges to women and youth that are compounded inaccessibility of physical party infrastructure, party information, and discriminatory attitudes within the parties. Although parties demonstrated some awareness of the need to increase opportunities for women, young people, and PWD, their proposals for redressing discrimination include quotas for women that fall well below that national standard of 35% representation for women as enshrined in the 2007 National Gender Policy, such as the 15% proposed by the PDP or the 20% proposed by ACCORD, and most party leadership clearly does not identify affirmative action for women, youth and PWD in parties as a priority. The parties also do not make a particular effort to ensure that women, youth and PWD are included in party decision-making processes.

PARTY CAPACITY: SPECIFIC TECHNICAL ISSUES.
At the level of technical capacity issues, the picture varies considerably between the largest two to three parties and the remainder of the registered political parties. In terms of national secretariats, parties range from the PDP with a huge secretariat staff to the smallest parties with 10 or fewer staff. The capacity of these secretariats also varies considerably. One key informant described party leaders as each having "allocations of jobs" at the secretariat, with the individuals placed in those jobs not being required to perform. Also, some parties for which

there was considerable commitment to the party's leadership or ideals, such as the CPC, were able to draw on considerable volunteerism to meet high labour demands during campaign and primary times.

Many of the parties expressed challenges in terms of their human resource capacity, especially at the state and lower levels. While it was difficult to do a thorough capacity assessment of secretariat staff and state party staff due to the limited time and scope for this assessment, many of the largest parties, such as PDP, APC and APGA include individuals with substantial experience and expertise. The largest parties clearly have the capacity to handle public relations, resource mobilization, and management of national party secretariats. Regrettably, some informants remarked that the parties are run as collections of individuals rather than unified secretariats working together for a joint purpose.

Some areas where parties have considerably less capacity include the following:

- Human resource capacity at the state and local level. The largest parties have local leadership that is politically strong at the community level or the state level but often lack key professional skills.
- Parties frequently fail to generate effective internal communication between their national and sub-national branches.
- Related to this challenge are parties' limited abilities in use and application of technology. Although some parties have demonstrated successful use of technology in campaigning, most party leadership, partly due partly to its age, have yet to take advantage of technological innovations like text messaging to party leaders and members for organisational and information sharing purposes, raising money through mobile money or online fundraising, and generating on-line policy debate on key party policy issues.

- Parties have also yet to attempt to build national, data-rich, and computerized membership databases, partly due to weak linkages between national, state, local government and ward party offices, and partly due to the political manipulations of party membership used by party candidates to exclude their opponents within the party.
- Developing a uniform, consistent and accessible way of recruiting, admitting, and managing members is also lacking, with a number of observers commenting that the PDP has made it extremely difficult for members to join and frequently manipulate membership when parties hold primaries.
- Parties raised concerns about their abilities to mobilize resources and raise funds, thereby limiting their activities that require significant resources. These concerns were voiced most strongly by the non-parliamentary parties.
- Parties have yet to demonstrate competence in research and analysis that looks at their own performance and develop clear plans and strategies that provide national frameworks for addressing their challenges and building the party
- Parties have yet to develop an inclusive and research-based policy and manifesto development process that provides a clear policy framework for them to govern; nor have parties developed a consistent way of monitoring and evaluating the extent to which their elected leaders are realising their manifestos during their terms of office
- Related to this, parties lack ideological or institutional identities outside their ethno-regional or religious affiliations, or their leading figures

PARTY SYSTEM LEVEL INTERVENTIONS.

At the level of the party system, several key challenges continue to restrict democracy party competition, including lack of consensus on the legal framework regulating political parties, poor relationships between parties and INEC, lack of civility and inter- party dialogue, lack of cohesion in political parties leading to frequent "cross carpeting" between parties, a lack of ideological and policy orientation in the contest for power between parties, significant barriers to the participation of women, youth and persons with disabilities in leadership and decision-making at the party level and at the party system level, and a limited ability of opposition parties to compete with the ruling party due to the lack of a level playing field. To address some of these challenges, it is hereby suggested that political Parties should consider the following possibilities for engagement:

1) To increase civility between political parties, and to encourage political parties to address electoral issues in a constructive forum, there should be an inter-party dialogue forum that consists of the parliamentary parties. To be effective, this forum needs to bring all the parliamentary parties together at the table, and ensure that both the ruling party and the opposition parties agree to take the issues raised at the forum seriously. Such a forum could help reduce electoral and political violence, develop an agenda for electoral reform and improved elections management, and build a culture of trust, tolerance and acceptance of diversity in Nigeria's charged political climate. This forum would not necessarily replace the existing forums of IPAC and CNPP, but would complement them as a space to address issues that need the presence of all of Nigeria's largest parties, whether on electoral issues, conflict management, legal reform, policy dialogue, or reducing hostility between competing political parties. To ensure that the inter-party forums are adequately representing all Nigerians, parties should ensure that their delegations include significant number of women, youth and persons with disabilities. The agenda for dialogue forums should also be inclusive to address electoral- and party-related concerns of particular interest to women, youth and PWD.

2) To improve trust between political parties and the INEC, there should be a regular liaison-meetings to address concerns of the parties and INEC. Such meetings could take place in conjunction with the inter-party dialogue forum recommended above, or the meetings could be held under different auspices. Frequent meetings involving INEC staff and top party leadership could begin to remove some of the mistrust that occurred as a result of the 2011 elections and prepare the ground for more positive relations in the run-up to the 2015 elections. Serious consideration should be given ,to involve a suitable local civil society organisation to convene such meetings or whether the parties and INEC would prefer another credible and neutral convener for the meetings. Like the inter-party dialogue forums, the liaison meetings should involve significant representation of women, youth, and PWD, and the specific concerns they are related to the electoral process.

3) To reduce excessive "cross carpeting" and begin to build party loyalty, there should be legal reforms (such as the ones proposed during the current constitutional review process) that limit the ability of political leaders to switch allegiances frequently between political parties. Although care should be taken not to restrict excessively ability to change party loyalty, the following reforms might support a process by which increased party loyalties can be built over time: i) a law restricting the ability of party leaders to switch parties once elected, forcing them to resign their seats if they switch party allegiances. Such a law would both limit defection and discourage party leaders from switching parties just to find a party that will make them a candidate on its ticket; ii) a law restricting party leaders who stand in one party's primary and lose from standing in another party's primary during the same election cycle. Such a law could prevent strategic defections and would help build party loyalty and party discipline. It might also build pressure for greater internal democracy within parties, and freer and fairer

primary elections; and iii) any other legal reforms that would discourage frequent switching of party allegiance without unduly constraining individual freedom of association.

4) To improve the competitiveness of the party system and create a more level playing field, there should be mechanisms that ensure that state resources are not used to the advantage of the incumbent in elections, and that all candidates get mechanisms for equal access to the media. Such an approach would require involvement from a governmental or civil society monitoring body (or both), either some sort of Political Party Registry Commission or INEC (which may be over-stretched already), or a suitable well- established, neutral and credible civil society monitor who could then provide information to an appropriate regulator. The monitors and regulators should closely monitor, assess, and publish the extent to which incumbents are using public resources during campaign periods. It should also closely monitor media houses to ensure that equal access is being provided, especially by state media. If incumbents are using public resources for campaign purposes, there should be penalties that are sufficient to disincentivise the use of public resources.

5) To encourage a policy-focused and issue-based campaign period serious consideration should be given to sponsoring and publicising widely a series of debates and town-hall meetings that engage parties and candidates in issue-based debate. Such a series of debates and town-hall meetings would provide candidates with much-desired publicity while also discouraging less policy-based forms of engagement. Ideally such engagements would begin well before the campaign to encourage the parties and candidates to develop ideology and policy positions before the elections. The debates would concentrate on arriving at and drawing out party policy positions rather than those of individual candidates. To support both the development of serious policy content and the public

appeal of the debates, such debates and town hall meetings would be co- sponsored by a policy research institute and a media house.

6) To build greater consensus on a legal framework for regulating parties, and support legal reforms to achieve a better legal framework, support should be given to dialogues and reform initiatives on areas including: party finance, party regulation, party internal democracy, proportional representation electoral systems, affirmative action for women, youth and PWDs in parties, and party regulatory options. The UNDP should also consider supporting campaigns that advocate for reforms that can provide for a more democratic framework for parties to operate and for citizens to use parties as avenues to participate in democracy.

To address the challenge of lack of participation by: a) women; b) youth; and c) persons with disabilities in leadership and decision-making in the party system and as candidates, serious support should be lent to working groups on gender, youth and disability issues to advocate for reforms such as: legal changes mandating affirmative action in political parties and among lists of candidates fielded by political parties; Providing reserved seats in national and local assemblies for marginalized groups; Development of agreements among all parties to engage marginalized groups at certain levels and based on certain principles; Adoption of non-discrimination and empowering policies by parties towards marginalized groups; Adoption of key policy issues of each marginalized group by leading parties in the party system; Public information campaigns to generate awareness on issues related to participation of marginalized groups in parties and politics, to generate support for initiatives.

INDIVIDUAL PARTY LEVEL INITIATIVES.

As noted in previous sections, parties also suffer from a number of internal capacity challenges. This is to help parties meet some of these gaps and key challenges, the following initiatives are recommended to help meet some of the key challenges:

1) Political parties should develop an international best practices model of how political parties strive to develop themselves, improve their capacity, incorporate marginalized groups into party activities and leadership, and popularize themselves to potential members. This would serve as a heuristic model against which a general assessment of political parties can be made.

2) Drawing on the best practices model, parties should consider supporting the conduct of a comprehensive evaluation to generate baseline data on a set of key indicators, including information on women, youth and PWD in the party, against which political party development can be measured. This evaluation can be used to track political party development over time and can also be used to provide public information on the status of political party development.

3) Parties should engage consultants to support them to carry out participatory SWOT self- analyses that encourage the parties to reflect on their current level of development and how they intend to build themselves during the coming years. Drawing on each of the self-analyses, each party should develop an action plan or strategic plan mapping out their priority areas for party development in the short- and medium-term. These will help orient the parties towards setting strategic goals that they can work together as a party. By setting their own priorities, the parties will feel a sense of ownership over their programming, and will identify priorities that are more relevant to them.

References

African Nationa Congress 50th National Conference, (1997). "Organisational Democracy and Discipline in the Movement", available at http://www.anc.org.za/show.php?id=308.

African Nationa Congress 50th National Conference, (1997). "Challenges of Leadership in the Current Phase. Discussion Document for the ANC National Conference", available at http://www.anc.org.za/show.php?id=307.

Anthony Butler (2000). "Tasks of the NDR and the Mobilisation of the Motive Forces." In How Democratic Is the African National Congress? Journal of Southern African Studies Vol. 31, No. 4, Fragile Stability: State and Society in Democratic South Africa (Dec., 2005), pp. 719-736 (18 pages) Published By: Taylor & Francis, Ltd.

ANC (2001). "Through the Eye of a Needle? Choosing the Best Cadres to Lead Transformation." Discussion document of the National Working Committee of the ANC, Umrabulo, Issue 11, available at http://www.anc.org.za/show.php?id=2945.

ANC (2002). "People's Power in Action" 51st National Conference: Preface to The Strategy and Tactics of the ANC 20 December 2002 available at http://www.anc. org.za/show.php?id=2496.

ANC (2003). "Here Comes the Sun – Drawing Lessons from Joe Slovo's 'No Middle Road'" African Communist, 163, First Quarter, available at http://www.sacp.org.za/main.php?ID=3046.

ANC (2007). "The State of the African National Congress", in: S. Buhlungu, J. Daniel, R. Southall & J. Lutchman (Eds.) State of the Nation: South Africa 2007. Cape Town: HSRC Press, 35–52.

ANC (2007). African National Congress Constitution. Amended and adopted at the 52nd National Conference, Polokwane. Johannesburg: African National Congress.

ANC (2010) (ed.). Paying for Politics: Party Finance and Political Change in South Africa and the Global South. Johannesburg: Jacana.

ANC (2011). "Black Economic Empowerment since 1994", in: Ian Shapiro and Kahreen Tebeau, (eds.), After Apartheid: Reinventing South Africa. Charlottesville VA: University of Virginia Press, 52–71.

ANC (2011). Sharpeville: An Apartheid Massacre and its Consequences. Oxford: Oxford University Press.

ANC (2012. "Statement of the National Executive Committee on the Occasion of the 100th Anniversary of the ANC", ANC Today, 13, 1.

ANC (2012). "Political Report to the 53rd National Conference of the ANC", Johannesburg, African National Congress 16 December 2012 available at http://www.anc.org.za/show.php?id=9989.

ANC (2013). "53rd National Conference Resolutions", Johannesburg, African National Congress 31 January, 2013. available at http://www.anc.org.za/docs/res/2013/resolutions53r.pdf.

ANC (2013a. The Idea of the ANC. Athens: Ohio University Press.

ANC (2013). "Modernising the ANC is not without its problems", Business Day, Johannesburg, 15 February, 2013.

ANC (2013). "NEC Subcommittees and the Teams of Deployees", available at www.anc.org.za/show.php?id=10017.

26 Elischer: Political Parties and Party Systems in Kenya 5051.

Abramson, P. R., & Claggett, W. (2001). Recruitment and political participation. Political Research Quarterly, 54(4), 905-916. Alinsky, S. D. (1972). Rules for radicals; a practical primer for realistic radicals. New York: Random House. Baumgartner, F. L., Beth L. (1998). Basic Interests: The importance of groups in politics and in political science. Princeton: Princeton University Press.

Ackerman, K. D. (2005). Boss Tweed. New York: Carroll and Graf Publishers.

Adcock, R. & Collier, D. (2001). "Measurement Validity: A Shared Standard for Qualitative and Quantitative Research," American Political Science Review 95, 2001, pp. 529-546

Adigwe, F. (1997). Essentials of Government for West African Students Nigeria:OUP Almond, G. A. (2000) Comparative Politics Today: A World View. India: Pearson Education Limited.

Ajulu, Rok (2002). Politicized Ethnicity, Competitive Politics and Conflict in Kenya: A His- torical Perspective, in: African Studies, Vol. 61, No. 2.

Albertus, Michael. (2012). "Vote Buying With Multiple Distributive Goods." Comparative Political Stud- ies 46(9):1082–1111.

Aldrich, J. H. (1995). Why Parties? The Origins and Transformation of Political Parties in America. Chicago: University of Chicago Press.

Allen and unwin Strikler, V. J. and Davies, R. (1996), "Political Party Conventions", in Magill, F.N. (ed.) International Encyclopedia of Government and Politics, London and Chicago: Fitzroy Dearborn Publishers.

ANC (1969). "First National Consultative Conference: Report on the Strategy and Tactics of the African National Congress", 26 April 1969, available at http://www.anc.org.za/show.php?id=149.

Angelo, P. (1988). Political Parties: Organization and Power. Cambridge: Cambridge University Press Azazi, O. (2012) 'NSA Blames PDP for Boko Haram Crisis'. Weeklytrust.com.ng April, 27.

Anstead, N. (2008). Internal Party Democracy in Europe and the United States: Different Models in a Changing Environment, Conference Paper, Political Studies Association, 1 - 3 April 2008, Swansea University

Arriola, Leonardo R. (2013). "Capital and opposition in Africa: Coalition building in multiethnic soci- eties." World Politics 65(02):233–272.

Arriola, Leonardo Rafael (2012). Multi-ethnic Coalitions in Africa: Business financing of opposition election campaigns. Cambridge University Press.

Asunka, Joseph, Sarah Brierley, Miriam Golden, Eric Kramon and George Ofosu. (2017). "Electoral fraud or violence: The effect of observers on party manipulation strategies." British Journal of Political Science .

Austin Ranney, Governing: An Introduction to Political Science, Englewood Cliffs, New Jersey: Prentice-Hall, 1987, pp. 165–66.

Ayoade, John A. (1986). 'Ethnic Management in the 1979 Nigerian Constitution', Publius 16 (Spring). Berelson, Bernard, Paul Lazarsfield and William McPhee (1954) Voting: A Study of Opinion Formation in a Presidential Campaign. Chicago, IL: University of Chicago Press.

Bannon,Alicia et al. (2004). Sources of Ethnic Identification in Africa, in: Afrobarometer Working Paper No. 44.

Berendsen, B. (2008). Democracy and Development, Amsterdam, KIT

Berman, Bruce / Eyok, Dickson / Kymlicka, Will (2004): Ethnicity and Democracy in Africa. Oxford: Oxford University Press.

Bermeo, Nancy (2002). 'The Import of Institutions', Journal of Democracy 13 (April): 96–110.

Berry, J. M., Portney, K. E., & Thomson, K. (1993). The Rebirth of Urban Democracy. Washington, D.C.: Brookings Institution.

Bibliography

Biezen van, I. (2004). How Political Parties Shape Democracy: Perspectives from Democratic Theory, Birmingham, University of Birmingham.

Biezen, I. V. (2004). 'How Political Parties Shape Democracy' Centre for the Study of Democracy Working Paper, UC Irvine. Http:// escholarship.org/uc/item/17p1m0dx Dahl, R. A. (2000) 'A Democracy Paradox?'. Political Science Quarterly, Vol. 115(1). P.38

Blydenburg, J. C. (1971). A controlled experiment to measure the effects of personal contact campaigning. American Journal of Political Science, 15, 365-381.

Bob-Milliar, George M. (2012). "Political party activism in Ghana: Factors influencing the decision of the politically active to join a political party." Democratization 19(4):668–89.

Bobo, K. A., Kendall, J., & Max, S. (2001). Organizing for social change: Midwest Academy manual for activists. Santa Ana, Calif.: Seven Locks Press. Brady, H. E.,

Bogaards, Matthijs (2003). Counting Parties and Identifying Dominant Party Systems in Af- rica, in: European Journal of Political Research, No. 43, pp. 173-197.

Brady, H. E., Verba, S., & Schlozman, K. L. (1995). Beyond SES: A Resource Model of Political Participation. American Political Science Review, 89(2), 271.

Branch, T. (1988). Parting the waters: America in the King years, 1954-1963. New York: Simon and Schuster.

Bratton, M and Van de Walle, N. (1994) Neopatrimonial Regimes and Political Transitions in Africa, World Politics, Vol. 46, No. 4 (Jul., 1994), pp. 453-489, The Johns Hopkins University Press

Bratton, Michael. (2008). "Vote Buying and Violence in Nigerian Election Campaigns." Electoral Studies 27(4):621–32.

Bratton. Michael / van de Walle, Nicolas (1997). Democratic Experiments in Africa. Regime Transitions in Comparative Perspective. United Kingdom: Cambridge University Press.

Brewer, M. D. (2010). "The Evolution and Alteration of American Party Coalitions", in: L. S. Maisel & J. M. Berry(eds.): The Oxford Handbook of American Political Parties and Interest Groups. New York: Oxford University Press.

Brierley, Sarah and George Ofosu. (2014). "The presidential and parliamentary elections in Ghana, De- cember 2012." Electoral Studies 35:362–405.

Briggs, Ryan C. (2012). "Electrifying the base? Aid and incumbent advantage in Ghana." The Journal of Modern African Studies 50(04):603–24.

Broder, D. S. (1972). The Party's Over: The Failure of Politics in America. New York: Harper & Row.

Brodsgaard, Kjeld, and Zheng Yongnian. The Chinese Communist Party in Reform. London: Routledge, 2006.

Butler A. (2005). "How Democratic is the African National Congress?" Journal of Southern African Studies, 31, 4, 719–36.

Campbell, A., Converse, P. E., Miller, W. E., & Stokes, D. E. (1960). The American Voter. Chicago: University of Chicago Press.

Cardy, E. A. (2005). An Experimental Field Study of the GOTV and Persuasion Effects of Partisan Direct Mail and Phone Calls. The ANNALS of the American Academy of Political and Social Science, 601(1), 28.

CCCPC Party Literature Research Office (comp.). Selected Important Literature since the 13th CPC National Congress (II). Beijing: People's Publishing House, 1992, (in Chinese).

Charter and Bylaws of the Democratic Party of the United States 2012. Washington, D.C.: Democratic National Committee.

Chege, M. (2007). Political Parties in East Africa: Diversity in Political Party Systems, Stockholm, IDEA.

Chhibber, Pradeep / Kollman, Ken (2004). The Formation of National Party Systems. Prince- ton: Princeton University Press.

Cho, W. K. T. (2003). Contagion Effects and Ethnic Contribution Networks. American Journal of Political Science, 47(2), 368.

Cho, W. K. T., Gimpel, J. G., & Dyck, J. J. (2006). Residential concentration, political socialization, and voter turnout. Journal of Politics, 68(1), 156-167.

Churchill, W. (1963). The Great Democracies, Bantam Books.

Claggett, William, Jeffrey Loesch, W. Phillips Shively and Ronald Snell (1982). 'Political Leadership and the Development of Political Cleavages: Imperial Germany, 1871–1912', American Journal of Political Science 26.

Coakley, John (ed.) (1993). The Territorial Management of Ethnic Conflict. London:

Cohen, C. J., & Dawson, M. C. (1993). Neighborhood poverty and African American politics. The American Political Science Review, 87(2), 286.

Collier, D. & Mahon, J. (1993). "Conceptual 'Stretching' Revisited: Adapting Categories in Comparative Analyses," The American Political Science Review 87, 1993, pp. 845-855.

Collier, Paul and Pedro C Vicente. (2014). "Votes and violence: evidence from a field experiment in Nigeria." The Economic Journal 124(574):F327–F355.

Collier, Paul and Pedro C. Vicente. (2012). "Violence, Bribery, and Fraud: The Political Economy of Elections in Sub-Saharan Africa." Public Choice 153(1–2):117–47.

Conroy-Krutz, Jeffrey. (2016). "Electoral campaigns as learning opportunities: Lessons from Uganda." African Affairs .

Constitution of Kenya Review Commission (2002). The People's Choice: The Report of the Constitution of Kenya Review Commission. Nairobi: The Constitution of Kenya Review Commission.

Corstange, Daniel. (2012). "Vote Trafficking in Lebanon." International Journal of Middle East Studies 44(03):483–505.

Cotter, C. P. & Hennessey, B. P. (n.d.): Politics Without Power: The National Party Committees. New York: Atherton Press.

Cox, G. (2010). Swing votes, core votes, and distributive politics. In Political Representation, ed. Stokes S. C. Wood E. J. & Kirshner A. S. Shapiro, I. Cambridge University Press pp. 342–358.

Cronin J. (1996). "Thinking about the Concept 'National Democratic Revolution'", Umrabulo, 1 (4th Quarter) available at http://www.anc.org.za/show.php?id=2968.

Dahl, R. (1971). Polyarchy: Participation and Opposition, New Haven: Yale University Press.

Delgado, G. (1986). Organizing the movement: the roots and growth of ACORN. Philadelphia: Temple University Press.

Diamond, Larry / Gunther, Richard (2001). Types and Functions of Parties, in: Diamond, Larry / Gunther, Richard (ed.), Political Parties and Democracy. USA: The Johns Hopkins University Press, pp. 1-39.

Diamond, Larry J. (1988). Class, Ethnicity and Democracy in Nigeria: The Failure of the First Republic. Basingstoke: Macmillan.

Dickson, Bruce J. Democratization in China and Taiwan: The Adaptability of Leninist Parties. Oxford: Oxford University Press, 1997.

Dickson, Bruce J. Red Capitalists in China: The Party, Private Entrepreneurs, and Prospects for Political Change. New York: Cambridge University Press, 2003.

Djupe, P. A., & Grant, J. T. (2001). Religious institutions and political participation in America. Journal for the Scientific Study of Religion, 303-314.

Dode, O. R. (2010). 'Political Parties and the Prospects of Democratic Consolidation in Nigeria: 1999-2006'. African Journal of Political Science and International Relations, Vol. 4(5) Pp. 188-94

DPSA (2013). Public Administration Management Bill (Pretoria, Department of Public Service and Administration).

Driscoll, Barry. (2017). "Why Political Competition Can Increase Patronage." Studies in Comparative International Development pp. 1–24.

Dryzek, J. (2000). Deliberative Democracy and Beyond: Liberals, Critics, Contestations. Oxford: Oxford University Press.

Dudley, B. J. (1973). Instability and Political Order: Politics and Crisis in Nigeria. Ibadan: University Press, P. 38

Edsall, T. B. (2013). "Has the GOP Gone Off the Deep End?" New York Times online edition, July 17.

Eldersveld, S. J. (1956). Experimental Propaganda Techniques and Voting Behavior. The American Political Science Review, 50(1), 154-165.

Election '94 South Africa: The Campaigns, Results and Future Prospects. Cape Town: David Phillip and New York: St. Martin's Press.

Electoral Commission of Kenya (1997). 1997 Parliamentary Results by Constituency, in: www.eck.or.ke.

Electoral Commission of Kenya (2002). 2002 Parliamentary Results by Constituency, in: www.eck.or.ke.

Electoral Commission of Kenya (2005). 2005 Referendum Results by Constituency, in: www.eck.or.ke.

Elischer: Political Parties and Party Systems in Kenya 25

Ellison, C. G., & Gay, D. A. (1989). Black Political Participation Revisited: A Test of Compensatory, Ethnic Community, and Public Arena Models. Social Science Quarterly, 70(1), 101.

Erdmann, Gero (2007). Party Research: Western European Bias and the African Labyrinth, in: Basesau et al. (ed.), Votes, Money and Violence. Political Parties and Elections in Sub- Saharan Africa. Sweden: Elanders Gotab.

Erdmann, Gero / Engel, Ulf (2007). Neopatrimonialism Reconsidered: Critical Review and Elaboration of an Elusive Concept, in: Commonwealth and Comparative Studies, Vol. 45, No. 1, pp. 95-119.

Erlank, N. (2012). "Christianity and African Nationalism in South Africa in the First Half of the Twentieth Century", in: Arianna Lissoni et al (eds.): One Hundred Years of the ANC. Johannesburg: Witwatersrand University Press, 77–96.

EU Election Observation Mission, Kenya, - Final Report on the General Elections 27 December 2007

Fisher, J. and Eisenstadt, T. A. (2004). "Introduction: Comparative Party Finance." Party Politics, Vol. 10(6)

Fisher, R. (1994). Let the people decide: neighborhood organizing in America. New York: Toronto: Twayne Publishers ; Maxwell Macmillan Canada ; Maxwell Macmillan International.

Fisher, R. (2009). The people shall rule: ACORN, community organizing, and the struggle for economic justice. Nashville: Vanderbilt University Press.

Fisher, R., & Romanofsky, P. (1981). Community organization for urban social change: a historical perspective. Westport, Conn.: Greenwood Press.

Franck, Rafael and Ilia Rainer. (2012). "Does the Leader's Ethnicity Matter? Ethnic Favoritism, Education and Health in Sub-Saharan Africa." American Political Science Review 106(2):294–325.

Frank Cass. Cox, Gary (1997). Making Votes Count: Strategic Coordination in the World's Electoral System. New York: Cambridge University Press.

Fridy, Kevin. (2007). "The Elephant, Umbrella, and Quarrelling Cocks: Disaggregating Partisanship in Ghana's Fourth Republic." African Affairs 106(423):281–305.

Gallagher, M. and Marsh, M. (1988). Candidate Selection in Comparative Perspective: The Secret Garden of Politics. London: Sage Publications Ltd. Gosnell, H. F. (1968) Machine Politics: Chicago Model. Chicago: University of Chicago Press

Gans Morse, Jordan, Sebastian Mazzuca and Simeon Nichter. (2014). "Varieties of Clientelism: Machine Politics During Elections." American Journal of Political Science 58(2):415–32.

Gauja, A. (2006). Enforcing democracy? Towards a regulatory regime for the implementation of intra- party democracy, Canberra, Democratic Audit of Australia.

268

Gaventa, J., Smith, B. E., & Willingham, A. W. (1990). Communities in economic crisis: Appalachia and the South. Philadelphia, Pa.: Temple University Press.

Geertzel, Cheery (1970): The Politics of Independent Kenya. Nairobi: East African Publishing House.

Gerber, A. S., & Green, D. P. (2000a). The Effect of a Nonpartisan Get-Out-the-Vote Drive: An Experimental Study of Leafletting. The Journal of Politics, 62(3), 846.

Gerber, A. S., & Green, D. P. (2000b). The Effects of Canvassing, Telephone Calls, and Direct Mail on Voter Turnout: A Field Experiment. The American Political Science Review, 94(3), 653.

Gerring, J. (2006). Case Study Research: Principles and Practices, Cambridge: Cambridge University Press.

Gershtenson, J. (2003). Mobilization strategies of the Democrats and Republicans, 1956- 2000. Political Research Quarterly, 56(3), 293-308.

Ghana Center for Democratic Development. (2016). "Educating the Public on Voting on Policy Issues: Reducing Vote Buying in the Election 2016.".

Gimpel, J. G., Lee, F. E., & Kaminski, J. (2006). The Political Geography of Campaign Contributions in American Politics. The Journal of Politics, 68(3), 626.

Goertz, G and Mahoney, J. (2005). Two-Level Theories and Fuzzy-Set Analysis, in Sociological Methods Research; 33; 497, London, Sage.

Goldstein, K. M. (1996). Watering the Grassroots: Interest Groups, Lobbying, and Participation in America. University of Michigan, Ann Arbor, Michigan.

Goldstein, K. M. (1999). Interest groups, lobbying, and participation in America. New York, NY: Cambridge University Press.

Goldstein, K. M., & Ridout, T. N. (2002). The politics of participation: Mobilization and turnout over time. Political Behavior, 24(1), 3-29.

Goldstein, K., & Paul, F. (2002). Campaign advertising and voter turnout: New evidence for a stimulation effect. The Journal of Politics, 64(3), 721.

Goldworthy, David (1982). Ethnicity and Leadership in Africa: The 'Untypical' Case of Tom Mboya, in: The Journal of Modern African Studies, Vol. 20, No. 1, pp. 107-126.

Gonzalez-Ocantos, Ezequiel, Chad Kiewiet De Jonge, Carlos Meléndez, Javier Osorio and David W Nickerson. (2012). "Vote buying and social desirability bias: Experimental evidence from Nicaragua." American Journal of Political Science 56(1):202–217.

Gosnell, H. F. (1927). Getting out the vote: An experiment in the stimulation of voting.

Green, D. P., & Gerber, A. S. (2005). Recent Advances in the Science of Voter Mobilization. The ANNALS of the American Academy of Political and Social Science, 601(1), 6.

Gyimah-Boadi, E and E Debrah. (2008). Political Parties and Party Politics. In Ghana: Governance in the Forth Republic, ed. Baffour Agyeman-Duah. CDD-Ghana Digibooks Publishing.

Hague, R. and Harrop, M. (2007). Comparative Government and Politics, New York, Palgrave Macmillan.

Helmke, H. and Levitsky, S. (2004). Informal Institutions and Comparative Politics: A Research Agenda, in Perspectives on Politics, 2, pp 725-740

Herrnson, P. S. (2010): "The Evolution of National Party Organizations", in: L. S. Maisel & and J. M. Berry (eds.): The Oxford Handbook of American Political Parties and Interest Groups. New York: Oxford University Press.

Hima and Hima Osaghae, E. E. (1998) Crippled Giant: Nigeria since Independence. London: C. and Hurst Putnam, R. (1993) Making Democracy Work: Civic Traditions in Modern Italy. Princeton N.J: Princeton University Press.

Hodgkin, Thomas (1961). African Political Parties. United Kingdom: Penguin Books.

Holden P. & H. Van Vuuren (2011). The Devil in the Detail: How the Arms Deal Changed Everything. Johannesburg: Jonathan Ball Publishers.

Hon.(DR.)Mohammed Wakil, OON, FNIM, FCIA, CMC, FIMS, (UK), FCIML (USA), ACIS.

Hopkin, J. (2006). "Conceptualising Political Clientelism: political exchange and democratic theory." Paper presented at the Annual Conference of American Political Science Association (APSA), Panel: Conceptual Analysis: Unpacking Clientelism, Governance and Neoliberalism, Marriott, Loews Philadelphia and the Pennsylvania Convention Centre, Philadelphia, PA, 31st August – 3rd September.

Horowitz, Donald (1985). Ethnic Groups in Conflict. Berkeley, CA: University of California Press.

Horowitz, Donald (1991). A Democratic South Africa? Constitutional Engineering in a Divided Society. Berkeley, CA: University of California Press. Idasa (September 1998) 'Party Support and Voting Intention (I)'. Available at: www.idasa.org.za/pos/op99, on 1 October 1998.

Horowitz, Donald (2000) Ethnic Groups in Conflict. Berkeley: University of California Press.

Horowitz, Jeremy. (2016). "The Ethnic Logic of Campaign Strategy in Diverse Societies Theory and Evidence From Kenya." Comparative Political Studies .

Huckfeldt, R., & Sprague, J. (1992). Political Parties and Electoral Mobilization: Political Structure, Social Structure, and the Party Canvass. The American Political Science Review, 86(1), 70.

Huntington, S. P. (1968). Political Order in Changing Societies. New Haven, CT: Yale University Press.

Ichino, Nahomi and Noah L Nathan. (2013). "Do Primaries Improve Electoral Performance? Clientelism and Intra-Party Conflict in Ghana." American Journal of Political Science 57(2):428–441.

Idasa. Mozaffar, Shaheen (1995). 'The Institutional Logic of Ethnic Politics: A Prole- gomenon', in Harvey Glickman (ed.) Ethnic Conflict and Democratization in Africa, pp. 33–69. Atlanta, GA: African Studies Association Press.

Institute for Education in Democracy (2003). Enhancing the Electoral Process in Kenya. Nai- robi: The Institute for Education in Democracy.

Iyare, T. (2004). "An Overview of Political Parties in Nigeria", in Odion-Akhaine, S. (ed.) Governance: Nigeria and the World, Lagos: Center for Constitutionalism and Demilitarization (CENCOD), pp. 79 – 98. Kura, S. Y. B (2011) 'Political Parties and Democracy in Nigeria: Candidate Selection, Campaign and Party Financing in People's Democratic Party', Journal of Sustainable Development in Africa, Vol. 13(6). Pp. 268-98

Jablonski, Ryan S. (2014). "How aid targets votes: the impact of electoral incentives on foreign aid distribution." World Politics 66(02):293–330.

Jensen, Peter Sandholt and Mogens K Justesen. (2014). "Poverty and vote buying: Survey-based evidence from Africa." Electoral Studies 33:220–232.

Josh Maiyo (2008). *POLITICAL PARTIES AND INTRA—PARTY DEMOCRACY IN EAST AFRICA From Representative to Participatory Democracy* . unpublished Thesis

'Joseph LaPalombara and Myron Weiner (eds) Political Parties and Political Development, USA, Princeton University Press, 1968

Jockers, Heinz, Dirk Kohnert and Paul Nugent. (2010). "The successful Ghana election of 2008: A convenient myth?" The Journal of Modern African Studies 48(1):95–115.

Jones, Mark / Mainwaring, Scott (2003) The Nationalization of Parties and Party Systems: An Empirical Measure and an Application to the Americas. USA: Kellogg Institute for In- ternational Studies.

Jordan, Pallo (2011). "ANC: On a Century of Movement", Mail and Guardian, 23 December 2011.

Joseph, R. (1997). Democratization in Africa after 1989: Comparative and Theoretical Perspectives", Comparative Politics, Vol. 29, No. 3, Transitions to Democracy: A Special Issue in Memory of Dankwart A. Rustow. (Apr., 1997), pp. 363-382.

Kadima, Denis / Owuor, Felix (2006). The National Rainbow Coalition, in: Kadima, Denis (ed.), The Politics of Party Coalitions in Africa. South Africa: Konrad Adenauer Founda- tion, pp. 179-221.

Kahn, S. (1991). Organizing, a guide for grassroots leaders. Silver Spring, Md.: National Association of Social Workers.

Kahn, S. (1994). How people get power. Washington, DC: National Association of Social Workers.

Karume, Shumbana (2003). Factional Intrigues and Alliance Politics. The Case of NARC in Kenya's 2002 Elections, in: Journal of African Elections, Vol. 2, No. 2, pp. 1-11.

Karvonen, L. (2007). Legislation on Political Parties: A Global Comparison", in Party Politics Vol. 13. No.4 pp. 437–455; London: Sage

Kasfir, Nelson (1976). The Shrinking Political Arena. Participation and Ethnicity in African Politics with a Case Study of Uganda. Berkeley: University of California Press.

Katz, R. S. (1997). Democracy and Elections. Oxford, Oxford University Press.

Kavanagh, D. (2003). Party Democracy and Political Marketing: No Place for Amateurs? Paper Presented at the Conference on Political Communications in the Global World, at Mainz, 30-31 October 2003.

Key, V. O., Jr. (1956). American State Politics: An Introduction. New York: Alfred A. Knopf.

Key, V. O., Jr. (1964). Politics, Parties, and Pressure Groups. Fifth Edition. New York: Thomas Crowell.

Kirchheimer, O. (1966). The transformation of the Western European Party Systems", in Political Parties and Political Development, ed. J. La Palombra and M Weiner (Princeton, NJ: Princeton University Press) pp. 177-200.

Knoke, D. (1990). Organizing for collective action: The political economies of associations. Hawthorne, NY: Aldine de Gruyter.

Kramer, G. H. (1970). The effects of precinct-level canvassing on voter behavior. Public Opinion Quarterly, 34, 560-572.

Kramon, Eric and Daniel N. Posner. (2016). "Ethnic Favoritism in Education in Kenya." Quarterly Journal of Political Science 11(1):1–58.

Kramon, Eric J. (2016). "Electoral Handouts as Information: Explaining Unmonitored Vote Buying." World Politics .

Kramon, Eric. (2017). Money for Votes: The Causes and Consequences of Electoral Clientelism in Africa. New York: Cambridge University Press.

Krassa, M. A. (1988). Context and the Canvass: The Mechanisms of Interaction. Political Behavior, 10(3), 233-246.

Kuenzi, Michelle and Gina MS Lambright. (2010). "Who votes in Africa? An examination of electoral participation in 10 African countries." Party Politics .

La Raja, R. J. (2010). "Party Nominating Procedures and Recruitment – State and Local Level", in: L. S. Maisel & J. M. Berry (eds.): The Oxford Handbook of American Political Parties and Interest Groups. New York: Oxford University Press.

Ladner, A. and Brändle, M. (1999.) Does Direct Democracy Matter for Political Parties? An Empirical Test in the Swiss Cantons, in Party Politics, Vol. 5, No. 3, 283-302, London, SAGE.

Lazarsfield, Paul, Bernard Berelson and Hazel Gaudet (1948). The People's Choice: How the Voter Makes Up His Mind in a Presidential Campaign. New York: Columbia University Press.

Leighley, J. (2001). Strength in numbers?: The political mobilization of racial and ethnic minorities. Princeton, N.J.: Princeton University Press.

Lemay, M. C. (2001) Public Administration. California: Wadsworth Lively, J. (1975) Democracy Britain: Western Printing Service Ltd Mainwaring,

Levitsky, Steven and Lucan A Way. 2010. "Why democracy needs a level playing field." Journal of Democracy 21(1):57–68.

Li, Qiang. Ten Chapters on the Social Strata. Beijing: Social Sciences Academic Press, 2008, (in Chinese).

Lieberthal, Kenneth. Governing China: From Revolution through Reform, translated by Hu Guocheng and Zhao Mei. Beijing: Social Sciences Academic Press, 2009.

Lijphart, Arend (1985). Power Sharing in South Africa. Berkeley, CA: University of California Press. Lijphart, Arend (1993) 'The Politics of Transition in South Africa: Report of a Faculty Seminar', PS: Political Science and Politics 26.

Lijphart, Arend (1994). Electoral Systems and Party Systems: A Study of Twenty- Seven Democracies, 1945-1990. Oxford and New York: Oxford University Press.

Lindberg, Staffan I. (2003). "'It's Our Time to" Chop'": Do Elections in Africa Feed Neo-Patrimonialism rather than Counter-Act It?" Democratization 10(2):121–140.

Lindberg, Staffan I. (2007). "Institutionalization of party systems? Stability and fluidity among legislative parties in Africa's democracies." Government and Opposition 42(2):215–241.

Lindberg, Staffan I. (2010). "What accountability pressures do MPs in Africa face and how do they respond? Evidence from Ghana." Journal of Modern African Studies 48(1):117–142.

Lindberg, Staffan I. (2013). "Have the cake and eat it The rational voter in Africa." Party Politics 19(6):945–961.

Linz, J. (2000). Totalitarian and Authoritarian Regimes. London, Lynne Rienner.

Lipset, S. M. (2001). Cleavages, Parties and Democracy", in Lauri Karvonen and Stein Kuhnle (Eds) Party Systems and Voter Alignments Revisited, pp. 3–9. London, Routledge.

Lipset, Seymour / Rokkan, Stein (1967). Party Systems and Voter Alignments. New York: The Free Press.

Lipset, Seymour Martin and Stein Rokkan (1967). 'Cleavage Structures, Party Systems and Voter Alignments: An Introduction', in Seymour Martin Lipset and Stein Rokkan (eds) Party Systems and Voter Alignments: Cross-National Perspec- tives. New York: Free Press.

Lipset, Seymour Martin. Consensus and Conflict, translated by Zhang Huaqing et al. Shanghai: Shanghai People's Publishing House, 1995.

Lodge T. (2004). "The ANC and the Development of Party Politics in Modern South Africa", Journal of Modern African Studies, 42, 2.

Lodge, Tom (1999). Consolidating Democracy: South Africa's Second Popular Election. Johannesburg: Witwatersrand University Press and the Electoral Institute of South Africa.

Magaloni, Beatriz, Alberto Diaz-Cayeros and Federico Estévez. (2007). Clientelism and portfolio diversi- fication: a model of electoral investment with applications to Mexico. In Patrons, clients, and policies: Patterns of democratic accountability and political competition, ed. H. Kitschelt and S. Wilkinson. Cambridge Univ. Press pp. 182–205.

Maisel, L. S. & Berry, J. M. (eds.) (2010): The Oxford Handbook of American Political Parties and Interest Groups. New York: Oxford University Press.

Maisel, L. S. & Brewer, M. D. (2012). Parties and Elections in America: The Electoral Process. Sixth Edition. Lanham, MD: Rowman & Littlefield Publishers.

Makinda, S.M. (2003). Reclaiming Democracy for Africa: Alarming Signs of Post-Democratic Governance", Conference Paper, African Studies Association of Australia and the Pacific, 2003 conference proceedings.

Maliyamkono, T.L. and Kanyongolo F.E. (2003). When Political Parties Clash, Dar es Salaam, ESAURP.

Mann, T. E. & Ornstein, N. J. (2012). It's Even Worse than It Looks: How the American Constitutional System Collided with the New Politics of Extremism. New York: Basic Books.

Manning C. (2005). Assessing African Party Systems After the Third Wave, in Party Politics Vol. 11 No. 6 pp 707-727. London, Sage.

Maphai V. & Gottschalk K. (2003). "Parties, Politics and the Future of Democracy", in: D Everatt & V Maphai (eds.): The Real State of the Nation. Johannesburg: Interfund, 51–74.

Marschall, M. J. (2004). Citizen Participation and the Neighborhood Context: A New Look at the Coproduction of Local Public Goods. Political Research Quarterly, 57(2), 231-244.

Marwell, G. O., Pamela E.//Prahl, Ralph. (1988). Social Networks and Collective Action: A Theory of the Critical Mass. III. American Journal of Sociology, 94(3), 502- 534. Massey, D. S. (2007). Categorically unequal: The American stratification system. New York: Russell Sage Foundation.

Matlosa, K, (2005). An Overview of Political Parties Development in the SADC Region: Challenges for Intra-Party Democracy, EISA-IDEA. Paper Presented at a Workshop on Internal Functioning of Political Parties: Fostering Intra-party Democracy in Tanzania, 30th September 2004, (not yet published, cited with author"s permission).

Mattes, Robert (1995). The Election Book. Cape Town:

McAdam, D. (1982). Political process and the development of Black insurgency, 1930- 1970. Chicago: University of Chicago Press.

McMahon, E. R. (2001). The Role of Political Parties in Democratic Development in Africa: Part of the Problem or Part of the Solution? Centre for Democratic Performance, New York, Binghamton University.

McMahon, E. R.(2004). Catching the "Third Wave" of Democratization?: Debating Political Party Effectiveness in Africa Since 1980, African and Asian Studies, Volume 3, Numbers 3-4, pp. 295-320(26), Brill.

McNulty, J. E. (2005). Phone-Based GOTV--What's on the Line? Field Experiments with Varied Partisan Components, 2002-2003. The ANNALS of the American Academy of Political and Social Science, 601(1), 41.

Meinhardt, H, and Patel, N, (2003). Malawi's Process of Democratic Transition: Analysis of Political Developments Between 1990 and 2003, KAF, Malawi.

Michels, R. (1968). Political Parties: A Sociological Study of the Oligarchical Tendencies of Modern Democracy, The Free Press - Macmillan, New York and London.

Modern Political Party Management - What Can Be Learned from International Practices?

Mondros, J. B., & Wilson, S. M. (1994). Organizing for power and empowerment. New York: Columbia University Press. Morris, A. D. (1984). The origins of the civil rights movement: Black communities organizing for change. New York : London: Free Press ; Collier Macmillan.

Morse, A. D. (1896). 'What is a Party?' Political Science Quarterly, Vol. 11(1), Pp. 60 – 78. Nnoli, O. (2003) Introduction to Politics. Revised 2nd Edition, Enugu: PACREP.

Motlanthe Kgalema (2005). ANC Secretary General's Organisational Report. ANC National General Council, June.

Musambayi, K. (2006). After the Floods-The Rainbow: Contextualising NARC"s Election Victory- Lessons Learnt and the Challenges Ahead", in Chris Maina Peter and Fritz Kopsieker (Eds) Political Succession in East Africa: In Search of a Limited Leadership, pp 13-51. Nairobi: Kituo Cha Katiba.

Mutahi, Patrick (2005). Political Violence in the Elections, in: Herve Maupeu et al. (ed.), The Moi Succession. Nairobi: Transafrica Press.

Nathan, Noah L. (2016). "Does Participation Reinforce Patronage? Policy Preferences, Turnout, and Class in Urban Ghana." Forthcoming, British Journal of Political Science .

Ndegwa, Stephen (2003). Kenya: Third Time Lucky, in: Journal of Democracy, Vol. 14, No. 3, pp. 145-158.

NDI Schattschneider, E. E. (1942). Party Government. New York: Holt, Rinehart and Winston.

Nellis, John (1974). The Ethnic Composition of Leading Kenyan Government Positions. Upp- sala: The Scandinavian Institute of African Studies.

Netshitenzhe J. (2003). "The Courage to Search for the New: Personal Reflections on Joe Slovo's 'No Middle Road'", African Communist, 163 First Quarter, available at http://www.sacp.org.za/main. php?ID=3046.

New Patriotic Party. (2006). Polling Station Manual for the New Patriotic Party Ghana.

Nichter, Simeon. (2008). "Vote Buying or Turnout Buying? Machine Politics and the Secret Ballot." American Political Science Review 102(1):19–31.

NIMD, (2004). A framework for Democratic Party Building, The Hague.

NIMD, (2008). The Dutch Political System in a Nutshell, NIMD, The Hague.

Niven, D. (2001). The limits of mobilization: Turnout evidence from state house primaries. Political Behavior, 23(4), 335-350.

Norrander, B. (1991). Explaining Individual Participation in Presidential Primaries.The Western Political Quarterly, 44(3), 640-655.

Ntalaja, G. N. (2000) 'Democracy and Development in Africa'. African Centre for Democratic Governance, Abuja, Nigeria

Nugent, P. (1999). 'Living in the Past: Urban, Rural and Ethnic Themes in the 1992 and 1996 Elections in Ghana', Journal of Modern African Studies, Vol. 37 (2), Pp. 287 – 319.

Nugent, P. (2001c), "Ethnicity as an Explanatory Factor in the Ghana 2000 Elections", Issue, Vol. XXIX (1/2), Pp. 2-7.

Nugent, Paul. (2007). Banknotes and Symbolic Capital: Ghana's Elections Under the Fourth Republic. In Votes, Money and Violence: Political parties and elections in Sub-Saharan Africa, ed. G. Basedua M., Erdmann and A. Mehler. Elanders Gotab AB.

Oberschall, A. (1973). Social conflict and social movements. Englewood Cliffs., N.J.:

Ogude, James (2002). Political Ethnicity in the Democratization Process in Kenya, in: African Studies, No. 61, pp. 209-221.

Ojukwu, C. and Olaifa, T. (2011). 'Challenges of Internal Democracy in Nigeria's Political Parties: The Bane of Intra-Party Conflicts in The People Democratic Party of Nigeria' Global Journal of Human Social Science, Vol. XI (III). Pp. 25-34

Okuku, J. (2002). Ethnicity, State Power and the Democratisation Process in Uganda, Nordic African Institute, Uppsala.

Olaniyi, J. O. (2001). Introduction to Contemporary Political Analysis, 2nd Impression, Lagos: Fapsony Nig Ltd.

Oloo, A. G. R. (2007). The Contemporary Opposition in Kenya: Between Internal Traits and State Manipulation, in Kenya: The Struggle for Democracy (Eds. Godwin Murunga and Shadrack Nasong"o) Codesria, Dakar.

Omodia, S. M. (2010). 'Political Parties and Party Politics in the Nigerian Fourth Republic', Trakia Journal of Sciences, Vol. 8(3). Pp. 65-69

Omotola, J. S. (2004). "The 2003 Nigerian Second Election: Some Comments", Political Science Review, Vol. 3 (1&2), pp. 127 – 38. Omotola, J. S. (2008) 'Democracy and Constitutionalism in Nigeria Under the Forth Republic, 1999-2007' Africana, Vol. 2(2)

Omotola, J. S. (2009). 'Nigerian Parties and Political Ideology', Journal of Alternative Perspectives in the Social Sciences, Vol. 1(3), Pp. 612-34

Omotola, J. S. (2010). 'Political Parties and the Quest for Political Stability in Nigeria' Taiwan Journal of Democracy, Vol. 6(2), Pp. 125-145.

Osaghae, E. E. (1994). 'Sustaining Democratic Values in Africa: The Moral Imperative", in Omoruyi, O et 'al eds. Democratization in Africa: Africa Perspective Vol. 1, Benin City:

Paget, Daniel. (2017). Rally Supporters and Canvass Swing Voters: Segmented Targeting in Tanzania. In Working Paper.

Parry, J., Barth, J., Kropf, M., & Jones, E. T. (2008). Mobilizing the Seldom Voter: Campaign Contact and Effects in High-Profile Elections. Political Behavior, 30(1), 97-113.

Picard L. (2005). The State of the State: Institutional Transformation, Capacity and Political Change in South Africa. Johannesburg: Wits University Press.

Piven, F. F., & Cloward, R. A. (1979). Poor people's movements: why they succeed, how they fail. New York: Vintage books.

Polsby, N. W. (1983). The Consequences of Party Reform. New York: Oxford University Press.

Prentice-Hall. Oliver, P. (1984). "If You Don't Do it, Nobody Else Will": Active and Token Contributors to Local Collective Action. American Sociological Review, 49(5), 601-610.

Ragin, C. (2000). Fuzzy-Set Social Science, Chicago: University of Chicago Press.

Rakner, Lise and Nicolas Van de Walle. (2009). "Opposition weakness in Africa." Journal of democracy 20(3):108–121.

Randall, V. (2007). 'Political Parties in Africa and the Representation of Social Groups' in Mathias Basedau, et'al eds. Votes, Money and Violence. Sweden: Nordic African Institute. Pp 82-104

Randall, V. and Svåsand, L. (2002). "Party Institutionalization in New Democracies," Party Politics. Vol. 8 Pp. 5–29;

Randall, Vicky and Lars Svåsand. (2002). "Political parties and democratic consolidation in Africa." Democratization 9(3):30–52.

Reisch, M. (2008). Intervention with Communities: John Wiley & Sons, Inc.

Reitzes, D. C., & Reitzes, D. C. (1987). The Alinsky legacy: alive and kicking. Greenwich, Conn.: Jai Press Inc.

Republic of South Africa (1996). Constitution of the Republic of South Africa. Act 108 of 1996. Pretoria: Republic of South Africa.

Reynolds, Andrew (1999). Election '99 South Africa: From Mandela to Mbeki. Cape Town: David Phillip and New York: St. Martin's Press.

Reynolds, Andrew and Ben Reilly (1997). The International IDEA Handbook of Electoral System Design. Stockholm: International Institute for Democracy and Electoral Assistance.

Richard Joseph, R. (1997). Democratization in Africa after 1989: Comparative and Theoretical Perspectives, Comparative Politics, Vol. 29, No. 3, Transitions to Democracy: A Special Issue in Memory of Dankwart A. Rustow, pp. 363-382, Brill.

Robinson, James A and Ragnar Torvik. (2009). "The Real Swing Voter's Curse." The American Economic Review 99(2):310.

Rosberg, Carl / Nottingham, John (1966): The Myth of Mau Mau: Nationalism in Kenya. Nai- robi: East Africa Publishing House.

Rosenstone, S., & Hansen, J. M. (1993). Mobilization, Participation, and Democracy in America. NY: Macmillan.

Royko, Mike (1971). Boss: Richard J. Daley of Chicago. New York: Dutton.

Rubin, H. J., & Rubin, I. (2008). Community organizing and development. Boston: Pearson/Allyn & Bacon. Saegert, S. (2006). Building Civic Capacity in Urban Neighborhoods: An Empirically Grounded Anatomy. Journal of Urban Affairs, 28(3), 275-294.

S. and Shugart, M. S. (1997). "Conclusion: Presidentialism and the Party System." In Mainwaring, S. and Shugart, M. S. (Eds.)

Presidentialism and Democracy in Latin America. New York: Cambridge University Press.

Salih, M.A. M., Ed. (2003). African political parties: Evolution, institutionalism and governance. Sterling, VA: Pluto Press.

Salih, M.A. M., Ed. (2007). Political Parties in Africa: Challenges for Sustained Multiparty Democracy, Stockholm, IDEA.

Sampson, R. J., Morenoff, J. D., & Gannon-Rowley, T. (2002). Assessing "neighborhood effects": social processes and new directions in research. Annual Review of Sociology (pp. 443(436)). Schlozman, K. L., Burns, N., & Verba, S. (1999). "What Happened at Work Today?": A Multistage Model of Gender, Employment, and Political Participation. Journal of Politics, 61(1), 29.

Sartori, G. (1976). Parties and Party Systems: A Framework for Analysis, Vol. I. London: Cambridge University Press.

Sartori, G. (1976). Parties and Party Systems: A Framework for Analysis, Cambridge and New York: Cambridge University Press.

Sartori, G. (2005). Parties and Party Systems: A Framework for Analysis, Colchester, ECPR.

Sartori, Giovanni (1994). Comparative Constitutional Engineering: An Inquiry into Structures, Incentives and Outcomes. New York: New York University Press.

Scarrow, S. (2000). "Parties without Members? Party Organization in a Changing Electoral Environment," in Russell Dalton and Martin Wattenberg, eds., Parties Without Partisans: Political Change in Advanced Industrial Democracies. Oxford: Oxford University Press, 79–101.

Scarrow, S. (2005). Political Parties and Democracy in Theoretical and Practical Perspectives: Implementing Intra-Party Democracy. Washington:

Scarrow, S. (2005). Political Parties and Democracy in Theoretical and Practical Perspectives: Implementing Intra-party democracy, National Democratic Institute.

Schattschneider, E.E. (1942). Party Government, New York: Holt, Rinehart and Winston.

Schedler, A. (2002). 'Elections Without Democracy: The Menu of Manipulation' Journal of Democracy, Vol. 13(2), Pp. 36- 50

Schlachter Morgenthau, Ruth (1964). Political Parties in French-Speaking Africa. Oxford: Clarendon.

Schlesinger, J. A. (1991). Political Parties and Winning of Office. Ann Arbor: University of Michigan Press. Schumpeter, J. S. (1954) Capitalism, Socialism and Democracy. London:

Schlozman, K. L., & Brady, H. E. (1995). Voice and equality: Civic voluntarism in American politics. Cambridge, MA: Harvard University Press. Walker, J. L. (1990). Political mobilization in America. Walker, J. L. (1991). Mobilizing interest groups in America: Patrons, professions, and social movements. Ann Arbor, MI: University of Michigan Press. Warren, M. R. (2001). Dry bones rattling: community building to revitalize American democracy. Princeton, N.J.: Princeton University Press.

Schlozman, K. L., & Tierney, J. T. (1986). Organized Interests and American Democracy. New York: Harper & Row. Shaw, C. (2004). The Campaign Manager: Running and winning local elections (3rd ed.). Boulder: Westview Press. Smith, J., & Zipp, J. F. (1983). The party official next door: Some consequences of friendship for political participation. The Journal of Politics, 45, 958-978. Thompson, K. (2001). From Neighborhood to Nation. Nashua, NH: University Press of New England. Tilly, C. (1978). From mobilization to revolution. Reading, Mass.: Addison-Wesley Pub. Co. Verba, S.,

Schlozman, K. L., & Verba, S. (1999). Prospecting for participants: Rational expectations and the recruitment of political activists. American Political Science Review, 93(1), 153-168.

Schröder, Günther (1998). The Multi-Party General Elections in Kenya. Nairobi: National Council of Churches of Kenya Service Overseas.

Selected Works of Jiang Zemin. Vols. 2 and 3. Beijing: People's Publishing House, 2006, (in Chinese).

Shambaugh, David. China's Communist Party: Atrophy and Adaptation. Washington, D.C., and Berkeley: Woodrow Wilson Center Press and University of California Press, 2008.

Simkins C. (2004). "Employment and Unemployment in South Africa", Journal of Contemporary African Studies, 22, 2, 253–78.

Slovo J. (1988). "The South African Working Class and the National Democratic Revolution." Umsebenzi Discussion Pamphlet. South African Communist Party, available at http://www.sacp.org.za/docs/history/ndr.html.

Statistics South Africa (1996). Census in Brief.

Stokes, Susan C, Thad Dunning, Marcelo Nazareno and Valeria Brusco. (2013). Brokers, Voters, and Clientelism: the puzzle of distributive politics. Cambridge University Press.

Stokes, Susan C. (2005). "Perverse Accountability: A Formal Model of Machine Politics with Evidence from Argentina." American Political Science Review 99(3):315–25.

Straus, Scott and Charlie Taylor. (2012). Democratization and Electoral Violence in Sub-Saharan Africa, 1990–2008. In Voting in Fear, ed. Dorina A. Bekoe. Washington, D.C.: United States Institute of Peace.

Suberu, Rotimi T. (1991). 'The Struggle for New States in Nigeria, 1976–1990', African Affairs 90, no. 361. Wehner, Joachim (2000) 'Fiscal Federalism in South Africa', Publius: The Journal of Federalism 30: 47–72.

Szwarcberg, Mariela. (2012a). "Political parties and rallies in Latin America." Party Politics .

Szwarcberg, Mariela. (2012b). "Uncertainty, Political Clientelism, and Voter Turnout in Latin America: Why Parties Conduct Rallies in Argentina." Comparative Politics 45(1):88–106.

Terence Ball, Richard Dagger, and Daniel I. O'Neill, Political Ideologies And The Democratic Ideal Tenth edition, New York, Routledge 2017

Teorell, J. (1999). A Deliberative Defence of Intra-Party Democracy" in Party Politics, Vol. 5, No. 3, 363-382, SAGE, London Thousand Oaks New Delhi

The Punch Editorial (2010). Politicizing Electoral Law, October 26, P. 14

Throup, David / Hornsby, Charles (1998). Multi-Party Politics in Kenya. USA: Ohio Univer- sity Press.

Transparency International (2013). Global Corruption Barometer [online] www.transparency.org /research/gcb/overview.

Tusasirwe, B. (2006). Political Succession in Uganda: Threats and Opportunities", in Chris Maina Peter and Fritz Kopsieker (Eds) Political Succession in East Africa: In Search of a Limited Leadership, pp 83- 108. Nairobi: Kituo Cha Katiba.

van de Walle, Nicolas. (2003). "Presidentialism and clientelism in Africa's emerging party systems." Journal of Modern African Studies 41(2):297–321.

Wahman, Michael. (2015). "Nationalized incumbents and regional challengers Opposition-and incumbent- party nationalization in Africa." Party Politics .

Wang, Chin-Shou and Charles Kurzman. (2007). The logistics: how to buy votes. In Elections for sale : the causes and consequences of vote buying, ed. Frederic Charles Schaffer. pp. 61–78.

Wang, Lihua, and Sun Qiongxian. "Retrospect and Summary on the Transformation of the Communist Party of China after the Founding of the PRC". Journal of Yunnan Administration College, 1 (2010), (in Chinese).

Wanjohi, N. G. (2003). Sustainability of Political Parties in Kenya, in Salih, M.A.M. (Ed) African political parties: Evolution, institutionalism and governance. Sterling, VA: Pluto Press.

Wanjohi, N. G. (2005). State of Political Parties in Kenya and the Transition to Democracy, in Democratic Transition in East Africa, Dar es Salaam, REDET.

Wantchekon, Leonard. (2003). "Clientelism and Voting Behavior: Evidence from a Field Experiment in Benin." World Politics 55(3):399–422.

Wayne, S. J. (2001). Is This Any Way to Run a Democratic Election? Boston; New York: Houghton Mifflin Co.

Weghorst, Keith R. and Staffan I. Lindberg. (2013). "What Drives the Swing Voter in Africa?" American Journal of Political Science 57(3):717–43.

Wei, Xiaodong. "Migrant Workers Are a New Social Stratum in China". Journal of Guangxi Institute of Socialism 3 (June 2009), (in Chinese).

White, T. H. (1965). The Making of the President 1964. New York: Athenaeum.

White, T. H. (1969). The Making of the President 1968: A Narrative History of American Politics in Action. New York: Athenaeum.

White, T. H. (1973). The Making of the President 1972: A Narrative History of American Politics in Action. New York: AthenaeumS

Widner, Jennifer (1992). The Rise of a Party-State in Kenya. Berkeley: University of Califor- nia Press.

Wielhouwer, P. W. (1999). The Mobilization of Campaign Activists By the Party Canvass. American Politics Research, 27(2), 177.

Wielhouwer, P. W. (2000). Releasing the Fetters: Parties and the Mobilization of the African-American Electorate. The Journal of Politics, 62(1), 206.

Wielhouwer, P. W. (2003). In Search of Lincoln's Perfect List: Targeting in Grassroots Campaigns. American Politics Research, 31(6), 632.

Wielhouwer, P. W., & Lockerbie, B. (1994). Party Contacting and Political Participation, 1952-90. American Journal of Political Science, 38(1), 211.

Wollinetz Steven (2002). Beyond the Catch-All Party: Approaches to the Study of Parties and Party Organization in Contemporary Democracies, in Gunther et al. (ed.), Political Parties. Old Concepts and New Challenges. Oxford: UK, Oxford University Press, pp. 147-168.

Wright, W.E. (1971). Party Process: Leaders and Followers, in Wright (ed.), pp 439-451

Xiao Gongqin, Great Transformation in China , Beijing: New Star Press, 2008, pp. 173-74.

Yaqub, N. (2002). "Political Parties and the Transition Process", in Onuoha, B. and Fadakinte, M.M (eds.) Transition Politics in Nigeria, 1970-1999, Lagos: Malthouse Publishers, pp. 118 – 134.

Yeich, S. (1996). Grassroots Organizing with Homeless People: A Participatory Research Approach. Journal of Social Issues, 52(1), 111-121.

Zabach, I. S. (2001). "Fundamentals of Strategy", Being the text of Lecture of the National War College, Abuja September, 16 1999 Constitution of the Federal Republic of Nigeria 2010 Electoral Act of the Federal Republic of Nigeria The Constitution of the People Democratic Party (PDP) The Punch, April 28, 2012

Zhao, Dejiang. Research on the Transformation of Ideology in Today's China: From the Perspective Based on Emerging Entrepreneurs. Beijing: Economic Science Press, 2009, (in Chinese).

Zheng, Yongnian, and Kjeld Brodsgaard. Bringing the Party Back In: The Party and Governance in China. Singapore: Eastern Universities Press, 2004.

Zheng, Yongnian. Chinese Communist Party as Organizational Emperor: Culture, Reproduction and Transformation. London: Routledge, 2010.

Zheng, Yongnian. The Chinese Mode: Experience and Paradoxes. Hangzhou: Zhejiang People's Publishing House, 2010, (in Chinese).

Zhou, Jianyong. "Theoretical Probe to the Transformation of the Contemporary Parties in the West". In Political Basis for the Growth of the Republic System. Comments on Politics by Fudan University, 7th ed. Shanghai: Shanghai People's Publishing House, November 2009, (in Chinese).

Zhu, Fu'en and Lin Dehao. "Sign of the Successful Transformation of Parties: Personal Understanding on the Decision of the 4th Plenary Session of the 17th CPC National Congress". Theoretical Exploration 2 (2010), (in Chinese).

Zipp, J. F., & Smith, J. (1979). The Structure of Electoral Political Participation. The American Journal of Sociology, 85(1), 167-177.

Printed in Great Britain
by Amazon